PAKISTAN'S SECURITY UNDER ZIA, 1977-1988

The Policy Imperatives of a Peripheral Asian State

Robert G. Wirsing

St. Martin's Press
New York

For Nancy, Aaron, Kurt, and Karl

© Robert G. Wirsing 1991

All rights reserved. For information, write:
Scholarly and Reference Division,
St. Martin's Press, Inc., 175 Fifth Avenue, New York, NY 10010

First Published in the United States of America in 1991

Printed in the United States of America

ISBN 0-312-06067-X

Library of Congress Cataloging-in-Publication Data

Wirsing, Robert.
    Pakistan's security under Zia, 1977-1988 : the policy imperatives of a peripheral Asian state / Robert G. Wirsing
      p.   cm.
    Includes bibliographical references (p.   ) and index.
    ISBN 0-312-06067-X
    1. Pakistan—National security. 2. Pakistan—Foreign relations.
I. Title.
UA853.P3W57   1991
355 .03305491—dc20   91-14643
                                                              CIP

CONTENTS

List of Tables iv
Preface v

1. The Security Environment: Introductory Perspectives . . . 1
    I. The international strategic context 3
    II. The domestic political context 10
    III. The debate over security policy 16
    IV. The argument of this book 20

2. The War in Afghanistan: The Interventionist Imperative . 25
    I. The reasons for intervention 26
    II. Pakistan's Afghan war policy 37
    III. Pakistan's refugee policy 42
    IV. The refugee issue in Pakistan's domestic politics . 44
    V. Pakistan and the Afghan resistance movement . . 53
    VI. The Geneva Settlement 63

3. The Arms Race with India: The Nuclear Imperative 81
    I. The military threat from India 84
    II. Nonnuclear alternatives 98
    III. The nuclear alternative 113

4. The Siachen Glacier Territorial Dispute with India: The Irredentist Imperative 143
    I. The territorial issues 145
    II. The military-strategic context 159
    III. Pakistan's counterboundary policy in Kashmir . 170

5. Conclusion: The Persistence of Insecurity 195

Index 209

LIST OF TABLES

1.1 Statistical Comparison of South Asian Countries (1985) . . 4
2.1 Distribution of Afghan Refugee Population in Pakistan in 1987 (by Province) 46
3.1 World Ranking of Selected Countries, 1985 (by Military Indicators) 88
3.2 Military Forces of India and Pakistan, 1984-85 90
3.3 Military Expenditures, India and Pakistan, as Percentage of Annual GNP, 1977-87 94
3.4 Arms Imports, India and Pakistan, in Value and as Percentage of Total Imports, 1977-87 95

PREFACE

The idea of writing this book began forming in my mind nearly a decade ago, in the early 1980s, in the course of research on ethnic separatism in Pakistan's western province of Baluchistan. It was already quite clear at the time that Pakistan's security was facing greater than normal pressures both from within the country and from without and, moreover, that Pakistani policymakers would be taxed to the utmost to cope with these pressures.

What was also clear, and a particular stimulus for this book, was that scholarly investigation of Pakistan's security problems and perspectives was sadly deficient. The deficiency was partly one of quantity: for a country of Pakistan's size and importance, there had been relatively little sustained and serious inquiry into its role in international affairs. Pakistani scholars, for their part, often found access to essential primary source materials blocked by government officials concerned far more with concealment than with appraisal of their activities. And the task of monitoring Pakistan's substantial and diverse international activities was simply too vast for the small band of Western scholars dedicated to the study of Pakistani politics and international relations.

The deficiency, however, was never just one of quantity. While there were notable exceptions, much that had been written about Pakistan's role in international affairs had dealt with Pakistan as a secondary or subordinate actor, rather than in its own terms as the central focus of investigation; and a great deal of what had been written had cast Pakistan as something of a pariah, more to be scolded, isolated, or punished than to be understood in its own right. Scholarship on Pakistan was handicapped, in other words, by the common practice of treating Pakistan simply as an offshoot of India or as an accessory to Great Power policy interests in the subcontinent. It was downright injurious to scholarship, however, for Pakistan to be the focus more often of political diatribe against its "uncivil" international behavior (in regard to nuclear weapons, for example) than of impartial efforts to understand its behavior.

It was with keen appreciation, then, of the need for research on Pakistan's international role that focused directly on Pakistan and was directed primarily toward understanding Pakistan's stakes in international affairs—*and the way in which Pakistanis perceived them*—that work on this book began in earnest by the middle of the decade. By then, the broad outlines of Zia's foreign policy were firmly established and the principal security problems with which this book is concerned—the war in Afghanistan, the conventional and nuclear arms race between India and Pakistan, and the boundary dispute between them over the Siachen Glacier in northern Kashmir—had all taken shape. My choice of these problems was deliberate. They were of obvious importance; and I decided early in the study that my objectives could be satisfied best by narrowing the scope of inquiry, rather than by attempting the meticulous chronicling of Pakistan's diplomatic history or a comprehensive survey of the entire landscape of its foreign policy interests.

Of critical importance to this study was dedicated exposure to the thinking of Pakistan's "foreign policy community"—the diplomats, generals, bureaucrats, professional analysts, politicians, intellectuals and journalists who in one way or the other contributed to the Pakistanis' collective understanding of their country's security situation. I did not satisfy all of my aspirations in this regard (for one thing, I met neither President Zia nor Sahabzada Yakub Khan, who served as Zia's Minister of Foreign Affairs from 1982 onward). But over the course of a dozen research visits to Pakistan between 1973 and the present (eight of them during the Zia period and one of these an 18-month stretch of residence in Pakistan), I conducted many scores of interviews with key decision-makers, their advisors, critics, and observers. Many of these interviews extended over several hours and involved multiple contacts. The analysis in this book relies heavily on these interviews, supplemented by a variety of secondary sources, accounts in newspapers, and official reports. Much of what I have to say about Pakistan's Afghanistan policy, for instance, is drawn from personal interviews with Pakistani military and civilian leaders, active and retired. These were extensively supplemented by personal observation during repeated visits to a variety of Afghan refugee camps as well as by numerous interviews with Afghan resistance leaders, foreign diplomats, and representatives of international (private and governmental) refugee relief agencies. My discussion of the Siachen Glacier dispute is based to a large extent on interviews with both Pakistani and Indian diplomats and military officers directly concerned with it, in addition to military-sponsored visits to the Siachen Glacier from both the Indian and Pakistani sides.

During the research and writing of this book, I have built up a debt to more people than I can single out for mention here, much less ever expect to repay. To the hundreds of Pakistanis, Afghans, Indians, and Westerners who generously and uncomplainingly subjected themselves to my meddlesome questions, I owe the greatest debt of all. To safeguard the confidentiality of the interviews, very few of these individuals are identified in the pages of this book. There would be no book without them, however, and to them I express my fullest gratitude.

For steadfast friendship, constant encouragement, and invaluable guidance through the labyrinthine passageways of Pakistani politics, I owe a truly enormous debt of thanks to Asaf F. Vardag. Erstwhile civil servant, now Senator, and always true Pakistani patriot, he bears responsibility for none of the opinions recorded in this book. Without his endlessly patient and wise counsel, however, I would have had far less confidence in expressing them. Others deserving of special mention for helping out and for provoking me to look at Pakistan in novel ways are Shafik Hashmi, Mir Abdul Aziz, Raja Ehsan Aziz, Agha Shahi, Hamid Yusuf, Azmat Hayat Khan, Ijaz Gilani, Inayatullah Khan, Theodore Mataxis, A. R. Siddiqi, Ayub Baksh Awan, Ahmed Hasan Dani, Ravi Rikhye, Samuel Baid, and Rajindra Sareen. I want to thank John Dixon, former director of the American Center in Peshawar, for simply spectacular hospitality and for helping me to get my bearings in that most fascinating city.

Also deserving of my deep appreciation are all those who at one stage or another gave financial support to the project. These would include the U.S. Army's School of International Studies at Fort Bragg, which generously funded foreign travel during my tenure at the school in the project's early years, 1982-84; the U.S. government's Fulbright Program, which granted consecutive lecturing and research awards in 1985-86; and the University of South Carolina, which awarded sabbatical leave in 1988. In its final stages, the project also benefited from a grant awarded in 1990 by the U.S. Institute for Peace for a separate study of conflict resolution in boundary disputes between India and Pakistan.

For their outstanding courtesy, encouragement, and generous provision of research facilities at various stages of the project, I am very grateful to the directors of the Institute of Strategic Studies in Islamabad, Noor A. Husain, Kamal Matinuddin, and Ross Masood Husain; the acting president (and his predecessor, the late A. I. Akram) of the Institute of Regional Studies in Islamabad, Bashir Ahmed; and the directors of the Institute for Defence Studies and Analyses in New Delhi, K. Subrahmanyam and Jasjit Singh. Their research librarians filled my hands with books; their administrative and research staffs freely gave of their time and knowledge. To them all, my lasting thanks.

In 1985-86, I was privileged to be appointed Visiting Fulbright Scholar to the Department of Political Science at the University of Karachi and, thereafter, to the Department of International Relations at Quaid-i-Azam

University in Islamabad. I thank the department chairmen at these institutions, Pervaiz Iqbal Cheema (Quaid-i-Azam University) and Manzooruddin Ahmed (Karachi), for their valued support and many kindnesses. I thank my former colleagues at both of these institutions for many hours of stimulating and frank discussion. On many occasions during the course of this project, I have benefited from the facilities and warm hospitality of the India International Center in New Delhi and the U.S. Education Foundation in Islamabad. To their directors and wonderfully competent and helpful staffs, my thanks.

I want to express my appreciation to the editors of *Asian Survey, Asian Affairs, Journal of South Asian and Middle Eastern Studies,* and *Strategic Studies* for granting me permission to draw from articles of mine published earlier in these journals.

I owe a special debt to Charles H. Kennedy, who read the entire manuscript with a practiced eye and made numerous helpful suggestions.

My editors at St. Martin's Press were Simon Winder and Lisa Goldberg. My thanks to them for superb guidance.

Lastly, to my wife Nancy and to our three boys, who were sojourners with me in Pakistan and who are the joy and inspiration in my life, this book is most affectionately dedicated.

Columbia, S.C., January 1991   R.G.W.

1

THE SECURITY ENVIRONMENT: INTRODUCTORY PERSPECTIVES

President General Zia ul-Haq ruled Pakistan from 5 July 1977, when he seized power in a bloodless coup from Prime Minister Zulfikar Ali Bhutto, until his death in a plane crash on 17 August 1988—a period of a little more than 11 years. This was a period of political turmoil and upheaval in South and Southwest Asia, especially in the crescent of states rimming the northwest quadrant of the Indian Ocean. Of this group of states—the so-called arc of crisis—Pakistan formed the geographic center. The pressure of momentous events was felt on all its borders.

When Zia came to power in 1977 at the age of 53, Iran was yet a monarchy and one of the "twin pillars" of Western strategy in the Gulf; Afghanistan was a backward and barely armed republic with only a minor role on the fringe of the East-West rivalry; and India, following Indira Gandhi's electoral defeat at the hands of the Janata party earlier the same year, had just embarked on a rare spell of detente in its relations with Pakistan. By the time of Zia's death, Iran had been convulsed by an Islamic revolution whose shock waves were felt throughout the Middle East and beyond, and then had fought Iraq in one of the bloodiest and most ruthless wars of the post-World War II era; Afghanistan had come under Marxist rule and been the setting for Soviet military intervention, the deaths in nearly 9 years of bitter warfare of as many as a million Afghans, and the flight to neighboring Iran and Pakistan of over 5 million others; Moscow had announced its stunning decision to withdraw its armed forces from Afghanistan; and India, restored in early 1980 to the hands of Pakistan's arch-nemesis, soon-to-be-assassinated Indira Gandhi, had entered the space age.

Thus, when Zia came to power, he inherited along with power a security environment on the edge of crisis and profound historical transition. A succession of developments, especially those in Iran and Afghanistan, fundamentally altered the security architecture of the region and created threats to Pakistan's security of a magnitude that was without precedent in Pakistan's history. Of course, Zia was not the first of his nation's leaders called upon to wrestle with extremely grave challenges to Pakistan's security. Three wars with India, a series of U.S.-imposed arms embargoes, the breakup of Pakistan, and a growing Indian nuclear weapons capability had clearly tested the statesmanship of his predecessors. Indeed, the country's unenviable security predicament had been the subject of robust debate among Zia's countrymen and their foreign supporters and detractors virtually since the country's founding. But none of those who ruled Pakistan before Zia had had to contend *simultaneously* with challenges to Pakistan's security of the scale, duration, and strategic complexity of those that confronted Pakistan in this period.

How and how well the Zia regime dealt with these challenges is the subject of this book. The subject is highly controversial, not only because the ramifications of the issues it addresses—that of nuclear proliferation, for instance—reach far beyond the borders of Pakistan, but because defense and security matters are extraordinarily entangled with the country's lengthy and largely unsuccessful search for a just and stable domestic political order. The Pakistan military itself has been a pivotal domestic as well as international political actor virtually since the country's founding, certainly since the then serving Commander in Chief of the Pakistan Army, General Mohammad Ayub Khan, was appointed Defense Minister in Prime Minister Mohammad Ali's cabinet in October 1954.[1] In the 11 years of Zia's rule, his multiple and, for most of the period, overlapping roles—Chief of Army Staff (COAS), Chief Martial Law Administrator (CMLA), and President—further obscured the distinction between civil and military authority.[2] Indeed, the imposition of martial law itself, which Pakistan has experienced on three occasions in its brief existence, is as easy to excuse in terms of foreign threats as it is to condemn in terms of protecting privileged elites and the domestic status quo. Everywhere domestic politics drives foreign policy to some extent. In Pakistan's case, it seems especially difficult at times even to distinguish between the two: the territorial boundaries between Pakistan and its neighbors are none too plain, and neither are the boundaries between domestic politics and international security.

Thus, we begin this book with an examination of both the international strategic and domestic political contexts of Pakistan's security policy, searching for the basic characteristics of each of them as well as trying to identify the more important, albeit sometimes subtle, connections between them. In this chapter, we also examine the broad contours of the debate over the country's external security policy that took place in Pakistan, and among Pakistan-watchers in other countries, during the Zia period. As we shall see, this debate concerned not only the question of the source of foreign threats, whether they sprang mainly from the global rivalry of the superpowers or from the regional rivalry between India and Pakistan, but also the related question of whether Pakistan's foreign security policy was a reaction mainly to internal (domestic) or external (foreign) pressures. The author will stake out his own views on these matters in the concluding pages of this chapter.

I. THE INTERNATIONAL STRATEGIC CONTEXT

Three fundamental conditions have characterized Pakistan's relationship to its international strategic environment since the country's formation in 1947: (1) a substantial imbalance of power between it and its most important regional rival, India; (2) a heavy reliance upon foreign allies to offset this regional imbalance; and (3) a persistent tendency for the reliability of these allies to be vitiated by Pakistan's own limited strategic appeal as well as by the existence of seemingly attractive strategic alternatives.

Strategic Asymmetry

India has been since independence the dominant power among the seven countries of the South Asian region. It has outstripped Pakistan, the only state in the region equipped to mount a serious challenge to India's regional preeminence, in practically every respect. In the middle of the 1980s, India accounted for about 77 percent of the region's population, 72 percent of its land area, 81 percent of its gross national product, 66 percent of its military manpower, and 77 percent of its military expenditures [see Table 1.1]. Its scientific and technological feats set it far apart from its neighbors.

In May 1974, it gave a convincing display of its nuclear weapons potential by detonating a plutonium-fueled nuclear device, with about the same yield as the Hiroshima bomb, at its Pokharan test site in the Rajasthan desert. In July 1980, it orbited an earth satellite, only the sixth nation on earth to succeed in doing so. In 1985, in feats of nuclear engineering only a handful of countries could manage, it commissioned its first indigenously built nuclear power reactor and its first fast breeder reactor. It was well ahead of Pakistan in the development of long-range missiles and rockets. It ranked about fifteenth in industrial production in the world; and it boasted, moreover, the Third World's largest pool of scientifically and technologically

Table 1.1
Statistical Comparison of South Asian Countries (1985)

	Area (km^2)	Pop. (mn)	GNP ($bn)	Milper(mn)	Milex ($bn)
Bangladesh	144 000	101.4	$ 15.10	.091	$ .256
Bhutan	47 000	1.3	0.12†		
India	3 288 000	767.7	218.50	1.515	7.732
Maldives	298	0.2	0.02‡		
Nepal	141 000	17.0	2.45	.025	.028
Pakistan	892 000	99.0	27.49	.644	1.856
Sri Lanka	66 000	16.0	5.85	.021	.170

GNP: Gross National Product (in current dollars) †1978 figure
Milper: Total armed forces ‡1980 figure
Milex: Annual military expenditure (in current dollars)

Source: U.S. Arms Control and Disarmament Agency, *World Military Expenditures and Arms Transfers 1988* (Washington, D.C.: U.S. Government Printing Office, June 1989) pp. 34, 46, 54, 56 &61; and (for Bhutan and the Maldives) Dieter Braun, *The Indian Ocean: Region of Conflict or 'Peace Zone'?* (New York: St. Martin's Press, 1983) pp. 200-1.

trained manpower. It also happened to command the world's fourth largest armed force.

As for Pakistan, it was hardly a strategic dwarf. Its rulers presided over the tenth most populous nation in the world and about the ninth largest armed force. Nevertheless, handicapped at the outset with about one-fourth as much territory and about one-eighth as much population as India, its efforts to challenge the might of its formidable neighbor had not been very successful. It failed to win any of the three wars fought with India, and in the third (1971) it was soundly defeated, its territory partitioned, and its population cut in half.

Pakistan's leaders have thus shaped its security policy in profound awareness of a severe regional imbalance of power. In none other of the third world's zones of intense regional conflict (the Middle East, Southeast Asia, Southern Africa, Central America) was the imbalance among the principal intraregional adversaries so stark and seemingly so unalterable. While Pakistan's propaganda mills have often magnified the Indian threat and attributed to India's leaders a lust for dismembering Pakistan unwarranted by available facts, there has always been inherent in the asymmetrical arrangement of the subcontinental balance of power the implicit danger of Indian hegemonial ambitions. Pakistan's security policy has always reflected this danger.

Strategic Dependence

Roughly two months after Pakistan gained its independence of Great Britain, the fledgling government of Governer General Mohammad Ali Jinnah dispatched a special emissary to Washington bearing a memorandum requesting a $2 billion loan from the United States. The loan was to be spread over 5 years and was to include over $500 million for Pakistan's defense. The extraordinary amount of the requested assistance was defended by pointing to Pakistan's geostrategic importance as guardian of the western gateway to the Indian subcontinent. The dominant factor in Pakistan's external and defense policy, said the memorandum, was "the proximity and vulnerability of Western Pakistan to Russia,...If Pakistan yielded to any external threat, the defence of India will become almost an impossibility." To be able to defend itself against such a threat, Pakistan needed

> to be economically developed and extensively improved, the existing air and military bases modernized and expanded, and new ones established, the production of essential arms and ammunitions enlarged and speeded up and better facilities created for the overhauling and maintenance of aircraft and other more advanced forms of machinery. Living conditons and training arrangements for regular troops will have to be improved, and an extensive system for training recruits will have to be introduced. With advancement of education, improved health conditions and a little better standard of life, and their traditional sense of pride and self-defence revived and stimulated, it is certain that the inhabitants of Pakistan will rise up to any occasion when the occasion does come. What is needed is finance, and more than that, a regular source of finance.[3]

Pakistan's request was promptly turned down and its emissary sent home essentially empty-handed. Washington was not then inclined to become Pakistan's "regular source of finance." By the standards of the day, the sum requested was immense and there were obviously numerous other claimants for U.S. support. The Cold War was still in its infancy; and Washington, conditioned to think of South Asia as Great Britain's defense responsibility, had hardly given thought at that time to Pakistan's potential role in an American-orchestrated Asian security system.

Jinnah's initial overture to the United States planted the seed, nevertheless, for what a few years later—aided significantly by a complete breakdown of the wartime alliance between Moscow and Washington, the communist takeover of China, and the outbreak of the Korean War—sprouted into a military alliance between the United States and Pakistan. As early as 1949, Pentagon planners were examining proposals to acquire operational use of military base facilities in Pakistan.[4] Contacts between the political and military leaders of the two countries increased considerably over the next several years. According to William Barnds, the Pentagon was given the go-ahead to negotiate a limited arms assistance program with Pakistan in December 1951.[5] In May 1954, Pakistan signed a Mutual Defence Assistance Agreement with the United States, according to which Washington undertook to provide military equipment and training to the Pakistani armed forces. In September 1954, Pakistan joined the U.S.-created Manila Pact (the South East Asia Treaty Organization/SEATO). And one year later, in September 1955, it joined the U.S.-backed Baghdad Pact (later the Central Treaty Organization/CENTO). By this time, Pakistan was being hailed as the eastern bulwark of the Northern Tier alliance against the Soviet Union, as the linchpin of the American collective security system in Asia, and as America's "most allied ally."[6]

Thus, almost from the moment of its birth as an independent state and with a single-mindedness rarely exceeded by other supplicants for Western aid, Pakistan sought to exchange its cooperation in the strategic encirclement of the Soviet Union in return for the West's cooperation in Pakistan's postindependence conflict with India. In exchange for the expected military, economic, diplomatic, and political benefits of strategic alliance with a nation vastly superior in power and wealth, in other words, Pakistan tacitly offered to relinquish the strategic independence it had gained, at least in principle, with the end of British colonialism. With few apparent misgivings, Pakistan's early leaders contrived to entangle the country in alliances and to establish it as a Western client on the rimland of Asia. To them, the notion of joint defense of the subcontinent with India—a regional alternative to foreign alliance—was practically a contradiction in terms. Neither did they have much confidence in neutralist and nonaligned alternatives. Instead, they settled upon an aggressively extraregional and internationalist strategy, alignment with the Western bloc of nations, driven by the necessity for "borrowing power" from abroad, as one author put it, in order to offset India's natural advantages within the region.[7]

Over the years, Pakistan has made substantial adjustments in its international alignments. For instance, when Washington's enthusiasm for its Pakistan connection began cooling in the early 1960s, Islamabad overcame its widely announced distaste for all things Marxist and began to forge a very close friendship with the People's Republic of China (PRC). In the wake of the 1965 war with India, with the unpleasant memory of the U.S. arms embargo still fresh in mind, Pakistan sought and received arms aid from the Soviet Union. When the United States failed to prevent India from exploiting the Bangladesh debacle in 1971, Pakistan launched a major effort to identify itself more closely with the Muslim Middle East, in particular with the conservative Arab states of the Gulf.[8] There has been no diminishment in the appeal of the extraregional internationalist strategy itself, however, which was as prominent in Pakistan's security policy under Zia—when Pakistan occupied the West's "frontline" against presumed Soviet adventurism in Afghanistan—as it had been in the 1950s.

Strategic Ambivalence

It has been Pakistan's distinct misfortune to have needed foreign allies far more than they have ever needed Pakistan. It has been Pakistan's additional misfortune to have as its principal adversary, India, an appealing strategic alternative to itself. Democratic, nonaligned, vast in size, and a potential Great Power, India inevitably intruded upon the strategic calculations of Pakistan's allies, tempting defection or at least inspiring a certain deference to India's regional aspirations in most of them. Pakistan's extraregional reach for allies has always exceeded its grasp. Its strategic dependence was never matched by the dependability of its alliance partners, upon most of whom the power realities of the subcontinent forced a troublesome ambivalence in outlook.

American ambivalence toward Pakistan was revealed early and repeatedly in the development of the U.S.-Pakistan relationship. Apparent almost immediately was U.S. reluctance to take sides in the conflict between India and Pakistan. When Governor General Jinnah dispatched his envoy to Washington in search of aid in October 1947, armed warfare was already in progress between India and Pakistan over the disputed territory of Kashmir. By January 1948, the danger that the Kashmir dispute would escalate into full-scale war between India and Pakistan was the focus of U.N. Security Council deliberations. In deference to U.N. efforts to bring about a negotiated end of the crisis, President Truman imposed what was termed an "informal embargo" on the export of military supplies to the belligerents, India and Pakistan, on 12 March 1948—hardly 7 months following the subcontinent's achievement of independence.[9] Several formal arms embargoes would follow this one, the first in 1965 at the time of the second Indo-Pakistan war, the last in 1979, only months prior to the Soviet armed intervention in Afghanistan.

While there were clearly periods in the history of U.S.-Pakistan relations (the mid-1950s, the 1980s) when Washington placed a high premium on its security links with Pakistan, there was a long stretch (1965-1979) in which Pakistan's standing among American security clients was obviously downgraded, an otherwise preoccupied Washington having temporarily relegated the South Asian region to the periphery of its security concerns.[10] Even following the Soviet military intervention in Afghanistan, with the price of Pakistan's cooperation with Washington apparent in the constant threat of Soviet retaliation, the plea for deference to Indian security sensitivities retained a strong band of supporters in the United States.[11]

It is true that China, at least, has been a remarkably steadfast ally of Pakistan. Pakistan fit comfortably in Beijing's anti-Soviet "counter-encirclement" strategy, and the Chinese offered Pakistan a convenient counterweight to India. Nevertheless, China's commitment to Pakistan was hardly unconditional, and the steps it took to aid Pakistan in Pakistan's disastrous war with India in 1971 prudently avoided risk to itself.[12] Pakistan's Middle East allies have supplied it with oil, money, a training ground for its soldiers, and massive remittances from its migrant workers. But they have had little to offer in the form of security guarantees.

Pakistan's experience with allies probably exhibits no better than other countries' experience the sad truth of the axiom that nations have permanent interests, not permanent friends. The ambivalence of Pakistan's allies may be harder to tolerate than usual, however, given Pakistan's early and sustained decision to accept strategic dependence as the price of countering Indian power. Be that as it may, Pakistanis often complain that the "friendship" received was not worth the price paid.

These three fundamental characteristics of Pakistan's relationship to its international strategic environment—strategic asymmetry, strategic dependence, and strategic ambivalence—were given exaggerated importance immediately before or during the Zia period by developments that created a security crisis throughout the Southwest Asian region and an intensification of threats to the security of Pakistan in particular. One such development was the sudden jeopardy to Pakistan's existing alliance framework and threat of international isolation that arose in the late 1970s.

Even during the Republican administration of President Gerald Ford strong pressures had been exerted to persuade Pakistan of the folly of its apparent drive to acquire nuclear weapons capability. On his last visit to Pakistan in August 1976, Secretary of State Henry Kissinger offered to sell Pakistan 100 high-performance A-7 jet fighters if Pakistan would agree to forgo its purchase of a nuclear reprocessing plant from France.[13] With the election of the Democrat Jimmy Carter to the White House in November 1976, however, Islamabad faced an administration strongly wedded to the nuclear nonproliferation cause and less enamored of the hard-line conception of East-West relations undergirding the U.S.-Pakistan alliance than had been any of its postwar predecessors. Drained of its ideological underpinning, the alliance all but collapsed: in June 1977, the Carter administration formally turned down Pakistan's request for the A-7s; in September 1978, it suspended economic and military aid to Pakistan in retaliation for Pakistan's planned purchase of the French nuclear reprocessing (plutonium) plant; and in April 1979, all but humanitarian assistance to Pakistan was terminated under provisions of the Symington amendment barring security assistance to any nonnuclear-weapon state that imported nuclear enrichment technology or equipment but failed to place all of its nuclear installations under international safeguards.

While the nuclear issue was thus driving a powerful wedge between Pakistan and its erstwhile American ally, events closer to home at about the same time were threatening to disrupt Pakistan's carefully nurtured ties with its coreligionist allies in the Middle East. The downfall of the Shah of Iran at the end of 1978 removed from Pakistan's western flank a like-minded regime that had joined with Pakistan in the American-sponsored alliance of Northern Tier states and that had directly aided Pakistan both in its wars with India and in crushing the domestic insurrection in Baluchistan in the mid-1970s.[14] It introduced in place of the Pahlavis a radical Islamic regime that openly threatened to export social revolution to neighboring Muslim states. And it led directly to a bitter war between Iran and Iraq that placed Pakistan's Middle East diplomacy under extraordinary stress and threatened to destroy its crucial economic and military ties with both sides in the dispute.

An even more negative development from Pakistan's security perspective in the late 1970s was the intensification of political hostility and military threat in its relationships with its two traditional adversaries, Afghanistan and India. The Marxist coup in Afghanistan in April 1978 brought to an abrupt end discussions between Islamabad and the Daoud regime in Kabul that had seemed to many to offer the best hope in years for a breakthrough in the traditionally chilly relationship between Pakistan and Afghanistan.[15] In place of expected progress toward settlement of the long-standing border dispute between them came renewed sharp invective and allegations by the Khalq regime in Kabul of Pakistani interference in Afghanistan's internal affairs. The rapid increase in Soviet assistance to Kabul and in the number of Soviet military advisors assigned to the Afghan armed forces deepened anxieties on the Pakistan side of the Durand Line, where the separatist "Pashtunistan issue" was always available for exploitation. When the first Soviet airborne and commando units landed at Kabul airport on Christmas Eve 1979, the Soviet threat, a staple of Pakistan's foreign policy for decades, materialized on Pakistan's northern border for the first time since Pakistan's founding.

Developments on Pakistan's eastern border in the early years of Zia's rule, albeit less dramatic, were hardly more reassuring. Soviet troops were barely across the Afghan border when Indira Gandhi was swept back into power in New Delhi in a landslide electoral triumph over the short-lived Janata government. Viewed by very many Pakistanis as their archenemy—the one who masterminded their country's breakup and crushing military defeat in 1971, Mrs. Gandhi replaced a government that had substantially accelerated the pace of normalization in India's relations with Pakistan.[16] Among her first acts upon returning to power was to approve a speech to be given by the Indian envoy to the United Nations, Brajesh Mishra, in which he excused the Soviet armed intervention in Afghanistan as a legitimate gesture, invited by a friendly Afghan regime in response to the meddlesome activities in the region of "some outside Powers."[17] Negotiations with the Soviet Union in 1980 soon yielded an arms import deal worth in the neighborhood of $1.6 billion—the largest in Indian history.[18]

Thus, by the time Zia had eliminated the principal domestic threat to his rule, Zulfikar Ali Bhutto, by hanging him in April 1979, confrontation had become the order of the day in Pakistan's foreign policy not only in its relations with its indispensable superpower ally, the United States, but in its relations with practically all of its regional neighbors. The ranks of its allies were diminishing at the very moment when the ranks of its enemies were swelling. Never before had Pakistan been quite so isolated and quite so theatened at the same time.

II. THE DOMESTIC POLITICAL CONTEXT

The imperfections of Pakistan's political system, from the frailty of its constitutions and parliamentary traditions to the inchoate character of Pakistani national identity itself, have been well documented and endlessly argued.[19] While Pakistan obviously shares these imperfections with many other states of the third world, the people of Pakistan have unquestionably paid a heavy price for them. Part of the price they have paid has been in the chronic instability and persistent injustices of the domestic political order. Another and not insignificant part of the price, however, has been in the realm of Pakistan's external security.

Pakistan's domestic political malaise affects its international security situation in essentially three ways: (1) it impairs the prestige, hence the appeal of (and trust in) Pakistan as an alliance partner; (2) it makes Pakistan more vulnerable to tactics of political destabilization engineered from abroad; and (3) it undermines domestic political support of national security policy objectives.

Impairment of Prestige

Pakistan's first three (pre-Zia) decades of political independence had won it very little praise either within Pakistan or internationally for skill in political engineering. On the contrary, by the time Zia came to power Pakistan had already compiled a lamentable record of constitutional failure, institutional weakness, interethnic violence, and military rule. It had implemented three federal constitutions (four, counting the Interim Constitution of 1972) and scrapped two; and it had lived twice under martial law. It had experienced two popular uprisings, one in East Pakistan and another in Baluchistan—the former having been particularly bloody and the only case of a successful secessionist insurrection in the postcolonial world. Its political parties, almost uniformly disorganized and fractionated, had never prospered. Its leaders, civilian and military alike, had shown little regard for civil rights. By the time General Zia arrived on the political scene, the despairing tone of both Western and Pakistani analysts of Pakistani politics was already a well-established tradition.

If anything, the despair grew even heavier in Pakistan's fourth (Zia) decade. Professor Stephen Cohen was not exaggerating when he said (in 1982) that "many Pakistanis and foreigners do not believe that Pakistan will survive in its present form beyond this decade."[20] In the later years of Zia's rule, especially following the outbreak of ethnic violence in urban areas of Sind province in spring 1985, commentaries on Pakistani politics in leading international journals and newsmagazines routinely bore such titles as "Pakistan: Living on the Edge," "Dateline Pakistan: A Passage to Anarchy?," "Pakistan: Chaos and Carnage," "The Approach of Anarchy," and "Pakistan: Bloodbath in the Streets."

Inevitably, Pakistan's seemingly chaotic domestic political situation became an issue in its foreign relations. This was particularly the case in the United States, where numerous commentaries came to ominous conclusions in regard to the fruitfulness of continued U.S. aid to Pakistan. Typical of these was a 26-page study of Pakistan's political condition published in January 1987 by the Washington-based and libertarian-inclined Cato Institute under the title "A Fortress Built on Quicksand: U.S. Policy Toward Pakistan." This widely-distributed study described Pakistan as "an extraordinarily frail ally—an impoverished nation with a history of political separatism and instability, governed precariously by a military strongman who faces mounting domestic opposition." Pakistan's weaknesses, said the author, had become "so severe that they threaten to plunge the country into chaos, perhaps culminating in the collapse of the state itself." Echoing Professor Cohen, the author expressed the view that Pakistan "will be fortunate if it survives as a political entity in the coming years." Faced with such circumstances, he concluded, the United States had no alternative but to terminate its military and economic aid programs in Pakistan and to disengage militarily from the region.[21]

Throughout the 1980s, similar views—some of them a parody of Pakistan's real circumstances—were aired repeatedly in the comments of congressmen and in the testimony of scholars and other private witnesses in public hearings whenever U.S. aid to Pakistan came up for congressional reauthorization. A male-dominated and repressive military dictatorship, with little left of plausible deniability in regard to its nuclear weaponization program, and awash in automatic weapons and narcotics, Pakistan offered a huge target for its many critics. Faced with a steady stream of bad publicity emanating from the host of energetic and influential human rights, feminist, antidrug, antinuclear, and antiforeign-aid groups that increasingly inhabited Washington, Zia's ambassadors in the United States must from time to time have yearned for the days when all they had to contend with was the pro-India lobby!

The bad publicity was more than merely a nuisance, however, in Pakistan's relations with the West. In fact, projecting an image abroad of stable and responsible domestic political leadership was an essential element in Pakistan's security policy. Some such image was required if Pakistan was to interest the United States and other of its allies in the sorts of long-term security assistance programs and guarantees without which the country's security might remain in jeopardy. Neither Pakistan's friends nor its foes, moreover, were likely to view its mounting nuclear-weapons capability with equanimity in the face of what appeared to be mounting domestic instability. An unruly domestic political situation undermined the trust in Pakistan both of its alliance partners and of its most likely adversaries.

Exposure to External Destabilization

Pakistan's internal political problems have been translated into external problems not only in the form of diminished international prestige, but also in the form of the country's increased vulnerability to external tactics of political destabilization. No less than other countries, Pakistan is vulnerable to an assortment of such tactics, ranging from malicious propaganda and disinformation campaigns to political subversion, assassination, and other clandestine operations. With growth in the amount and intensity of political dissidence and disaffection in the country, however, Pakistan's vulnerability to destabilization tactics has almost certainly increased.

The implementation of such tactics by Pakistan's adversaries was, of course, extremely difficult for outsiders to document. While central and provincial authorities in the Zia period routinely blamed foreign forces for instigating domestic political disorder and violence, in particular ethnic violence, they usually failed to name these forces. Moreover, hard evidence of interference was almost never made available. Incentives for foreign interference were usually plain enough; but so were the government's potential reasons for wanting to shift responsibility for domestic strife to a "hidden hand."

Pakistan's past experience with political destabilization campaigns against it seemed rather mixed. On the one hand, India was certainly involved very heavily and at the highest levels of decision-making in clandestine support of Bengali separatists in the months following outbreak of civil war in East Pakistan in March 1971.[22] On the other hand, neither India's motives then nor Pakistan's extraordinary vulnerability (in part geographic and to a considerable extent self-inflicted) were likely to be repeated in unison at any time in the foreseeable future. The Bangladesh episode, in other words, was to a large extent exceptional. Insofar as the Baluch tribal insurrection of the 1970s was concerned, most observers seemed agreed that Soviet and/or Indian aid to the rebellious Baluch tribesmen amounted to little, if anything.[23]

During the Zia years, foreign involvement in disturbances in the Sind and in terrorist bombings in the northern part of the country, especially in the North West Frontier Province (NWFP), was frequently alleged. Some skepticism in regard to the charges of foreign interference in the Sind was probably warranted: homegrown motivations for the political discontent and violence there were plentiful. There was little justification, however, for skepticism in regard to foreign involvement in the terrorist bombings. According to a U.S. Defense Department tally, roughly 90 percent of the estimated 777 acts of international terrorism committed worldwide in 1987 occurred in Pakistan.[24] Quite in contrast to the almost daily air- and groundspace violations of Pakistani territory by Soviet or Afghan government forces at the time, the terrorist bombings were unquestionably neither the accidental nor incidental byproducts of a war that had moved steadily closer to Pakistan's border. They were almost certainly intended as reprisals for Pakistan's substantial role in support of the Afghan resistance movement, and they very likely had as one of their paramount objectives the undermining of the Afghan resistance by fostering ill-will between the Afghan refugee population and its Pakistani hosts. We examine this problem in detail later in this book. For now, my objective has been simply to suggest that Pakistan's domestic instability made it a tempting target of hostile foreign machinations and that the instability, in this way too, seriously complicated the country's ability to cope with external security threats.

Loss of Popular Political Support

Another way in which Pakistan's domestic political problems have affected its external security situation has been to widen the dissensus over security policy between government and opposition within Pakistan, and thus to encourage disaffection from and to undermine popular support of national security objectives. The dissensus has always been present. Important regional and religious elements of the population opposed even the creation of Pakistan; and there was a significant division of opinion even in the early days of postindependence Pakistan in regard to the proper course for the country to follow internationally in light of regional circumstances and the country's capabilities and limitations.

Dissensus over policy has been magnified enormously over the years, however, by the government's long-term failure to legitimate its authority in the eyes of a large percentage of Pakistanis. The complete collapse of common security purpose relative to India that occurred between the eastern and western wings of pre-1971 Pakistan is the most glaring example of this failure. In that case, Bengali resentment of Punjabi domination of Pakistan overcame the bond of common Islamic identity that had led to the formation of Pakistan in the first place and that was supposed to guard Muslims in both wings of the country against the threat of Hindu domination. The government's failure to legitimate its authority has been just as apparent, however, in the profound disagreements that have developed among Pakistanis over virtually the entire range of their country's security policy in the years since 1971.

The link between Pakistan's long-term crisis of authority and widespread political rejection of its foreign security policy was tellingly revealed during the Zia period on Christmas Day 1986 at an unusual gathering of Pakistani notables called together in Islamabad by the late President. Over 150 prominent academics, journalists, lawyers, religious scholars, and a fair number of elder statesmen were assembled in the imposing new Presidency building and there, with Zia himself presiding, deliberated on a single question put to them by the President: "What," he asked them, "is the greatest problem facing the nation today and how is it to be resolved?" The nine groups into which the conferees were divided naturally came up with different responses. Group Seven, consisting mostly of a glittering array of once-powerful ex-officials in the country's military, diplomatic, and bureaucratic establishments, got the biggest headlines, however, by solemnly declaring "national survival" to be the core problem. It held threats to Pakistan both from abroad and from within, the latter including moral decay, hypocrisy, and corruption on an unprecedented scale, responsible for the country's present malaise. But in a scarcely veiled criticism of the gathering's presidential host, it emphasized that there could be no solution to the problem without replacement of the existing government by a fully civilianized regime supported by the people.[25]

Group Seven included a former foreign minister, an ex-ambassador to Moscow, an ex-ambassador to Washington, two former chiefs of staff of the Pakistan Army, a former chief of staff of the Pakistan Navy, a former chief of staff of the Pakistan Air Force, a retired three-star general (at the time director of the government-run Institute of Regional Studies), the then chairman of the board of governers of the government-run Institute of Strategic Studies, and an ex-chief of Pakistan's civilian intelligence—none of them known for radical political views. Had the gathering been more representative of the country's political leadership, it is certain that criticism of the government would have been far more energetic and far less veiled.

The truth of this last statement was forcefully demonstrated near the end of December 1985, one year prior to Zia's convocation, at a public seminar on the subject of the war in Afghanistan held at Lahore under the sponsorship of the popular daily newspaper *Jang*. The author was among the participants. The subject was obviously controversial, the auditorium was packed, and the principal invitees—including some of the top leadership of the Pakistan-based Afghan resistance movement as well as some of the best-known pro-Moscow leftist political leaders in the country—represented the widest conceivable array of political opinion in the country.

Some speakers heaped praise upon the Afghan guerrillas, or mujahideen, and one, in an especially immoderate address, called for a "thousand-year jehad" against the atheist communists in Kabul. Others, with nearly equal vehemence, condemned the war and Pakistan's role in it. When the late Mir

Ghaus Bux Bizenjo, the Pakistani leader of a Baluch nationalist party, charged that the Soviets had entered Afghanistan on the invitation of a friendly government, and that they had been forced to enter Afghanistan to deter aggressive American designs in the region, pandemonium broke out. Left- and right-wing party cadre led their supporters in frenzied efforts to outshout the other side. As tempers grew, Bizenjo and other opposition leaders were escorted from the building. Warning shots were fired by one side or the other's political supporters just outside the main entrance. With the audience thinned down and the more passionate speakers departed, the seminar returned to its formal deliberations. For the author, however, the country's acute ideological polarization over national security policy, and the problems the government of Pakistan faced in attempting to mobilize support for its policy, had just been unforgettably illustrated.

Understanding Pakistan's security predicament is thus in no small measure a problem of understanding both its domestic political, and its international strategic environments. The two intersect and overlap extensively. As we have seen, Pakistan's strategic environment is marked by conditions of strategic asymmetry, dependence, and ambivalence, all presenting major obstacles to Pakistan's policy ingenuity. At the same time, Pakistan's domestic political weaknesses have compounded the problem by making the country less appealing to its allies, more vulnerable to its enemies, and less capable of mobilizing its own citizens' support for its security policies.

Beyond this, however, understanding Pakistan's security predicament requires familiarity with the structure and content of the debate over security policy that has gone on virtually without interruption since the country's founding. We turn now to consider this debate in some detail.

III. THE DEBATE OVER SECURITY POLICY

The debate over Pakistan's security policy has been wide-ranging and has involved a large and ideologically mixed assortment of official and nonofficial observers, Pakistani and foreign. Over time, the specific content of the debate has changed as different issues have come into focus. At bottom, however, the debate has revolved around two fundamental questions: (1) whether Pakistan's international security policy was driven essentially by its domestic or international environment, and (2) whether, in the international environment, the dominant threat to Pakistan sprang from the global rivalry of the two superpowers or from the regional rivalry between India and Pakistan.

The Determinants of Security Policy: Domestic or International?

One side in the debate held that Pakistan's security policy was rooted primarily in the exploitative structure of domestic society, in the ambitions and self-interests of the country's military-bureaucratic-feudalist landlord oligopoly. This oligopoly, it was claimed, had diverted attention in the past away from domestic injustices by invoking the specter of foreign threats. It had welcomed the superpower rivalry into the region as a means for securing weapons, largely for the control of its own population, and for acquiring economic assistance for its own enrichment and to buttress the status quo. The military leadership was especially villainous. It had been responsible for Pakistan's past mistakes in security policy. Regime change (from military dictatorship to popular democracy) would mean a change in security policy. Domestic political reform was, therefore, the most promising approach to Pakistan's security problems. A more democratic Pakistan would very likely adopt a more neutral, nonaligned, and, hence, pacific security policy.[26]

From this point of view, Pakistan's seeming insecurity was essentially internal in origin, not really the product of its surroundings. As K. Subrahmanyam, erstwhile director of the Institute for Defence Studies and Analyses in New Delhi, put it, "Most of Pakistan's security problems, and the haunting sense of insecurity of the country's rulers are inherent in the nature of the Pakistani state and the relationship between rulers and ruled." India, he claimed, "can do nothing about it."[27] In fact, it was sometimes argued by adherents of this school of thought that external threats were actually welcomed by Pakistan's privileged groups, who cynically exploited them in order to sow doubts about the opposition's patriotism, to excuse repression, or as a way to lure foreign support to bolster the elites' own shaky domestic position. The domestic political crisis was said to fuel the security crisis on Pakistan's borders. Apart from having "deepened Pakistan's already impressive internal divisions by sharply restricting political activity and by neglecting the grievances of ethnic minorities," observed Mohammed Ayoob, the Zia regime's "desperate need for some kind of domestic legitimacy has also produced a foreign policy that has ringed Pakistan with powerful antagonists."[28]

The other side in the debate held that Pakistan's security policy responded essentially to pressures and threats in the country's external environment, in particular to the existence of marked discrepancies in the power capabilities between itself and its adversaries. By and large, Pakistan's large defense establishment and energetic efforts to obtain foreign political and military support could be explained by the size and nature of the foreign threats arrayed against it. These threats, it was pointed out, emerged from a basic clash of interests between Pakistan and its adversaries; they were in no sense fictional or contrived. In the past, Pakistan's *civilian* leadership had demonstrated irresponsibility in regard to the country's security and defense requirements, and it was itself largely to blame for the country's past military setbacks. Domestic political reform could not in itself do much to protect Pakistan against foreign threats. On the contrary, maintenance of military strength and careful cultivation of foreign alliances were the most promising approaches to Pakistan's security.

This perspective acknowledged that there was a domestic political crisis. It proposed, however, that the crisis owed its existence less to the actions or inactions of Pakistan's ruling class than to a regional geopolitical situation only partially of Pakistan's own making. From this point of view, there was a clear association between external security and domestic politics; but it was the former's influence on the latter which was emphasized. Pakistan's military establishment was said to exercise disproportionate influence in Pakistan in large part because it had to cope with what Stephen Cohen once described as "one of the most complex and multilayered strategic threat analyses of any state in the world."[29]

By those on this side in the debate, Pakistan was seen to be sandwiched between two highly threatening, if not malevolent, forces—an expansionist Soviet Union to the north and hegemony-driven India to the east. These two forces, singly or in concert, sought out Pakistan's zones of vulnerability and mounted (or at least threatened to mount) subversion within them. The survival of neither of these two powerful countries was in any jeopardy from Pakistan. Pakistan's survival, on the other hand, was plausibly threatened by both of them.[30] From this point of view, external insecurity inevitably altered Pakistan's domestic priorities and reduced domestic political options; democracy was hobbled in the interest of public order.

Viewed from this perspective, external insecurity compelled Pakistan, moreover, to expose itself to high risk situations on its borders (for example, by arming the Afghan resistance fighters) in order to assure its territorial integrity or even national survival. As Hoover Institution analyst Anthony Arnold expressed it in 1986, "the Soviet threat to Pakistan is in inverse proportion to the vigor and success of the Afghan resistance....As long as the USSR is unable to turn Afghanistan into a firm and stable stepping stone, Pakistan will enjoy a measure of security."[31]

The Dominant International Threat to Pakistan: Global or Regional?

Has the primary external threat to Pakistan come from within the South Asian region (from India)? Or has it mainly been extraregional in origin (that is, global, the result of superpower rivalry and its encroachment on the region)? One reply to these questions has been that Pakistan was essentially a pawn in a superpower game, a victim of its own weakness in a rivalry over which it had virtually no control. The superpower rivalry overshadowed Pakistan's regional rivalry with India, indeed magnified it by destabilizing the regional arms balance, that is, by provoking and subsidizing a dangerous and open-ended arms race.

Seen in this light, the regional rivalry was to a very great extent a byproduct of global strategic competition, not of any irreconcilable issues between the subcontinental rivals. The Soviet alliance with India and the U.S. alliance with Pakistan stemmed from their own strategic expediency, not from any fundamental interest of these powers in the development, safety, or well-being of the subcontinental societies. Absent superpower rivalry from South Asia and the region's natural and necessary impulses toward conflict mitigation and interstate cooperation would be released.[32]

An alternative reply to these questions has been that the dominant international threat to Pakistan was regional in origin and stemmed from the gross inequality in power between Pakistan and its rival, India. Between Pakistan and India, it was said, existed fundamental and essentially irreconcilable differences over territory, ideology, and strategic objectives. In fact, the very principles upon which these two states were founded—the one secular, the other Islamic—were themselves a constant, even if wholly unintended, threat to the social harmony or even existence of the other.[33]

Pakistan, a peripheral regional power that was yet too large and too well armed to be forced into submission, frustrated the regional and global ambitions of its much larger neighbor—the seemingly natural and inevitable postcolonial inheritor of regional domination. From this point of view, superpower involvement in the region was thus mainly the result of regional rather than global dynamics. Absent superpower rivalry, South Asia would still be a region in conflict and India, relieved of Western involvement on the side of its neighbor, would be even more of a threat to Pakistan.

A series of major changes in Pakistan's strategic and political environment coming at or near the end of the Zia period greatly intensified the debate over the country's security policy and sharpened the question of whether post-Zia Pakistan was capable of a fundamental break with past external security policy. The first of these changes was the apparent reduction in the intensity of the regional military threat to Pakistan that followed the Soviet military withdrawal from Afghanistan. Completed on schedule on 15 February 1989, the withdrawal lifted over 100 000 well-armed Soviet troops from territory immediately adjacent to Pakistan's poorly defended northwestern border.

The second of these changes was the increased fluidity apparent in the last few years in both global and regional strategic alignments. Movement toward detente in Sino-Soviet relations and dramatic warming in U.S.-Soviet relations, not to mention the potential for parallel changes in Indo-U.S. or Sino-Indian relations, were bound to spill over onto Pakistan's security domain by increasing the potential for a restructuring, whether for good or for ill, of its own alliance system.

The third of these changes was the restoration of civilian political control in Pakistan following the death of Zia in August and the subsequent general elections in December 1988. This change, which brought a youthful and popularly supported leader to power in Islamabad, seemed to some to herald a new international as well as domestic start for the country. In any event, it unquestionably supplied an opportunity for Pakistan to test the thesis relating political democracy to regional peace.

IV. THE ARGUMENT OF THIS BOOK

This book does not take a neutral position in regard to the two questions addressed above. Instead, it takes issue with those who have asserted that Pakistan's security problems arose fundamentally from self-inflicted domestic political wounds, that is, from the internal crises generated by the structural contradictions of an allegedly unnatural and authoritarian political entity. It allows for substantial domestic influence on security policy. And it holds Pakistani policymakers responsible for their mistakes. It argues, however, that external constraints have been the dominant shaping influence on Pakistan's external security policy.[34]

This book also takes issue with those who have contended that in Pakistan's international environment the dominant factor shaping national security policy was the global rivalry between the two superpowers, the United States and the USSR. It argues instead that the dominant influence on Pakistan's security policy has been the regional balance of power, that is, that the greater threat to Pakistan, hence by far the greater influence on its security calculations, arose from within the South Asian region and stemmed

The Security Environment: Introductory Perspectives 21

directly from the power imbalance present between Pakistan and its Indian neighbor.

This book argues that the dominance of the international environment, and of India within it, in Pakistan's security policy significantly increases the probability of interregime continuity in security policy. It thus discounts the significance for the country's security policy of a shift from military to civilian rule, arguing instead that a major byproduct of Pakistan's extraordinarily troublesome security predicament has been a regime-transcendant consensus within the policy-making community on the country's basic national interests, the primary threats to them, and the measures needed to defeat these threats. The argument in this book does not rule out change. It observes, however, that thus far in the post-Zia era there have been no major departures from Zia's foreign policies nor any dramatic breakthroughs in India-Pakistan relations the equivalent of those which now seem to be placing U.S.-Soviet and Sino-Soviet relations on rather new footing. On the contrary, India-Pakistan relations, propelled by their own set of policy imperatives, seem nowadays to be moving inexorably to a yet more dangerous level of conflict.

The imperatives of Pakistan's security policy are analyzed and assessed in the following chapters. Chapter 2 examines Pakistan's policy in the Afghanistan war (the imperative of intervention), Chapter 3 its arms race—conventional and nuclear—with India (the imperative of nuclear deterrence), and Chapter 4 its boundary conflict with India over the Siachen Glacier in northern Kashmir (the irredentist imperative). Chapter 5 concludes the book with some reflections on the policy implications of Pakistan's persistent insecurity.

NOTES

1. For background on the Pakistan military in politics, see Hasan-Askari Rizvi, *The Military and Politics in Pakistan 1947-86*, third edition (Lahore: Progressive Publishers, 1986); Mohammad Asghar Khan, *Generals in Politics, Pakistan 1958-1982* (New Delhi: Vikas, 1983); Stephen P. Cohen, *The Pakistan Army* (Berkeley: University of California Press, 1984); and Omar Noman, *Pakistan: Political and Economic History Since 1947* (London: Kegan Paul International, 1990).
2. One close observer of the Zia era has written that Zia's "long rule established two 'facts' in Pakistan's political development. The first was that future governments must never overlook the armed forces' power and influence in Pakistan." The second was that the armed forces "could no

longer govern without the explicit support of a cross-section of Pakistan's political elites." Shahid Javed Burki, "Pakistan Under Zia, 1977-1988," *Asian Survey* 28:10 (October 1988) 1099.
3. "Memorandum of the Government of Pakistan to US State Department on its requirements of financial and military assistance, October 1947," in K. Arif (ed.), *America-Pakistan Relations*, vol. I (Lahore: Vanguard Books, 1984) pp. 5-6.
4. See "Memorandum of the Joint Chiefs of Staff, 24 March 1949," in ibid., pp. 15-17.
5. William J. Barnds, *India, Pakistan, and the Great Powers* (New York: Praeger, 1972) p. 92.
6. For a stimulating account of the early years of the U.S.-Pakistan relationship from an Indian perspective, see M. S. Venkataramani, *The American Role in Pakistan* (New Delhi: Radiant Publishers, 1982).
7. Mohammed Ayoob, "India, Pakistan and Super-power Rivalry," *The World Today* 38:5 (May 1982) 198-9. For the view that Pakistani diplomats fashioned the strategic alliance with the United States with a far more clearheaded conception of their country's fundamental interests than was the case with their American counterparts, see Robert J. McMahon, "United States Cold War Strategy in South Asia: Making a Military Commitment to Pakistan, 1947-1954," *The Journal of American History* 75:3 (December 1988) 812-40.
8. See Marvin G. Weinbaum and Gautam Sen, "Pakistan Enters the Middle East," *Orbis* 22:3 (Fall 1978) 595-612.
9. "Memorandum of Secretary of State Marshall to President Truman recommending the imposition of an 'informal' embargo on export of military material to India and Pakistan, 11 March 1948," in Arif (ed.), *America-Pakistan Relations*, pp. 8-9.
10. See Stephen P. Cohen, "U.S. Weapons and South Asia: A Policy Analysis," *Pacific Affairs* 49:1 (Spring 1976) 49-69.
11. See, for example, Selig S. Harrison, "U.S. Policy in South Asia," in Stephen P. Cohen (ed.), *The Security of South Asia: American and Asian Perspectives* (Urbana: University of Illinois Press, 1987) pp. 134-40.
12. See Yaacov Y. I. Vertzberger, *China's Southwestern Strategy: Encirclement and Counterencirclement* (New York: Praeger Publishers, 1985) pp. 51-9.
13. Shirin Tahir-Kheli, *The United States and Pakistan: The Evolution of an Influence Relationship* (New York: Praeger, 1982) p. 90.
14. See Shirin Tahir-Kheli, "Iran and Pakistan: Cooperation in an Area of Conflict," *Asian Survey* 17:5 (May 1977) 474-90.
15. See, for example, Abdul Samad Ghaus, *The Fall of Afghanistan: An Insider's Account* (Washington, D.C.: Pergamon-Brassey's International Defense Publishers, 1988) pp. 140-7. Ghaus was Deputy Foreign Minister in the Daoud cabinet when the discussions occurred.
16. Raju G. C. Thomas, *Indian Security Policy* (Princeton: Princeton University Press, 1986) p. 114.

17. Thomas Perry Thornton, "India and Afghanistan," in Theodore L. Eliot, Jr., and Robert L. Pfaltzgraff, Jr., (eds.) *The Red Army on Pakistan's Border: Policy Implications for the United States* (Washington, D.C.: Pergamon-Brassey's International Defense Publishers, 1986) pp. 46-7.
18. *The New York Times,* 29 May 1980, p. A16, and 30 May 1980, p. A3.
19. See Lawrence Ziring, *The Enigma of Political Development* (Boulder: Westview, 1980); and Anwar Hussain Syed, *Pakistan: Islam, Politics, and National Solidarity* (New York: Praeger, 1982).
20. Stephen P. Cohen, "Pakistan," in Edward A. Kolodziej and Robert E. Harkavy (eds.), *Security Policies of Developing Countries* (Lexington, Mass.: Lexington Books, 1982) p. 111.
21. Ted Galen Carpenter, *A Fortress Built on Quicksand: U.S. Policy Toward Pakistan,* Policy Analysis No. 80 (Washington, D.C.: Cato Institute, 5 January 1987) pp. 3, 8, 11, 18.
22. See Surjit Mansingh, *India's Search for Power: Indira Gandhi's Foreign Policy 1966-1982* (Beverly Hills: Sage Publications, 1984) pp. 216-17; and Richard Sisson and Leo E. Rose, *War and Secession: Pakistan, India, and the Creation of Bangladesh* (Berkeley: University of California Press, 1990) pp. 177-205.
23. See, for example, Selig S. Harrison, "Nightmare in Baluchistan," *Foreign Policy* No. 32 (Fall 1978) 159.
24. *International Herald Tribune,* 16 December 1987, p. 3.
25. *The Muslim* (Islamabad), 27 December 1986.
26. For an earlier effort by the author to describe the contours of the security debate over Pakistan, see Robert G. Wirsing, "Pakistan's Security Predicament," in William L. Dowdy and Russell B. Trood (eds.), *The Indian Ocean: Perspectives on a Strategic Arena* (Durham: Duke University Press, 1985) pp. 317-37.
27. K. Subrahmanyam, *Indian Security Perspectives* (New Delhi: ABC Publishing House, 1982) p. 178.
28. Mohammed Ayoob, "Dateline Pakistan: A Passage to Anarchy?", *Foreign Policy* No. 59 (Summer 1985) 154.
29. Cohen, "Pakistan," p. 97.
30. Rodney W. Jones makes this point in "The Military and Security in Pakistan," in Craig Baxter (ed.), *Zia's Pakistan: Politics and Stability in a Frontline State* (Lahore: Vanguard, 1985) p. 79.
31. Anthony Arnold, "The Soviet Threat to Pakistan," in Eliot and Pfaltzgraff (eds.), *The Red Army on Pakistan's Border* p. 7.
32. G. S. Bhargava argues, for example, that the crux of India's security problem and a formidable barrier to a more compromising attitude in Islamabad is Pakistan's unwarranted amassing of military muscle with the assistance of the United States, France, China, and others. "Devoid of external military aid and free of involvement by outsiders," he avers, "Pakistan would be more likely to settle all disputes, including Kashmir, on a realistic basis of give and take." *South Asian Security After Afghanistan* (Lexington, Mass.: Lexington Books, 1983) p. 123.

33. Barry Buzan, "A Framework for Regional Security Analysis," in Barry Buzan and Gowher Rizvi (eds.), *South Asian Insecurity and the Great Powers* (New York: St. Martin's Press, 1986) p. 15.
34. A recent study that makes the case for the primacy of external constraints in the making of national security policy is Michael Mandelbaum, *The Fate of Nations: The Search for National Security in the Nineteenth and Twentieth Centuries* (New York: Cambridge University Press, 1988). Five of Mandelbaum's six case studies deal with stable and prosperous democracies, a factor which obviously may help to account for his judgment that these countries "have been more sensible and prudent [in the choice of security policies], even when unsuccessful, than they have often been retrospectively judged." (7)

2

THE WAR IN AFGHANISTAN: THE INTERVENTIONIST IMPERATIVE

At the time of the Marxist coup that overthrew the government of President Mohammad Daoud Khan in Kabul in late April 1978, the martial law regime of General Zia ul-Haq was about 10 months old. When elements of the Soviet Red Army toppled the government of Marxist leader Hafizullah Amin and forcefully occupied Afghanistan in late December 1979, Zia had already been in power in Pakistan for two and a half years. By the time of Zia's death in August 1988, an agreement signaling the end of Soviet military intervention in Afghanistan had been signed and the Soviet troop pullout was well under way. Zia's tenure in office thus encompassed all of the first decade of Marxist rule in Afghanistan and all but the final 6 months of the 9 years and 50 days that elapsed between the Soviet Union's entry into Afghanistan and the withdrawal of its last soldier on 15 February 1989.

The Afghanistan war presented Zia and his advisors with Pakistan's most formidable foreign policy problem. For one thing, it sharply increased Pakistan's enmity with its traditional Afghan adversary. For another, it placed the armed might of a superpower on Pakistan's doorstep. And thirdly, its human impact, even by modern standards, was simply devastating. Before the Soviets departed, an estimated one-third of the Afghan population had fled the country, as many as 1.3 million (9 percent) had been killed in the war, and another 11 percent had become internal refugees. According to a Swiss study, the war's death rate ranked among the highest in history, exceeding even the estimated 8.6 percent death rate experienced by the Soviet Union in World War II.[1] Inevitably, the war's byproducts spilled over into Pakistan. Most of the refugees fled to Pakistan; and, as the war ground on, Pakistan suffered literally hundreds of air and ground attacks on guerrilla bases in Pakistan's border areas as well as almost daily terrorist bombings against civilian targets. The war was impossible to ignore, in other words, and every policy decision made in regard to it bore potentially grave consequences as much for Pakistan's internal as for its external situation.

The Pakistan government's decision at an early stage in the Afghanistan war to take an active role in opposing the Soviet military occupation of Afghanistan eventually enabled Pakistan to play a key role in deciding the outcome of the war. Pakistan's lengthy border with Afghanistan supplied the West with its only practical access to the resistance forces. As distributor of massive quantities of Western aid to the resistance, Pakistan was able to exert strong influence over the pattern of hostilities inside Afghanistan. As the principal advocate for over 3 million Afghan refugees, victims of the war's ruthless inhumanity, it helped to focus the collective wrath of world opinion against the Soviet Union and its Afghan clients. Moreover, as the principal diplomatic surrogate for the resistance in efforts to resolve the conflict through international negotiations, it also had a major hand in shaping a settlement.

Islamabad's decision to protest the Soviet action and, in time, to give indispensable support to the Afghan resistance unleashed a torrent of controversy in Pakistan that continues to this day. Questions were raised whether Pakistan's intervention in the war really served the national interest; whether the extent and forms of intervention adopted by Pakistan placed the country's security at excessive risk; whether the war could have been settled sooner and on better terms; and whether the war's aftermath might prove Pakistan's apparent victory Pyrrhic. In this chapter, we reflect upon these questions by examining the motivations behind Pakistan's intervention in the Afghanistan war, the character of its policy toward the war, the war's impact upon Pakistan, and the meaning for Pakistan of the Geneva settlement.

I. THE REASONS FOR INTERVENTION

Within days of the Soviet military occupation of Afghanistan, General Zia convened a meeting of senior officials in Islamabad to deliberate on Pakistan's response. A draft policy statement had been prepared for their consideration by Foreign Minister Agha Shahi, who had returned hurriedly from an official visit to Teheran. In a day-long meeting, Shahi laid out for the high-powered participants the options available to Pakistan.[2] According to Shahi's later rendering of these options, Pakistan at the time had only three:

1. to confront the Soviet Union directly by participating in the Afghan resistance;

2. to acquiesce in the fait accompli imposed by the Soviet Union with all its attendant security and political implications;
3. to protest the Soviet action for its violation of accepted international norms in the international forums of the United Nations, the Islamic Conference and the Non-Aligned Movement short of a confrontation with this superpower, while seeking to strengthen Pakistan's security politically and [in terms of] its defensive capability but without aligning itself with one side or the other in the superpower contention.[3]

The first option, given the disparity in military power between Pakistan and the USSR, was flatly unrealistic and was quickly dismissed. The second was not without attraction; but Shahi argued against it, saying that acquiescence (1) was not in conformity with Pakistan's public diplomacy in support of noninterference norms of international behavior; (2) would mean tacit acceptance of Soviet troops on Pakistan's border—a potentially permanent and heavy liability; and (3) risked setting a dangerous precedent in the region for a later act of intervention against Pakistan by India.

"Pakistan," said Shahi, "preferred the third option. It was," he said,

> the one dictated by the geopolitical circumstances of the region. Admittedly, this course was difficult to sustain, especially in the deteriorating political climate of East-West relations. *The emotional urge to demonstrate Islamic solidarity in full measure had to be restrained as a military solution to the problem was out of the question. The only hope of withdrawal of the Soviet forces lay in mobilising the force of international public opinion and concerting political and diplomatic pressure against the Soviet military intervention.*[4]

The third (political) option was indeed Pakistan's *overt* choice; and in its public statements throughout the 1980s the Zia government rarely deviated from it. Though in time evidence to the contrary grew quite overwhelming, Islamabad consistently maintained that its material involvement in the war was strictly humanitarian and that it relied wholly on political and diplomatic pressure to force the Soviets out. Quietly, however, but simultaneously, Islamabad chose to supplement the third option with a fourth, the *covert* support of the Afghan guerrillas' military struggle against both Kabul's and Moscow's forces in Afghanistan. Missing from Shahi's inventory, this option clearly carried greater risk than the third; and the implementation of it was no doubt only made haltingly as the resistance itself developed momentum. As we shall see, however, it represented more of an augmentation than a radical departure from Pakistan's policy toward Afghanistan in the preceding decade. Evidently, Shahi's apparent desire to forestall Pakistan's having to align itself with either side in the East-West struggle and his expressed confidence in the power of outraged world opinion were not shared with equal fervor by Zia and the rest of the decision-making elite. For most of them, it seems, the imperative of intervention in Afghanistan's war overrode the prudent counsel of the Foreign Office.

The reasons for the momentous Pakistani decision to become involved, overtly *and* covertly, on the side of the resistance in the Afghanistan war were multiple. Three reasons stand out in published analyses of this period: (1) defending the integrity of Pakistan's border with Afghanistan; (2) mitigating the severity of the Soviet military and political threat to Pakistan; and (3) increasing Pakistan's access to the political, military, and economic benefits of alliance with the West. These obviously overlap to some extent. Nevertheless, analysts differ very significantly in the importance they attach to one or another of them. The differences have profound and continuing implications for Pakistan's security policy. We begin our discussion by examining Pakistan's border dispute with Afghanistan—the least often emphasized but, in my judgment, a necessary condition for Pakistan's intervention in the Afghanistan war.

"Pashtunistan" And The Border Dispute With Afghanistan

Well over half of Pakistan's international border is contested by its neighbors. On Pakistan's eastern border in Jammu and Kashmir, no permanent international boundary has ever been agreed between India and Pakistan, whose armed forces are presently arrayed on either side of a 478.5-mile United Nations-supervised Line of Actual Control. Some 200 miles of Pakistan's northern border with the People's Republic of China, from the trijunction of Pakistan, Afghanistan, and China's Xinjiang province to the Karakoram Pass (in Ladakh), was delimited amicably by treaty between Pakistan and China in 1963, but India has consistently denounced the treaty as illegitimate.[5] As for Pakistan's western border, the 1510-mile Durand Line that was negotiated between Sir Henry Mortimer Durand and the Afghan ruler Amir Abdur Rahman Khan at the height of British imperialism in 1893, Afghanistan has never officially accepted it. The Afghan quarrel with Pakistan over it profoundly embittered the relationship between the two countries and gave their foreign policies a basically hostile orientation. Pakistan, it is well to recall, is the only ex-colonial state to have experienced a successful secessionist movement (in Bangladesh)—one that cost it over half of its population. For obvious reasons, then, securing the integrity of its borders and gaining international recognition of them are matters that have been given the highest priority in Pakistan's foreign policy from the moment of its birth.[6]

Conflict over the Durand Line surfaced between Afghanistan and Pakistan at the time of British withdrawal from the subcontinent in 1947. Threatened by Britain's departure with permanent loss of the 3 to 4 million Pashtuns dwelling on the Pakistan side of the line, the Afghanistan government initially tried to persuade the British to renegotiate the boundary. When that failed, Kabul denounced the Partition Plan and demanded that the Pashtuns east of the Durand Line be given the choice of independence. The British, however, went ahead with a scheduled referendum that limited the Pashtuns' choice to union either with Muslim Pakistan or with Hindu India—a choice that left no serious doubt in regard to the outcome. Thus frustrated in their efforts to undo the Durand Line, Afghanistan's rulers fell back on support for Pashtunistan, an appeal for Pashtun self-determination that apparently had the support of leading Indian Congress party leaders, including Mahatma Gandhi, and that Pakistanis have all along felt was thinly veiled Afghan irredentism.[7] Ever since then, the Pashtunistan issue has placed a heavy burden on Pakistan's relations with Afghanistan.[8]

Definitions of Pashtunistan vary. In its most innocuous form, it amounts to little more than renaming of the Pashtun-majority North West Frontier Province (NWFP) and local autonomy within Pakistan.[9] In its more extreme formulations, however, it envisions a fully independent Pashtun state between Afghanistan and Pakistan. Geographically speaking, it may be limited essentially to the present boundaries of the NWFP or embrace all of Pakistan west of the Indus River and south to the Arabian Sea.[10]

Although the Afghanistan government undoubtedly sought to gain political mileage by wielding the Pashtunistan issue in international forums, its support for Pashtunistan was never simply a bargaining ploy or diplomatic stunt. On the contrary, the roots of Pashtunistan lay deep in Pashtun nationalism, in the ethnic pride stemming from Pashtun political domination of Afghanistan for the past two centuries, and in the drive for modern military power.[11] They lay also in the vulnerability implicit in Afghanistan's landlocked geographic situation and in its inevitable preoccupation with the problem of access to trade, transit, and migratory routes.[12] To some extent, Kabul's support for Pashtunistan may have been a defensive reaction reflecting anxiety arising from its own polyethnic complexion. While maps of Pashtunistan were circulated that showed many non-Pashtun groups (Nuristanis, Hazaras, Chitralis, Brahuis, and Baluch) within its proposed boundaries, the Afghanistan government had from the beginning been noticeably careful to exclude from Pashtunistan its own Pashtuns, lest the claim for Pashtunistan result inadvertently in a truncated Afghanistan (or in a Greater Pakistan). Were political amalgamation ever to come, Olaf Caroe warned darkly some years ago, "Peshawar would absorb Kabul, not Kabul Peshawar."[13]

Pakistani apprehensions in regard to Pashtunistan, in turn, had fairly deep roots of their own. The independent-minded Afridis, Waziris, Orakzais, Mohmands, and other Pashtun tribes that inhabited the remote tribal belt straddling the border between Afghanistan and Pakistan had never been brought fully under control by the British, even after years of determined military operations against them. Even now the Pashtun tribesmen inhabiting Pakistan's Federally Administered Tribal Area (2.2 million in number in 1981) cling to an autonomous—and quite ambiguous—political status that has few parallels on this planet. Given the circumstances, their political loyalty to Islamabad—and vulnerability to the blandishments of Pakistan's enemies—has always been problematic.

By the time Zia ul-Haq came to power in 1977, mutual distrust stemming largely from the border dispute was already well entrenched between Afghanistan and Pakistan. Cross-border violence, trade and transit disputes, and virulent government propaganda campaigns were the norm in the period from 1947 to 1963. Twice in that period (1955, 1961) diplomatic relations were severed. Daoud's forced resignation from the office of Prime Minister in 1963, the result in part of widespread dissatisfaction in Afghanistan with his hard-line and economically costly Pashtunistan policy, produced a temporary hiatus in the dispute. With the overthrow of the monarchy and Daoud's return to power in July 1973, however, the Pashtunistan issue again cropped up in Afghanistan-Pakistan relations. Daoud's return happened to coincide with a serious domestic political crisis in Pakistan pitting Prime Minister Zulfikar Ali Bhutto against opposition party governments in the two provinces bordering on Afghanistan—the NWFP and Baluchistan. Kabul was accused of inciting violence in both provinces and of backing an insurrection that broke out in Baluchistan in 1973. Relations between the two countries were severely strained.

Bhutto reacted with an enterprising set of border policies that fell under two broad headings: (1) mobilization of a covert Afghan antigovernment guerrilla force, drawn largely from Afghanistan's growing Islamic fundamentalist movement, to conduct military operations inside Afghanistan; and (2) stepped-up efforts to integrate Pakistan's border tribal areas into Pakistan.

The War In Afghanistan: The Interventionist Imperative

According to retired Major General Nasirullah Babar, ex-governor of the NWFP and inspector general of the Frontier Corps when these policies were implemented, the Pakistan government brought the first of the guerrilla fighters from Afghanistan to Pakistan in October 1973, only months following Daoud's successful coup. "We had an interest," he said, "in Afghanistan's stability. We wanted a party through which we could influence events in Afghanistan. There had been some explosions in the Frontier province of Pakistan. My advice to Bhutto was that Pakistan should take some countermeasures."[14] The mujahideen were brought to Pakistan for training in groups of thirty or forty. Armed with automatic weapons, most were reinfiltrated back into Afghanistan, left in place against the day when their services might be required. For a while, according to Babar, the Bhutto government even kept in readiness near a Pakistani airbase in the NWFP a small mujahideen-manned armored force that could be airlifted for surprise guerrilla attacks against targets inside Afghanistan.

As it turned out, the only major military operation in which Bhutto's Afghan guerrilla force ever engaged proved militarily disastrous. The mujahideen raiding parties pitched against administrative headquarters and police outposts in scattered areas of Afghanistan in July and August 1975 were easily routed. They succeeded neither in inciting a popular uprising nor in provoking an Afghan army mutiny. Many of the raiders surrendered to the government. Of those who fled, many were captured and hundreds executed. Some made their way back to Pakistan.[15]

Paralleling the Bhutto government's mobilization of an Afghan resistance force were its efforts to accelerate the integration into Pakistan of its own Pashtun tribal periphery. This Bhutto sought to accomplish with an array of state-sponsored initiatives in the border tribal belt that included beefed up administrative machinery, expanded road-building programs, extension of voting rights, and sharp increases in government allocations for economic development. Departing from customary practice, Bhutto himself paid a number of well-publicized visits to the tribal areas. In these visits, he insisted on holding mass public meetings, thus capitalizing on his populist talents by appealing directly to the tribesmen over the heads of their tribal leaders. According to one of Bhutto's chief advisors in tribal matters at the time, Bhutto's objective in all of this was to reduce the tribesmen's vulnerability to Afghanistan's machinations by eliminating the tribal belt's traditional autonomy.[16]

Bhutto's aggressive policy in regard to the border question clearly increased the pressures on Afghanistan and very likely helped to stimulate Kabul's movement toward accommodation. On this point, Pakistanis and

Afghans seem agreed. The account of Afghanistan-Pakistan relations during the Bhutto period given by Abdul Samad Ghaus, who was Deputy Foreign Minister of Afghanistan under President Daoud, is especially revealing in this connection.

According to Ghaus, Kabul's intervention in the Baluch and Pashtun areas of Pakistan was as flagrant as was alleged by Islamabad. "Afghanistan could not remain indifferent to what was happening [in these areas]," he writes, "especially since representatives and deputations from tribal areas were continuously coming to Kabul to seek help and guidance. They received ample moral and material help from the Afghans, as they had in the past. So far as guidance was concerned, the government made it clear that, whatever the Pashtuns and their leaders decided about their future, Afghanistan would accept and support their stand." Ghaus also acknowledges the impact of Bhutto's policies on the mood of Kabul's policy makers. "As time passed," he says, "the government of Afghanistan, wary of Pakistan's hostile intentions, highlighted by the Panjsher incident of the summer of 1975 among others, and anxious to secure favorable conditions both internally and externally for speedy economic development (which was expected to be substantially financed by Arab and Islamic countries very friendly to Pakistan), became inclined to seek deescalation of the tensions between Afghanistan and Pakistan."[17] Whereas in late 1974 Bhutto talked of possible war with Afghanistan,[18] by late 1975 preliminary discussions were under way that led ultimately to an exchange of official visits to one another's country by Bhutto and Daoud in summer 1976.

These visits seemed to offer some promise that Pakistan and Afghanistan might find grounds for a permanent settlement of the border dispute. In the two rounds of discussions, the Pakistanis pressed hard for Afghanistan's formal abandonment of the Pashtunistan claim and for its recognition of the Durand Line as Afghanistan's international frontier with Pakistan. In the communiqué issued on conclusion of Bhutto's visit to Kabul in June, the problem of the "naughty *s*," stemming from the traditional Afghan insistence that the tension between the two countries be described in terms of a singular difference over Pashtun self-determination and not, as Pakistan claimed, as the product of multiple difference*s* affecting *both* countries' interests, was resolved in Pakistan's favor.[19]

Bhutto's overthrow in July 1977 interrupted the progress of the talks, but apparently only temporarily. Zia seems very quickly to have established excellent rapport with President Daoud, and in Daoud's visit to Pakistan in March 1978, a strong basis for further steps toward reconciliation seems to have been reached.[20] Within a few weeks of Daoud's return to Kabul, however, the Communist coup had destroyed both Daoud and his regime and had launched a new, and far from friendly, chapter in Afghanistan-Pakistan relations.

Over the objections of key advisors,[21] President Zia journeyed to Kabul in September 1978, only a few months following the Communist coup, in an effort to persuade the leadership of the People's Democratic Party of Afghanistan (PDPA) to revive the bilateral talks. His effort was futile. Armed resistance to the Communist regime mounted during the winter months and refugees began pouring into Pakistan. The first guerrilla training camps and supply routes into Afghanistan were developed at that time—that is, less than a year following the 1978 coup.[22] By the early spring of 1979, Zia had clearly given up on the PDPA regime and had resumed his predecessor's support for the Afghan mujahideen.

To summarize, it is clear that the border dispute between Pakistan and Afghanistan was a fundamental impediment to peaceful relations between them. The issue of Pashtunistan aroused intense emotions on both sides of the Durand Line and allowed little room for compromise. Since 1947, neither government had strayed very far from its initial position. This was as true of Pakistan as it was of Afghanistan. In particular, no significant difference was visible between the Afghanistan policy of the Pakistani leaders Bhutto and Zia.

Zia inherited from Bhutto Pakistan's conciliatory policy in regard to the border dispute, and he abandoned it when Kabul reverted to its traditional hostility. Ideological opposites though they may have been, the "fundamentalist" Zia and the "socialist" Bhutto *both* saw advantage for Pakistan in giving support to the mujahideen cause. For both Zia and Bhutto, in other words, coercive diplomacy, in the form of covert military intervention aimed at destabilizing the regime in Kabul, ultimately prevailed.

Zia's resumption of support for the Afghan resistance preceded by at least seven or eight months the Soviet military intervention in Afghanistan. By the time of that intervention, however, the Soviet Union's political and military role in Afghanistan was already highly visible. Zia's action in regard to Afghanistan, even at that time, therefore, seems likely to have been motivated increasingly by concern for Moscow's and not only for Kabul's motives.

Left to its own resources, Afghanistan had never been able to put the Durand Line in serious jeopardy. Reinforced by the might of a superpower, however, Kabul's territorial ambitions had to be seen in a new light. From an irritating border dispute, Pakistan's problem with Afghanistan was rapidly turning into a major security threat. Zia's critics have often contended, however, that he seized upon this threat to disguise other, less savory motives. The issue deserves closer inspection.

Soviet Threat or Western Aid Bonanza?

In the immediate aftermath of the Soviet military intervention in Afghanistan at the end of 1979, the war in Afghanistan might well have seemed to some in Islamabad to contain a silver lining.[23] Pakistan was then relatively isolated internationally. Peeved with Islamabad's alleged nuclear weapons program, the Carter administration, for example, had imposed an aid ban on Pakistan in 1978 and again in 1979. Execution by Pakistan of the fallen Prime Minister Zulfikar Ali Bhutto in April 1979, following doubtful court proceedings, had drawn widespread criticism from many nations. In November 1979, after an enraged mob had burned down the U.S. Embassy in Islamabad in reaction to rumored American involvement in an attack on a religious shrine in Saudi Arabia, relations between the United States and Pakistan reached their lowest point ever. Pakistan's economy was in a shambles, and its military was armed with antiquated equipment. Thus, in one sense at least, Moscow's decision to intervene militarily in Afghanistan came as welcome relief to Pakistan. It brought the West promptly to Pakistan's rescue with promises of renewed economic and military assistance; and it also quickly boosted Pakistan's sagging prestige. By providing sanctuary for Afghan refugees in Pakistan and by serving as a pipeline for arms to the Afghan resistance forces operating inside Afghanistan, Pakistan was able eventually to transform its reputation from international rogue to good Samaritan.

Pakistani leaders were undoubtedly tempted from time to time to exaggerate the regional (and global) strategic implications of the Soviet military presence in Afghanistan. Nevertheless, the Soviet threat to Pakistan was not simply a convenient fiction concocted in Islamabad for the sake of coaxing aid from Washington. Apart from the palpable threat arising from the proximity of Soviet forces to the Pakistan border, Moscow's military action in Afghanistan had, after all, transgressed a norm of East-West relations—the nonuse of regular Soviet troops in conflicts outside the Soviet bloc—that had stood since World War II. Coming so soon after the collapse of the Pahlavi regime in Iran, with which Pakistan had been closely allied for years, Soviet military intervention in Afghanistan clearly jeopardized not only Western but Pakistani interests in the Gulf as well. Pakistan-Soviet relations had never been good.[24] On the contrary, the Soviet Union had enjoyed a close and continuing military relationship with Pakistan's chief adversary, India, for almost a quarter of a century. With Soviet forces lodged directly on its long, porous, and poorly guarded border with Afghanistan, itself a traditional enemy of Pakistan, Pakistan's strategists had to contend with the increased potential for Soviet subversive activities among Pakistan's numerous dissident political groups.

Actions taken at the time by the Zia regime reveal that Pakistan's leaders recognized the Soviet military occupation of Afghanistan in December 1979 for what it was—a catastrophe. In the roughly 18 months' interval *following* Soviet intervention but *prior* to the U.S.-Pakistan security assistance pact announced in June 1981, the Pakistan government, in conformity with Shahi's third option, led world protest against the Soviet action, securing resolutions demanding Soviet withdrawal from Afghanistan from the Organization of the Islamic Conference (OIC), the Non-Aligned Movement (NAM), and the United Nations General Assembly. Well *before* the Soviet intervention, moreover, the Pakistan army, in conformity with the fourth—covert—option, was training Afghan guerrillas.[25] There is evidence, indeed, that Islamabad was facilitating a modest level of *American* covert assistance to the mujahideen resistance movement fighting the Communist regime in Afghanistan by late spring 1979—a half year before the Soviet intervention took place, 2 years before the U.S.-Pakistan security agreement was signed.[26]

The Zia regime had many faults. Indifference to developments in Afghanistan was not one of them. The argument that Pakistan might not have become involved in the Afghanistan war at all had it not been for the temptation of Western arms and economic assistance is not supported either by the logic of the situation or by available evidence. As a senior Pakistani bureaucrat remarked in a conversation with the author in Islamabad in 1989, "the Soviet intervention in Afghanistan in December 1979 was unprecedented, vastly increasing the threat to Pakistan. Pakistan didn't need to be shoved into the war. Any government of Pakistan would have reacted in the same way."

Let me hasten to add that there is equally little reason to believe that Pakistani leaders saw Armageddon looming at the time on the country's western border. Strategic analysis in Pakistan had never, in fact, given much weight to the likelihood of a significant Soviet expansionist drive in the direction of Pakistan; and the presence of Soviet troops in Afghanistan in the 1980s does not seem to have overturned that assessment.

More characteristic of Pakistani strategic thinking were the findings of a comprehensive interagency study of the regional security environment said to have been undertaken by the Pakistan government in 1973, in the early stages of the Bhutto regime. This study, according to a senior official who participated in it,[27] concluded that the region was entering a period of turmoil and change that would increase Pakistan's security problems, but that probable Soviet pressures in the region would be directed more against the Southwest than South Asian area. The study visualized Iran as the principal focus of Soviet concern, and it identified the Iranian port city of Chah Bahar on the Arabian Sea as a more likely target of Soviet adventurousness than Pakistan's own Baluchistan coast. The study observed that the potential for Indo-Soviet military collusion would have to be taken into account in all post-1971 planning. In general, however, it discerned a basic shift to the Gulf in terms of regional strategic conflict and held that Pakistan would *not* be a key objective of Soviet aggression. According to the official, the Bhutto government interpreted the overthrow of King Zahir Shah and Daoud's recapture of power in Afghanistan in 1973 as confirmation of the study's basic conclusions. In this official's judgment, this study still stood as a basic guideline to the country's foreign policy well into the Zia era.

Daoud's overthrow in 1978 no doubt came as a shock to Pakistan. Whatever promise for reconciliation there had been in the bilateral talks that were then under way was abruptly shattered. The rapid buildup in Soviet advisors that followed seemed bound to complicate relations between Kabul and Islamabad even more. There is no evidence, however, that the Zia regime, either then or even after the Soviet military takeover in Kabul, expected the Soviet Union to move militarily against Pakistan. In fact, in the period immediately prior to Soviet military intervention, and in no small measure because of the Carter administration's forceful signaling of its displeasure with Pakistan's nuclear weapons program, Islamabad had actually been moving to repair relations with Moscow. Standing in its way was its remaining membership in an American-sponsored, anti-Soviet security pact, the Central Treaty Organization (CENTO).[28]

In March 1979—almost a year following the Marxist takeover in Afghanistan and 9 months prior to the Soviet invasion—Pakistan announced its withdrawal from CENTO, in the words of the then Foreign Affairs Advisor (later Foreign Minister) Agha Shahi, "to soften the edge of Soviet-Pakistan relations." CENTO, he said, had become "politically counterproductive"; leaving it might "lessen the points of friction" with the USSR.[29]

Thus, it seems highly unlikely that Pakistanis shared the same level of anxiety about Soviet expansionism in the region as had developed in the United States by the end of the 1970s. Whereas U.S. observers increasingly invoked the frightening specter of an aggressive and expansionist Soviet

Union bent on extending its influence if not its territorial limits to the warm waters of the Arabian Sea,[30] Pakistan's leaders at the time of the Soviet intervention in Afghanistan, according to Agha Shahi, "did not think the USSR would attack Pakistan."

Pakistan's leaders certainly did fear the broad implications of the Soviet action in Afghanistan, however, and not only because it was bound to unleash Kabul's hostility for Pakistan. Pakistanis were quick to recognize that what had a "silver lining" for them had one also for India. In many ways, the most disabling feature for Pakistan of the Soviet military occupation of Afghanistan was not, in fact, the presence of Soviet military forces on the Pakistan border so much as the feared impact of the Soviet presence on Pakistan's older adversary, India. This factor, as will shortly become evident, had profound influence on Pakistan's evolving Afghan policy.

II. PAKISTAN'S AFGHAN WAR POLICY

While Pakistan's conception of the Soviet threat thus differed very significantly from the conception then very widespread in the United States, we have seen that the war in Afghanistan was certainly understood by Pakistan's policymakers as a threatening development, not simply as America's war, in other words, but also as their own. A crucial element in Pakistan's war policy, however, was that the war not come to be seen abroad *solely* as Pakistan's war. It appears that Pakistan's leaders felt that if they were to accept the costs and the risks of hosting Afghan refugees and their heavily armed resistance organizations on Pakistani soil, it was essential to share the costs and ensure themselves against the risks by enlisting maximum international support for their war policy. This meant, first of all, appealing for symbolic expressions of support through such instruments as OIC and UN resolutions on the war, as well as for material support for the refugees, whether from multinational, national, or private donors. Second, given the differing motivations of potential donors, it meant giving publicity not only to Pakistan's humanitarian role, but also to the anticommunist and Islamic character of the Afghan resistance. Third, it meant systematic internationalization of the search for a settlement, including the conduct of indirect talks under UN auspices, insistence on international guarantees of the settlement, and frequent consultation with key allies at every stage in regard to the negotiations. Finally, it meant that Pakistan's single most important international supporter, the United States, would be pressed to give tangible assurances of its commitment to Pakistan's own security.

Pakistan's compulsion to enlarge the international stake in the war no doubt helps to account for Islamabad's rejection of the Carter administration's $400 million aid offer, made in early 1980. It may also help to account for its insistence on the Reagan administration's consent to sell Pakistan the General Dynamics F-16A fighter-bomber, in spite of its high cost and the ready availability of the much cheaper Northrup F-20 fighter-interceptor, as a condition of the 1981 agreement. Knowing full well the price Washington would have to pay in its relations with New Delhi for selling Pakistan its most advanced combat aircraft, Islamabad viewed the sale at least in part as a potent symbol of America's commitment to the struggle in Afghanistan.[31]

The Afghanistan war was thus not supposed to become exclusively Pakistan's war. Neither was it to be fought too zealously—or to be fought inside Pakistan. Apart from internationalization, then, Pakistan's policy objective seems to have been to maintain a discreet, low-profile level of support for the resistance that strictly limited its own overt engagement and avoided unnecessary provocation of the Soviets. The plausibility of its denials of involvement was to be sustained. Pakistan's policy was to preserve as strict control over mujahideen conduct of the war in Afghanistan as was possible, primarily through the introduction of Pakistani military advisors into combat planning and operations and through its near monopoly of weapons supply, as well as over mujahideen political operations in Pakistan and abroad. Soviet/Afghan violations of Pakistan's border were to be absorbed as the price of Pakistan's involvement. Spread of the war beyond the border area, however, was to be strenuously avoided. From the Pakistani perspective, better a long—perhaps even a losing—war than a war fought on Pakistani territory.

Pakistan's policy toward the war was thus founded first and foremost on a prudent regard for its own security. The signs of its self-interest were everywhere to be seen: in Islamabad's reported reluctance, for example, to go along with Washington's long-delayed direct humanitarian aid program, a program that seemed to threaten Pakistan's control over the direction of the war;[32] in Islamabad's efforts to control the news output from Afghanistan;[33] in Islamabad's apparent willingness to risk Washington's displeasure by pursuing a more conciliatory line with Kabul in the Geneva negotiations;[34] as well as in Islamabad's strenuous efforts to maintain at least the appearance of nonalignment.

The reasons for Pakistan's efforts to limit its engagement in the Afghanistan war were not hard to identify. First, Pakistani strategists continued to view India, rather than Soviet-backed Afghanistan, as the foremost military threat to Pakistan. The Soviet military occupation of Afghanistan had dramatically enlarged the traditional Afghan threat to Pakistan without, however, eliminating the threat from India. Indeed, it had raised the disturbing possibility of concerted Indo-Soviet action meant to intimidate, destabilize, or even dismember Pakistan. At the time, such an eventuality did not seem altogether remote. Soviet specialist Peter Duncan put it thusly:

> After the April 1978 revolution in Afghanistan, India's hostility to Pakistan provided Moscow with a potential advantage. At times when the Soviet Union wished to put pressure on Pakistan to prevent it from aiding the Afghan resistance, it could hold out the threat of joint Soviet-Indian pressure on Pakistan on two fronts. However difficult this would have been in practice, given India's jealous preservation of its independence, the threat of such pressure may have been a factor constraining Pakistan's actions in relation to Afghanistan.[35]

From Islamabad's perspective, an inevitable consequence of the successive seizures of the Wakhan Corridor of Afghanistan by the Soviets (1980) and of the Siachen Glacier in northern Kashmir by the Indians (1984) was practical enhancement of the potential for Indo-Soviet defense collaboration.[36] The substantial asymmetry in arms plus the general instability in Pakistan's overall geopolitical environment thus helped to preclude excessive risk-taking on Pakistan's Afghanistan border.

Second, Pakistan's strategic planners under Zia were compelled to allow for the strong possibility that Soviet "presence" in Afghanistan would form a permanent part of the security architecture of the area. Depending on the outcome of the war, Soviet presence might retain a lesser or greater military component; Afghanistan's nonalignment might or might not be restored. Until Soviet leader Mikhail Gorbachev's surprise offer on 8 February 1988, to begin withdrawing Soviet troops from Afghanistan within 60 days of the signing of a settlement between Kabul and Islamabad, Pakistanis were in no position to gamble on Soviet goodwill. At no time during the war did military defeat *of* the Soviet army seem possible. At least short-run military defeat of the mujahideen forces *by* the Soviet army, on the other hand, seemed at all times possible. Having failed for 40 years to dislodge Hindu India from the Muslim-majority state of Jammu and Kashmir, Islamabad harbored few illusions about either its own or the Afghan guerrillas' capacity to drive Marxist USSR out of Muslim Afghanistan.

At the time, the security implications of Gorbachev's evolving design for the restructuring of Soviet society were grasped hardly at all in the United States, much less in Pakistan.[37] What then seemed most relevant to Pakistan's leadership was the distinct possibility that Moscow, were it to tire of Pakistan's meddling in Afghanistan, might choose to create havoc in Pakistan.

Third, and notwithstanding propaganda about the transnational Islamic "holy war," there was a deeply entrenched ambivalence about Afghanistan in the outlook of Pakistani decision-makers. In contrast with the often romantic view of the Afghan guerrillas apparent among some Western supporters of the liberation movement, Pakistanis inevitably viewed their Afghan allies with a certain amount of detachment, not to mention suspicion. Pakistanis recognized that Afghanistan and Pakistan, regardless of whoever was ruling in Kabul at a particular time, had always been adversaries. For reasons already reviewed above, Islamabad's marriage with the Afghan resistance forces was clearly born of necessity at least as much as of desire.

Fourth, Pakistanis naturally feared that international material and moral support for the Afghan cause might prove transitory. Their fear was well grounded. In early 1987, Charles Dunbar, then special assistant for Afghanistan in the Department of State, observed in a widely circulated article that, all along, international concern for Afghanistan had been relatively hollow and ritualistic, deferential to the Soviet Union, and premised on the expectation of the guerrillas' ultimate defeat. Only two nations, Egypt and Saudi Arabia, had broken diplomatic relations with the Kabul regime. For most purposes, it—*not* the guerrillas—represented Afghanistan throughout the world. The world viewed the Afghan guerrilla struggle, he wrote, "not as a national liberation movement, but as a politically purposeless exercise by fractious groups of tribal warriors."[38] Sooner or later, international fatigue over the problem of Afghanistan was expected to set in, and Pakistan had to be prepared for that eventuality. Avoiding its own overexposure in the war was a part of that preparation.

Pakistan's fear of being stranded stemmed, above all, from the uncertainty of its security ties with the United States. This is surprising, in a way, since Zia enjoyed a very close and friendly relationship with the Reagan administration, and at no point in the 8 years of that administration did the U.S.-Pakistan relationship appear under any great strain. The seeming inconstancy of American policy in the region had left Pakistanis much bemused on a number of earlier occasions, however, and very few expected the present state of affairs to last for long. For now we set aside this problem of American "commitment" to Pakistan. It is far too complex and controversial to be dealt with adequately here. We take it up in greater detail in Chapter 3.

A fifth and final reason for Pakistan's efforts to limit its engagement in the war was concern for the potential domestic political consequences of its war policy. Pakistan's involvement in the war unquestionably strained the goodwill of Pakistani citizens; and domestic opposition to Pakistan's role in the conflict was fairly widespread. Precisely how widespread was difficult to measure, however, and exaggeration was plentiful on both sides of the issue. Zia's allies claimed that Pakistan's support for the Afghan resistance was popular with Pakistanis, who were said to identify strongly with their Islamic coreligionists across the border. Zia's opponents claimed, equally vociferously, that Islamabad had yielded control of its regional policy to a foreign superpower and that domestic support was limited to right-wing religious fundamentalists. The truth was bound to be more complicated than either side represented it. The war's fallout on Pakistan was enormous, in any event, and clearly served to put the government on the defensive over its Afghan policy.

Apart from the focus upon limiting its own engagement, Pakistan's Afghan policy throughout the Zia period remained remarkably unconvincing about long-term objectives. These were said by Islamabad to be the withdrawal of Soviet forces, the restoration of Afghanistan's independence and nonaligned status, and the repatriation of the Afghan refugees. None of these objectives lay within Pakistan's capability to accomplish on its own, however; and until Gorbachev in 1988 removed all doubts about the pullout of Soviet troops, they were not expressed with much conviction.

In private, Pakistan's bureaucratic and military leadership was extremely skeptical that the Afghan resistance could ever forcefully evict the Soviets from Afghanistan. The best that Pakistan could achieve, it seemed, was to prevent the premature collapse of the Afghan rebel forces and thus to help delay Soviet consolidation of its control over Afghanistan. But if this was Pakistan's real objective, it was transparently short-term. No wonder, then, that some Pakistanis concluded that Pakistan had no long-term goals at all in Afghanistan, that it had made a terrible blunder to have gotten entangled in the war in the first place, and that it had been trapped by its reliance upon foreign support into the reckless "bleeding" of the Soviet Union on behalf of Washington's own global strategic purposes.[39]

Part of the explanation for the seeming confusion over Pakistan's long-term objectives in Afghanistan was due, no doubt, to the partially contingent nature of its objectives, to the obvious need, in other words, to keep in step with the objectives, whether declared or undeclared, of Islamabad's leading benefactors. Soviet withdrawal from Afghanistan, they said, was essential; but it was never entirely clear how far they would be willing to go (critics said only "to the last Afghan") to advance that objective. Part of the explanation was due, additionally, to the extreme caution that was forced upon Pakistan in this war by virtue of its relative weakness. Wholly lacking in the military capability that would have been required to settle by itself the issue of Afghanistan's future on the battlefield, Pakistan naturally sought to avoid foreclosing nonmilitary options. This led to an anomalous but largely unavoidable duality in Pakistan's policy. By this I mean Pakistan's public stance that its overt leadership of the international protest against the Soviet military intervention and of world humanitarianism on behalf of the refugees, in spite of the magnitude of its covert military assistance to the mujahideen, represented the sum total of its Afghan policy. This stance, which required a virtual thicket of official denials to be put out about the covert side of Pakistani aid, seriously understated the extent of Pakistan's military confrontation of the Soviet Union.

To clear up some of the confusion, we turn now for a closer look at the two faces of Pakistan's policy—first at the humanitarian aid of the Afghan refugees and then at the military aid of the Afghan resistance movement. Along the way, we pay particular attention to the controversy generated in Pakistan about the refugees. Nothing better illustrates the way in which Pakistan's domestic politics and its security policy were intermingled with one another—and not necessarily to the disadvantage of the latter—than this problem.

III. PAKISTAN'S REFUGEE POLICY

Pakistan's Afghan refugee policy, developed in the earliest phases of the refugee influx and sustained without significant change throughout the Zia period, had three conspicuous characteristics. First, the refugees were warmly welcomed, granted territorial sanctuary and material support, and accorded maximum rights under international refugee conventions. In these respects, Pakistan's policy was notably liberal. Its refugees were relatively free to settle where they wished; by and large, they—not the government of Pakistan—chose the district and the camp in which to dwell, or whether to live in the camps at all. In Pakistan, the Afghan refugees were given substantial access to local resources. They were free, for instance, to find employment, to bring in their vehicles from Afghanistan and to use them on Pakistani highways, and to travel within Pakistan and abroad with very limited restriction.

Second, international relief organizations were also warmly welcomed and given a leading and highly visible role in support of the refugees. In sharp contrast to the practice of neighboring Iran in regard to its own vast refugee influx, Islamabad gave a friendly reception to over forty foreign private voluntary agencies (VOLAGS), not to mention a large assortment of foreign governmental and international relief agencies, that established headquarters in Pakistan.[40]

Third, the refugees' voluntary and unimpeded repatriation to Afghanistan was stipulated as the ultimate goal of Pakistan's policy and as an essential element of any negotiated settlement.

The reasons for Pakistan's strongly prorefugee orientation were relatively transparent. In the first place, the refugees, especially in the first few years of the influx from Afghanistan, were quickly and with relatively little friction absorbed into Pakistan. This made restrictions on their settlement and mobility both cumbersome and unnecessary. In fact, as we will take note of below, the refugees more often than not were a socioeconomic boon to the areas in which they settled.

In the second place, the prominence of international relief agencies was important as a tangible emblem of the international community's commitment to Pakistan's Afghanistan war policy. Having exposed itself to Soviet retaliation, Islamabad was loath to allow the impression to spread abroad that the war and its assorted heavy burdens were somehow Pakistan's to shoulder alone. In effect, these agencies served Pakistan as hostages against the erosion of international interest in the war, while also affording opportunity for Pakistan to publicize its humanitarian role and thus to compensate for its somewhat lean international reputation in the field of human rights.

An even more important reason for the warmth of Pakistan's welcome for international relief organizations, however, was pecuniary. By any standard, maintaining over 3 million refugees was bound to be expensive; and for Pakistan, faced with already staggering economic pressures of its own, taking on single-handedly the task of economic support of that many refugees was a daunting proposition to say the least. It was extremely important for Pakistan, therefore, that the international community carry the lion's share of the financial burden. Throughout the Zia period, that, in fact, is what the international community did.

Official Pakistani estimates of the total annual economic cost of maintaining the refugees in the mid-1980s generally ran around Rs 6 billion—an amount that converted roughly into about $1 million per day. In literally scores of statements and publications, Islamabad publicized this figure, claiming its own share to be about half (Rs 3 billion).[41] Strictly speaking, however, Pakistan's share never came close to 50 percent; the great bulk of relief came, in fact, from programs managed by two agencies of the United Nations—the UN High Commissioner for Refugees (UNHCR) and the World Food Programme. Nearly half of Pakistan's presumed 50 percent share was said by the government to be paid out in the form of a cash maintenance allowance (up to Rs 350 per refugee family per month). The evidence is overwhelming, however, that this allowance—which would have amounted by 1988 to about $120 million per year—was rarely if ever paid.[42]

In the third place, Pakistan's stress on the refugees' right to repatriation was obviously consistent with Islamabad's understandable concern that the burden of the refugee influx not become permanent. More than that, however, Islamabad sought to bind the international community morally and legally to the refugees' support, whether or not they ever returned to Afghanistan. The possibility always existed that the entire burden of maintaining the refugees might one day shift to Pakistan as a result of diminished international interest in the war. Establishing the refugees' right of return was a convenient measure for defeating "donor fatigue."

There is little doubt that Pakistan played its overt humanitarian role in the war well. It won nearly universal admiration for its generous and hospitable treatment of the refugees. It succeeded in getting the international community to bear the largest share of the refugees' financial burden. And it built into the Geneva accords a strong international commitment to an equitable solution of the refugee problem. These were considerable accomplishments. Seen from this perspective, the refugee influx was by no means an entirely negative development. Indeed, in terms of Pakistan's foreign relations, as a Pakistani physician in a refugee hospital in Peshawar commented, the refugee problem was a "good" problem.[43]

From the perspective of Pakistan's domestic politics, of course, the impact of the refugee influx was much more problematic and a source of intense political controversy. Particularly widespread was the argument that the Afghan refugees, whatever might be their social and economic impact on Pakistan, were a political time bomb and a major embarrassment to the government. The argument deserves close scrutiny.

IV. THE REFUGEE ISSUE IN PAKISTAN'S DOMESTIC POLITICS

In midsummer 1987, Afghan refugees in Pakistan were officially estimated to number 3.45 million—almost 3.5 percent of Pakistan's entire population and the largest refugee population in the world.[44] They were settled in 325 camps, most of them in rural areas of the two provinces—the NWFP and Baluchistan—adjoining the border between Pakistan and Afghanistan. Their flight from Afghanistan had begun over a decade earlier following the Marxist takeover in Kabul in April 1978. Since then, the scale of their misfortune had grown steadily.[45] By the end of Zia's rule, the influx of refugees had been substantially reduced. Nevertheless, the continuing presence of the refugees in Pakistan had emerged as one of the most contentious political issues in the country.

The Afghan refugees had been an issue in Pakistan's domestic politics virtually from the moment they first began to cross the border into Pakistan.[46] Practically everything about them—their numbers, their popularity among Pakistanis, their prowess as fighters, their impact on the economy, their fidelity to Islam, their desire to return home—had been inflated, distorted, or underrated at one time or another in the ongoing controversies over Pakistan's proper role in the Afghanistan conflict. Circumstances surrounding the refugee influx were hardly conducive to systematic study of anything about them, least of all their political impact in Pakistan. Implicit in these circumstances, however, was the great likelihood that their impact varied considerably from province to province and, within the provinces, from group to group and from district to district. Subtle differences of this kind, though bound to engage the attention of those charged with framing Pakistan's refugee policy, rarely entered the political debate. The nature and extent of these differences, and the political significance of them, are the focus of the following discussion.

North West Frontier Province

Of Pakistan's four provinces, hardest hit by the war in Afghanistan was the NWFP. It was the principal conduit for foreign-supplied military equipment to the Afghan resistance forces as well as the main staging ground for guerrilla operations inside Afghanistan. Its refugee camps provided military manpower and, in some cases, served as training facilities for the rebel guerrillas fighting Soviet/Afghan forces. Much of the heaviest fighting in the war went on in border areas of Afghanistan immediately adjacent to this province. As a result, it bore the brunt of frequent cross-border artillery shellings and air attacks.[47] It was also the principal target of retaliatory terrorist bombings. In 1986, for example, the NWFP experienced 143 fatalities or nearly 95 percent of a countrywide total of 151 deaths in such bombings.[48] Inevitably, the violence claimed Pakistani citizens as victims along with the Afghan refugees.

The refugee influx was clearly heaviest in the NWFP. This province held 247 (76 percent) of the 325 refugee camps in Pakistan in 1987 and about 2.15 million (68 percent) of the total refugee population [see Table 2.1]. There were refugees in most parts of the province, large numbers of them in ten of the twelve so-called settled districts of the province as well as in seven

Table 2.1
Distribution of Afghan Refugee Population in Pakistan in 1987 (by Province)

Province	Number of refugees	Percent
NWFP	2 150 460	68.1
Baluchistan	812 332	25.7
Punjab	175 188	5.5
Sind	18 674	.6
TOTAL:	3 156 654	100.0

Source: Adapted from Kamal Matinuddin, "Afghan Refugees: The Geo-Strategic Context," paper presented to the Fourth International Conference on Refugees in the Islamic World, Bellagio, Italy (October 1987) 36.

of the eight Federally Administered Tribal Areas (FATA) of the tribal belt. In a few districts, including Peshawar, containing the provincial capital, the refugees nearly equaled in number the indigenous population. In Kurram Agency, well over half of the population consisted of refugees. In fact, in the NWFP roughly every seventh person was a refugee; in the tribal belt, in particular, the proportion was closer to one in three or four.

Obviously, a human influx of this magnitude could not occur without heavy cost to the host society. The refugees were fierce competitors with indigenous Pakistanis for jobs. They undermined the earning power of unskilled Pakistani workers; and they threatened to displace Pakistanis entirely from the transport industry and from a number of petty trades. They drove up rents, spread disease, felled scarce timber, and overgrazed their flocks on common lands. They overflowed hospitals and other public facilities. Above all, they threatened to upset the established provincial political order and to deepen the antagonism that already existed between local right- and left-wing forces.

No doubt, the militant right-wing Jama'at-i-Islami Pakistan (JIP) party was among the political beneficiaries of the refugees' presence in the NWFP. By virtue of its close rapport with the martial law authorities then ruling in Islamabad, the JIP was certainly well placed in the early years of the influx to convert the refugees into a major political resource. According to its critics, the party profited in particular from its position astride the aid pipeline to the refugees. Enormous patronage lay at its disposal, it was alleged, due to its ability to influence government appointments to the provincial Afghan

Refugee Commissionerate, a bureaucratic colossus in Peshawar employing upward of 6000 Pakistanis and financed almost entirely by an agency of the United Nations (the UNHCR). The Commissioner of Afghan Refugees in the NWFP from 1980 until 1983, Sheikh Abdullah Khan, became the center of a storm of controversy when allegations surfaced in the Western press that he was using the Commissionerate's considerable resources to benefit the Jama'at's "fundamentalist" allies among the mujahideen.[49] In the opinion of some observers, the Jama'at employed its mujahideen clients in semicovert and violent battles against leftist opposition groups in the Frontier's rough-and-tumble politics.[50] There was even some speculation that the Jama'at would one day use its mujahideen "army-in-waiting" to take power by force in Islamabad.

The political left in the NWFP reacted to these allegations with an attack centering upon the government's refugee policy. In particular, the leadership of the Awami National Party (ANP) demanded an end to Islamabad's backing of the Afghan rebels and acceptance of Kabul's terms for the speedy repatriation of the refugees. ANP followers seemed to share their leaders' perspective. In a poll taken in 1987 by the Pakistan Institute of Public Opinion (PIPO), some 66 percent of ANP respondents, the largest percentage of any political party in Pakistan, expressed themselves against Pakistan's continued support of the Afghan mujahideen.[51]

Although the ANP was the standard-bearer of Pashtun nationalism in the NWFP, it unquestionably represented only a minority—some would claim a dwindling minority—of the Frontier's voters. On the other hand, opposition to Islamabad's refugee policy was certainly not confined to the ANP. In fact, in spite of the bonds both of Islamic faith and Pashtu language, support of the refugees seemed for practically all parties to have gradually become a substantial liability in provincial politics. Demands for the externment of the refugees from Peshawar and for their confinement to the refugee camps were routinely voiced by a broad spectrum of community and political leaders.[52] Apparently, even the staunchly Islamist JIP's local youth organization in Peshawar adopted an antirefugee position in 1987.[53] Confessed a top figure in the moderate Tehrik-i-Istiqlal party, himself a Pashtun with strong prorefugee leanings: "No Pashtun wants refugees or mujahideen to stay in Pakistan....The government's argument that the Afghans are our brothers carries no weight with the Pashtuns of the Frontier."[54]

Privately, even government officials in the NWFP admitted that Pakistani hospitality for the refugees was being stretched to its limits. Typical was the statement of a senior bureaucrat, a man with many years of experience in the tribal belt and himself a Pashtun, that "99 percent of the people of the Frontier are sick of the refugees. I have never met anyone in the tribal areas who wanted the refugees to stay in Pakistan....The 'cultural affinity' argument is used by the Government to dismiss allegations of friction between refugees and locals. In truth, the cultural likenesses only go so far in maintaining good relations....There is no deep sense of community between the refugees and the locals."[55]

Local tolerance for the refugees was thus far from unlimited in the NWFP. Neither, however, were the limits of tolerance particularly narrow. In fact, available evidence seemed to indicate that the refugees, while not exactly front-runners in popularity, generally provoked ambivalent—and often quite positive—feelings among the residents of the Frontier. For this, there were several reasons. First, the refugees were a powerful stimulus to the growth of markets in backward areas of the province and an abundant source of cheap labor in a labor-scarce environment.[56] Second, their influx unquestionably produced a bonanza for local propertied classes and shopkeepers, especially in the cities, as well as for the medical, legal, and teaching professions. Third, observers were nearly all agreed that the refugees were exceptionally law-abiding, and that refugee-caused disturbances were generally minor and very infrequent. According to the District Commissioner of Refugees for Peshawar district, a man with 60 refugee camps and nearly 500 000 refugees under his jurisdiction, the refugee crime rate for the whole district had been lower during his 3 years of service than the rate for just one police subdistrict (*thana*) of Peshawar district serving only 200 000 indigenous Pakistanis.[57]

Even the strongest antagonists of the government's refugee policy, including ANP leader Khan Abdul Wali Khan, conceded that the refugees were decent and industrious people, and that there had been almost no serious disputes in the Frontier between refugees and the settled population.[58] Ironically, Pakistani admiration for the refugees seemed to account for some of the resentment of them. As one Pakistani political leader put it, the Afghan refugees were seen as a threat by the local population precisely because they were virile, hardworking, honest, thrifty, strong, and courageous—and thus capable of moving in and taking over from the locals everywhere in the province.[59] Even more ironic, perhaps, was the fact that public opinion, in spite of the NWFP's proximity to the war in Afghanistan, seemed more strongly supportive of the Afghan mujahideen in that province than elsewhere in the country. PIPO nationwide polling results in 1987 revealed, for example, that Pakistan's Pashtu-speakers, who are mainly concentrated in the NWFP, ranked near the top of respondents expressing support of the guerrilla forces.[60]

Baluchistan

The province of Baluchistan clearly bore a heavy share of the refugee burden stemming from the war in Afghanistan. By the middle of 1987, the refugee influx into Baluchistan had climbed to over 800 000 registered refugees, yielding the same ratio of refugees-to-Pakistanis (roughly 1 in 7) that we found in the NWFP [see Table 2.1]. In at least one district (Chaghai), the refugees outnumbered the local Pakistani population; and in some others their number approached half. Though to a vastly lesser extent than the NWFP, Baluchistan suffered frequent Soviet/Afghan border violations; and its catalogue of economic and environmental ills resulting from the refugees' presence was as lengthy as that of the Frontier. Popular feeling against the refugees, it seemed, was even stronger in Baluchistan than in the NWFP. Polling data in 1987 indicated, for example, that Baluchi-speakers expressed the strongest sentiments of all Pakistanis in favor of withdrawing support from the mujahideen.[61]

In some respects, the political challenge posed by the refugees to the existing political order in Baluchistan was even more severe than in the NWFP. Even before the onset of the refugee influx, the indigenous Baluchi-speakers were very likely a minority, or nearly so, in their own province.[62] With the addition of the refugees, the overwhelming majority of whom were Pashtu-speaking, the threat to the province's already fragile ethnic balance was still greater.[63]

The demographic threat was only one element, however, of the refugees' political challenge to the indigenous Baluch. Baluch nationalists had fought an unsuccessful insurgency against Islamabad in the 1970s, during the course of which the Baluch had suffered heavy casualties and material losses.[64] After the Baluch defeat in 1977, the leader of the most militant of the insurgent tribes, Khair Bux Marri, chose self-exile, ultimately winding up in Afghanistan. There he and a few thousand Baluch guerrillas found refuge under the new PDPA regime in Kabul. Naturally, this alliance found little favor with the newly born Afghan mujahideen. Between them and the Baluch nationalists there soon grew an inevitable and very deep divide. Thus, in contrast with the situation in the NWFP, where there were cultural bonds and a certain amount of ideological similarity to promote solidarity between the refugees and the indigenous Pakistanis, neither was much in evidence in Baluchistan, at least insofar as the Baluch were concerned.

Somewhat suprisingly, perhaps, the friendship between Baluch nationalists and Soviet-backed Kabul, in fact, had very little material impact on the refugees. One reason for this was that the refugees in Baluchistan, unlike those in the Frontier, were concentrated in camps located almost entirely in one part of the province—the northern and Pashtun-settled tier of districts closest to Afghanistan, thus effectively isolating them from the Baluch, who were numerically dominant in the sprawling province's more southern districts.[65] Another reason was that the "Pashtun belt" of the province, built up over the years by a steady stream of Pashtu-speaking migrants heading south in search of opportunity, lay between the Baluch and their would-be political supporters in Afghanistan. Pashtuns in this area, heirs to a long tradition of rivalry with Baluch tribesmen, had strong political, in addition to ethnic and ideological, reasons for befriending the incoming refugees. In the tacit alliance thus formed between the indigenous Pashtuns and the refugees, Islamabad discovered a powerful antidote to Baluch nationalist impulses in the province. At least temporarily, the refugees were actually a useful political asset for Islamabad in Baluchistan, neutralizing otherwise unruly elements in the province. In part due to the presence of the refugees, the "nightmare in Baluchistan" predicted by an American writer in 1978 never materialized.[66]

Sind

The influx of Afghan refugees into Pakistan had far less direct impact on the Sind, the province geographically most distant from the country's border with Afghanistan, than on either Baluchistan or the NWFP. The only one of Pakistan's four provinces without any refugee camps, its refugee population was relatively small and concentrated mainly in Karachi. According to government statistics, registered refugees in the Sind in mid-1987 numbered fewer than 19 000 [see Table 2.1]. The actual number of Afghan refugees in the Sind was practically impossible to ascertain, in fact, for it consisted largely of unregistered refugees difficult to distinguish from Pakistani Pashtuns already settled in the area in large numbers. An estimate made in 1986 by the head of Pakistan's central refugee relief agency put the total of unregistered refugees in *both* the Sind and Punjab at no more than 50 000.[67]

The impact of the Afghan refugees on the Sind was probably more political than anything else, and in this respect their impact was clearly disproportionate to their numbers. Their arrival in the Sind happened to coincide with a steep increase in regionalist militancy in the province involving subnational groupings of Sindhis, Urdu-speaking Mohajirs (of Indian descent), Biharis (from Bangladesh), Punjabis, and Pashtuns. A widespread and violent antigovernment Sindhi agitation swept the province in autumn 1983; but it remained confined mainly to rural areas and consequently involved few if any of the Afghan refugees. In spring 1985, severe interethnic riots erupted in urban centers in the Sind, especially in Karachi and Hyderabad, and these were repeated in the next few years with both increasing frequency and ferocity. These disturbances involved mainly Urdu-speaking Mohajirs and Biharis on one side and Pashtun migrants from the NWFP, said to number anywhere from 1 to 2 million in Karachi alone, on the other. Though hard evidence was almost never produced, there were increasing allegations in the Pakistani press in this period that the Afghan refugees, widely seen as the political allies of the migrant Pashtun population, themselves were mainly responsible for the lawlessness, drug and gun smuggling that had spread alarmingly in the province in the course of the war. In December 1986, when Sind police razed Karachi's sprawling Sohrab Goth neighborhood in what the police claimed was a sweep for contraband arms and narcotics, the Afghan refugees domiciled in that area were for the first time accused of direct involvement in the rioting.[68]

Hostility toward the Afghan refugees was thus not an insignificant matter in the Sind. There were complaints against their influx into both urban and rural areas of the province; in addition, there were frequent demands for their externment from the province. Nevertheless, given the relatively modest size of the Afghan refugee element in most parts of the Sind, the hostility for refugees seemed far more a byproduct of preexisting ethnoregionalist rivalries and antigovernment sentiment than a direct result of the refugee influx itself.

Punjab

Of Pakistan's four provinces, undoubtedly the one to suffer the least from the Afghan refugee influx was the Punjab. There were, according to an official estimate, about 175 000 registered refugees in the province in mid-1987 [see Table 2.1]. For a number of reasons, however, their presence was hardly even noticed by the great bulk of Punjabis. Firstly, they were housed entirely in about twelve camps in the Isakhel subdistrict of Mianwali district in western Punjab. In accordance with terms of an agreement reached in late 1982 with the Punjab provincial government, these camps were methodically laid out well in advance of the refugees' arrival and a maximum ceiling of 200 000 was set on the number of refugees to be permitted to resettle in them.[69] The Indus River cuts Mianwali district into two parts. The part containing Isakhel subdistrict as well as the Afghan refugee camps lies on the west bank of the river, where it juts into the southern end of the NWFP. This part of Mianwali district is Pashtu-speaking. Politically, it was dominated by the fundamentalist Jamiat-ul-ulema-i-Islam party (JUI), a group generally prorefugee in orientation. It is wholly separated from the Punjabi-speaking part of the district on the east bank of the river. Thus, both in its manner and location refugee resettlement in the Punjab was little likely to provoke much controversy among Punjabis.

Secondly, outside of Mianwali district there were few Afghan refugees to be found in the Punjab. According to a Western diplomat posted in Lahore, there were no more than 2000 Pashtu-speakers (including *both* indigenous Pashtuns and Afghan refugees) in the entire city of Lahore—the Punjab's largest city with a population over 4 million—in 1987. In other cities of the Punjab, he said, there were even fewer.[70] The paucity of refugees in the Punjab was no doubt in some measure a result of the refugees' own choice: their numbers, after all, were greatest in those parts of the country—the NWFP, northern Baluchistan, and Karachi—where there were large numbers of their ethnic kin, the Pashtu-speaking Pashtuns, to provide welcome and support. The thinness of their ranks in the Punjab was also due, however, to the deliberate curbs placed on their interprovincial movement by the government of Punjab.[71] The Punjab is ethnically the most homogeneous of Pakistan's provinces and the refugees were relatively easy to spot, round up, and return to the NWFP.

Thirdly, neither the Afghan refugees nor the Afghanistan war itself was a major political issue in the Punjab. According to a diplomatic source, the war typically was not brought up for discussion on the floor of the Punjab provincial assembly on more than 5 occasions in a year's time. There had been a few terrorist bombings in the province, he said, but they did not seem to have made much of a dent in public attitudes toward the refugees. Insofar as foreign policy was concerned, he added, the threat from India was a far more salient issue in the Punjab than the threat from Afghanistan.[72] Public opinion surveys seemed to support his argument. In a 1987 poll, for example, more Punjabi-speakers expressed themselves in favor of continued Pakistani support of the Afghan mujahideen than were opposed.[73]

Critics of the government sometimes suggested that the Punjab's relatively benign view of the refugees stemmed from the huge economic and political benefits that had come to the province by virtue of Pakistan's "frontline" role in America's anti-Soviet strategy in the region. The Punjab prospered, it was said, while the minority provinces bled. This argument may have been ideologically tainted, of course. In any event, it was nicely summed up in the metaphor, attributed to ANP leader Khan Abdul Wali Khan, likening the refugees to a giant cow, the Frontier having hold of its horns, the Punjab of its teats!

From the above, one can conclude that the link between the Afghan refugees and Pakistan's internal politics, while clearly problematic, was multifaceted and resistant to facile generalization. The situation certainly did not warrant the judgment that Pakistanis were moving en masse to blanket disapproval of the refugees' presence in the country. On the contrary, Pakistanis were evidently not of one mind on the subject, with disapproval appearing strongest in the Sind and Baluchistan, weakest in the NWFP and Punjab. Ironically, proximity to the war seemed to have no decisive effect on how Pakistanis collectively felt about the refugees; in fact, where the impact was harshest, feelings toward them appeared relatively positive.

One should of course bear in mind here that unequivocal data of any kind on this issue simply didn't exist in Pakistan. The simple fact that the issue was many-sided (that Pakistan was a sanctuary, for example, both for noncombatant refugees and the jehad-waging guerrilla forces) obviously rendered the task of measuring popular sentiment about it unusually difficult. As we have seen, Pakistanis seem to have given strong backing to government support for the refugees, but their support of the guerrillas was a good bit less spectacular. In reality, of course, "refugees" and "guerrillas" were overlapping categories not very easily disentangled in a survey questionnaire. Polling data, in fact, were quite limited. Loud objection to the refugees' presence was raised by practically the entire leadership of the political opposition in the country; but one could not be certain that the leaders fully commanded the sentiment of the rank and file.

Most significant, perhaps, was the fact that Pakistan's most populous and powerful province, the Punjab, seemed relatively immune from the negative consequences of the refugee influx. On this issue, at least, the Punjab was not much of a headache for Islamabad. Indeed, the Punjab's relative indifference both to the Afghanistan war and to its harmful consequences in the three minority provinces freed the government's hand considerably in regard to managing the issue in those areas. In terms of domestic politics, in other words, Islamabad's refugee problem, while clearly not a "good" problem, wasn't such a bad one, either.

V. PAKISTAN AND THE AFGHAN RESISTANCE MOVEMENT

We have seen that Pakistan's Afghan policy was overtly pointed at mobilizing international political and diplomatic opposition to the Soviet military occupation of Afghanistan as well as at providing sanctuary and material relief for the massive refugee exodus. We have taken note, however, that

Pakistan's Afghan policy had another face. This was its (nominally) covert military support of the Afghan resistance movement. Scarcely concealed from public awareness even in the first years of the war, Pakistan's clandestine aid of the rebels eventually grew so massive that it became virtually impossible to conceal. Consistently denied by Islamabad, its covert assistance was in fact (and from the outset of the war) the centerpiece of Pakistan's policy upon which everything else depended. It generated much more heated domestic political controversy than did Pakistan's care of the refugees, some quarters in Pakistan charging that Islamabad was not doing enough to aid the guerrilla struggle, others that it was doing far too much. To the extent it motivated the ultimate Soviet decision to exit from Afghanistan, it was hugely successful.

Militarily, Pakistan supported the resistance in numerous ways. It provided the guerrilla forces with sanctuary, unrestricted access to the refugee camps for recruitment, and almost complete freedom of movement across the international border. It consented to act as the principal conduit for arms supplies coming from Egypt, China, the United States, and elsewhere.[74] Its army, furthermore, imparted intelligence, training in weapons, as well as operational and logistical support to the guerrillas. The army's operational guidance of the mujahideen extended well beyond instruction. Beginning at a fairly early point in the war, selected officers and enlisted men of the Pakistan army's commando-trained Special Services Group (SSG) were detached from regular duty, given special training and assigned to guerrilla units for operations inside Afghanistan. They participated directly in hundreds of reconnaisance, sabotage, and combat operations against both Soviet and Afghan government forces.[75]

As noted earlier in this chapter, Pakistan's military support of Afghan mujahideen groups began before Zia came to power. Marxist takeover of Afghanistan in April 1978 dramatically accelerated development of the resistance movement as also the pace of Pakistan's military involvement in it. By April 1979, months prior to the Soviet military intervention, Soviet media were accusing Pakistan of infiltrating into Afghanistan Pakistani troops disguised as Afghans, of operating twelve training camps for the resistance on Pakistani soil, and of harboring on Pakistani soil American and Chinese military instructors who had, they said, already embarked on the training of 1000 mujahideen.[76] By the end of 1980, both Kabul and Moscow media were alleging the existence of thirty such camps, staffed by Pakistani and a variety of other foreign instructors, and the number of alleged camps grew steadily thereafter.[77] Even allowing for exaggeration both in the number and quality of camps, a network of camps for training guerrillas clearly already existed inside the Pakistani frontier even before the Soviet military intervention; and following Soviet intervention, as the war spread and intensified, the network undoubtedly spread with it.

Management of Pakistan's covert programs of military support of the Afghan resistance was lodged in the country's top national security agency, the army's Directorate for Inter-Services Intelligence (ISI). Formed in 1949 as an external-oriented military intelligence organization, the ISI by the 1970s had grown into a sprawling intelligence superagency with responsibility for domestic as well as foreign intelligence. For long the target of intense criticism from Zia's domestic political opponents, the ISI acquired vast new powers from its commanding role in funneling as much as $2.5 billion in U.S. aid to the Afghan rebels following the Soviet move into Afghanistan in 1979.[78] Lieutenant General Akhtar Abdul Rahman Khan, Director General of the ISI for most of the Zia period, was widely regarded as a key ally of Zia in the making of Pakistan's Afghan policy and as one of the most powerful men in the country.[79]

Viewed from whatever angle, the covert side of Pakistan's involvement in Afghanistan was both long-term and massive. Oddly, however, for this aspect of its role in the Afghan war Pakistan rarely got much praise. Many published accounts of the war by Western analysts, even those favorably disposed to Pakistan, largely or wholly ignored the subject of its covert role. And when the subject was addressed, Pakistan was often described as an impediment to the guerrilla movement rather than as a benefactor of it. The milder sorts of criticism focused on Islamabad's ambivalence toward the resistance, on its reticence to become involved in advance of solid assurances of foreign backing, and on the steps it took to lessen the risks of reprisal. These characteristics, as outlined above, were no doubt present. The mistake of many observers was to report them, often in exaggerated terms, and nothing else, as well as to take Islamabad's public postures as clear indication of its policy. One volume published in 1981 suggested, for example, that the Pakistanis were as much concerned with confiscating weapons destined for the resistance as with supplying them to it. Its authors wrote that "at Pakistan border checkpoints weapons are routinely confiscated. Yet arms sales to Afghans are not prevented. Smuggling across Afghan's borders has long since become institutionalized." They conceded that Pakistan's "announced policies against arms movements may therefore serve primarily to avert Soviet retaliation rather than to block actual shipments." They concluded rather gloomily, however, that "such evidence as we have suggests that they [the Pakistanis] have not clamped down totally, despite their official protestations. Much more significant, however, has been their discouragement of assistance from other governments, which has the effect of seriously limiting the amounts and kinds of supplies that can get through to the mujahidin."[80]

More serious criticism was directed at Pakistanis for diverting to their own use shipments of supplies meant for the Afghan resistance. In commenting on the vital importance of outside assistance for the survival of the resistance, the author of one book, for example, faulted in particular the distribution system that had been erected for supplying foreign arms to the mujahideen. "In theory," he said, "the weapons are passed on to the Pakistanis for distribution to the Afghans." The Pakistanis, however, reluctant to act too openly as an arms conduit, had "prevented too many heavy or sophisticated weapons from slipping through." Instead, "Pakistani officials, with the connivance of certain Afghan 'resistance' circles, have helped themselves to the shipments, allowing brand-new Kalashnikovs to be replaced by old Chinese-made Pakistan army issue rifles. Crates of new combat boots leaving the port of Karachi arrive at their destination in the form of second-hand rejects. Machine guns simply disappear en route to reappear for sale in the weapons bazaars."[81] Islamabad naturally maintained a discreet silence over such reports; and hard evidence of direct Pakistani involvement in illicit activity of this kind was hard to find. Most estimates of the amounts involved were highly speculative; but judging from numerous comments made to the author by Pakistanis with firsthand knowledge of the Pakistani trade in contraband arms and supplies, the 1987 estimate in a leading American newsmagazine that Pakistani middlemen, including high-ranking military officers, were skimming off 30 percent or more of covert U.S. aid to the guerrillas, may not have been much exaggerated, if at all.[82] Diversion of arms and corruption on a simply colossal scale, by Pakistanis among others, were among the war's more prominent characteristics. Any doubt about this had vanished within a few years of the war's onset. Also vanished by then was any reason to doubt allegations of major involvement in these practices by top-ranking officers of the Pakistan army, especially ISI officers.

The Afghan resistance itself, however, was clearly less bothered by these charges than were Western writers. Resistance leaders themselves were among those who profited; and the problem of arms in Afghanistan in any event was at all times much more one of quality than one of quantity. Moreover, Western writers rarely took account of the fact that corruption, as colossal as it undoubtedly was, was still only one of many characteristics of Pakistan's engagement in the war. Senior Afghan resistance leaders interviewed by the author in Peshawar in 1986, for example, almost uniformly disparaged the civilian Pakistani *provincial* adminstration of the refugee program, calling it corrupt, grossly inefficient, and often downright hostile to the resistance movement. At the same time, however, they expressed extremely high praise for the assistance rendered to them by the central government in Islamabad and by the Pakistan army. The military advisors with whom they worked most closely they described, in particular, as professional, dedicated to the mujahideen cause, and honest. One guerrilla intelligence officer with advanced education confided to the author, for instance, that the Pakistanis—upon whom the guerrillas, he said, were wholly dependent for arms—were after all taking a major risk in provoking the Soviets. According to him, if some in the Pakistani military were diverting to their own use some of the arms meant for the Afghan resistance forces, they deserved the arms and he felt no resentment against them.[83]

The most serious charge leveled against Pakistan, however, was that its policy toward the Afghan guerrillas was ideologically motivated and that this, unlike the possibly forgivable sin of greed, was a basic threat to the integrity and ultimate success of the resistance movement. What was generally meant by this was that Zia, who seemed to be a zealous promoter of Islamization in Pakistan, favored the so-called "fundamentalist" over the "traditionalist" mujahideen organizations, thus contributing to the existing problems of disunity within the resistance as well as to the sense of alienation that was said to be growing between the resistance as a whole and the masses of the Afghan people. There were numerous corollaries to this charge—that Zia was himself an Islamic fundamentalist, that he saw a fundamentalist-ruled Afghanistan as Pakistan's best defense against future security threats from that direction, that weapons and supplies were parceled out to the mujahideen on the basis of ideological rather than performance criteria, and, finally, that Islamic militancy was a more divisive than unifying force in Afghan society.

These charges began to be made at a very early point in the war and they quickly acquired considerable popularity both among Pakistanis and foreign observers. They never lost their popularity and, indeed, in some quarters—especially the Pakistani print media—acquired the status almost of dogma. Not enough is known either of the motivations or methods of the Zia regime to rule these charges entirely out of consideration. The weight of available evidence, however, seems tilted against them.

Most easily dismissed of them is the claim that Zia was himself an Islamic fundamentalist and thus naturally moved Pakistan's foreign policy in that direction. The word "fundamentalist," in fact, fit Zia very poorly, no matter what meaning was given to it. In the first years of his regime and for understandable reasons, Zia relied on the Islamist elements in Pakistan, in particular the Jama'at-i-Islami party, for political support. Prominent Jama'at leaders, such as Professor Khurshid Ahmad, served in Zia's cabinet under martial law in the period 1978-79, and played an important, albeit informal, advisory role in the government thereafter. The Jama'at, which at the time had a bitterly antagonistic relationship with virtually the entire political opposition in Pakistan, had itself very little to choose from. Though Zia's much-publicized efforts to introduce an Islamic Order in Pakistan fell far short of the Jama'at's expectations, he was far preferable to the likely alternatives and his all-important Afghan policy was largely to the Jama'at's liking.[84] In most respects, however, Zia was mainly a disappointment to Pakistan's right-wing Islamists. The reasons for this were explained particularly well by a Pakistani academic with close links to the Jama'at. "Zia," he said,

> was a middle-class average Pakistani. He was not a fundamentalist, but a secularist and pragmatist. He stood between the two worlds of East and West, no doubt, but he was basically what Pakistanis call a "deshi"—one who is at home in Pakistan, at home in the Urdu language, religious but not fanatically as depicted in the West. In 1977, he recognized the political utility of Islam and coopted it. Always, however, his first concern was his own political survival, not the propagation of Islam. Zia was a man of no vision, no programs, Islamic or otherwise. He was incapable even of imagining a project for spreading Islamic influence from Pakistan to Afghanistan and beyond. Zia was above all else a man of the status quo! His children were wholly secular. His closest military intimates, including [ISI Chief] Akhtar and [Vice Chief of Army Staff] Arif, were secular. Zia was comfortable with secularists, not with fundamentalists....Zia did not want a fundamentalist Afghanistan any more than he wanted a fundamentalist Pakistan. What he wanted in Kabul was a regime that would combine elements of the mujahideen in a way that would exclude the radical pro-Pashtunistan elements, including the loyalists of ex-King Zahir Shah.[85]

Whether Zia nevertheless showered more attention and benefits on the fundamentalist mujahideen groups than on their traditionalist rivals is a more difficult question to answer. There were at least six mujahideen groups already based in Peshawar at the time of the Soviet invasion. These multiplied substantially following the invasion, but they were soon winnowed to seven main parties. Of these seven, four were commonly classed as fundamentalist or Islamist, three as traditionalist or moderate.[86] Some were much more successful than others in securing outside assistance. In particular, some of the fundamentalist groups enjoyed the very valuable patronage of Pakistan's Jama'at-i-Islami party. All seven, however, were recognized by the Pakistan government and all seven were unquestionably materially aided by it.

In parceling out aid to the mujahideen, Islamabad appears to have been motivated largely by *raison d'état*. French scholar Olivier Roy's comments in this regard are instructive. "The extent to which ideological affinities determined the preferences of the Pakistan government," he wrote in a well-regarded study of the Afghan resistance first published in 1985,

> has long been overestimated. In fact, the Pakistan government has not especially supported the Islamists, but has brought in other organisations to assist it in meeting its responsibilities. Relations with the Islamist parties are handled by means of the Pakistan *jama'at*, while the army has dealt directly with the moderate parties. Any special treatment that the Islamists did receive would have come through certain highly placed members of the *jama'at*, such as the commissioner for refugees in the north-west province [i.e., Sheikh Abdullah]. The Islamist section which was particularly favoured was the Hizb, which had close ties with the Pakistan *jama'at*, both parties being predominantly Pashtun. Relations between the *jama'at* and the Afghan Islamists were established on a firm footing as long ago as 1965 by Pakistani Pashtun...But, while the policies of General Zia and those of the *jama'at* pursued the same goals until the spring of 1983, they did so for different reasons. The stance taken by the *jama'at*—and in this it resembles all the other Islamist organisations—is dictated by purely ideological considerations, underpinned by a network of personal relations; it recognises only the alliance of the Islamist parties and, like the Saudis, requires that the appearance of unity should be maintained since it believes this to be a visible expression of the *umma*. Its preferred leaders were Sayyaf and Hekmatyar. Zia's government maintained an even-handed attitude towards the two alliances, hoping to control the resistance by avoiding any imbalance in favour of the Islamists; in this it was not moved by any ideological considerations.[87]

Notwithstanding Islamabad's apparent ideological evenhandedness, however, there is little doubt that the bulk of weapons and supplies, during most of the Zia period, did wind up in the hands of the fundamentalist mujahideen. In part, this was a consequence of an association between the government of Pakistan and the fundamentalist leaders, in particular Burhanuddin Rabbani, Gulbuddin Hekmatyar, and Yunus Khalis, reaching back to the Bhutto regime in the 1970s. This association had intensified during the 20 months between the Marxist revolution in Afghanistan in April

1978 and the Soviet move into Afghanistan in December 1979. In contrast, the traditionalist groups joined the movement after the Soviet invasion and were thus less well established as aid claimants.

The favored position of the fundamentalist groups was even more the consequence, however, of differences in the performance of the two wings of the movement. In the judgment of virtually all informed observers, right- and left-wing and including even their harshest critics, the fundamentalist groups by and large were the most effectively organized, most highly motivated, and best led of the mujahideen.[88] Moreover, while their own claims in this regard were often highly fanciful, they seem to have done most of the fighting. Quite apart from any ideological sympathies, in other words, Zia's pragmatism would have inclined him to favor the fundamentalists.

A large part of the dispute over Zia's alleged favoritism toward certain mujahideen groups had little to do, in fact, with the rivalry between the fundamentalist and traditionalist wings of the movement, as such, but with the controversial role in the resistance movement of one of the fundamentalist chiefs—Gulbuddin Hekmatyar. Charismatic leader of the Hezb-i-Islami Afghanistan (Afghanistan Islamic Party), Hekmatyar was one of those who launched the mujahideen movement against the Daoud regime with Pakistan's support in the early 1970s. Ideologically radical, Hekmatyar was widely credited with having created the most effective and smooth-running political organization in the movement, with a relatively sophisticated public relations section and a solid core of disciplined and ideologically committed subordinates. His critics in Pakistan, including many within the resistance itself, accused him of an extraordinary range of misconduct, including homosexuality, ruthless torture and killing of his adversaries within the resistance, and even collaboration with the Soviet Union. "A man of few scruples," wrote Girardet,

> Hekmatyar has aroused violent antagonism among his fellow compatriots. He is regarded as ruthless, uncompromising and devious, or as one foreign observer noted "dictatorship material at its worst," and is often accused of trying to establish his own hegemony at the expense of the Afghan resistance. The Hezb has been associated with the assassination of scores of political adversaries in Pakistan and Afghanistan and is known to operate its own jails, where kidnapped mujahed opponents have been tortured and killed.... Above all, many resistance detractors hold Hekmatyar responsible for consistently undermining mujahed groups in the field....Both outside observers and reliable resistance sources have witnessed armed Hezb assaults against fellow mujahideen, even in the midst of battle with the Soviets....Hekmatyar disclaims all responsibility for such attacks, either disowning them completely or maintaining that his supporters are not

involved. His stab-in-the-back methods, however, have led many to believe that he is working in tacit co-operation with the Soviets.[89]

Hekmatyar's unsavory reputation was not simply the result of the Afghans' culturally acquired fondness for character assassination. Nor was it solely a product of his detractors' ideological bias, a charge which Hekmatyar's lieutenants freely hurled at his opponents. On the contrary, even Hekmatyar's supporters in Pakistan generally conceded that he was no saint. In his defense, however, they insisted that his personal characteristics were largely irrelevant in the context of the war, moreover, that far too much was being made in the Western press of internecine feuds among the mujahideen groups. With perhaps less than full conviction, they tended to dismiss these as inevitable struggles over turf.[90]

By far the most damaging charge leveled against Hekmatyar was that the Hezb, supposed by many to be the recipient of a disproportionate share of external aid, mainly stockpiled the weapons for a future showdown with the other resistance leaders and rarely did any fighting against the Soviets. Olivier Roy, among others, was quite emphatic on this point. "The strategy of the Hizb," he said,

> consisted in avoiding direct contact with Soviet troops and in establishing firm bases, like the famous camp of Allah Jirga, which was more or less an enclave in Pakistan territory. (Here the Hizb put on a display for the benefit of journalists who were short of time, and stored a formidable arsenal which might prove useful in any post-war conflict, *since its present-day military involvement was nil.*) Places where the Hizb has established a presence are, in general, situated on the main lines of communication of the resistance and not of the Soviet army..., and at regular intervals the Hizb has organised a full blockade of [rebel-controlled] Panjshir.[91]

Roy's statement is puzzling because he does not explain why a government (in his words) "not moved by any ideological considerations" and "more favourable to the resistance than any conceivable replacement would be" would still continue to sponsor a guerrilla organization as wholly crippling to the resistance as Roy says the Hezb was.[92] Only a government much less committed to the Afghan resistance movement than Zia's, it seems, would pursue such a self-defeating course of action. In any event, Roy's viewpoint has been fiercely contested not only by spokesmen of the Hezb-i-Islami, but by many Pakistani and outside observers of the resistance struggle interviewed by the author in Pakistan.[93] Included among these were some with both long-term and intimate knowledge of Pakistan's covert military ties to the mujahideen. Their appraisals of the Hezb's war-fighting potential and practice were admittedly far from uniform. Some insisted that Hekmatyar outshone all of the other leaders, that he was effective militarily inside Afghanistan, that he was the target of particularly virulent propaganda, and that the suggestion that he was stockpiling arms in Pakistan for use against other mujahideen was unworthy of comment. Others conceded only that the Hezb did its "fair share" of the fighting against the Soviet/Afghan forces. Still others maintained that the fundamentalists, in general, unquestionably did most of the fighting but that the Hezb had gradually lost its place as front-runner among them. Hardly anyone with extensive knowledge of guerrilla operations in Afghanistan, however, took a position quite as negative as Roy's.

Gulbuddin Hekmatyar was unquestionably an enigmatic figure, and this is not the place to attempt to unravel the seeming contradictions that abound in regard to his role in the Afghan war. Adequate information in regard to his role—or in regard to Pakistan's material support of him—at the moment simply does not exist in the public domain; and much that has been written about him is highly subjective, based on extremely limited observation of both the man and his organization, and often seems largely partisan in inspiration. Much the same may be said of Zia's supposed favoritism toward Hekmatyar, allegations of which are far more common than evidence in support of them. Until this war's many complexities, including the mainly hidden pattern of linkages between foreign governments and the government of Pakistan, between the government of Pakistan and the Peshawar-based mujahideen parties, and between them and the war-fighting commanders in the field inside Afghanistan, are better investigated, all such allegations must necessarily be treated with considerable caution.

Generally speaking, Pakistan's covert role in the Afghan war in the Zia period was not well understood in the West and even less well appreciated. This was in part the result, as pointed out earlier, of Pakistan's official denials of military involvement and the related difficulty of gaining access to credible information in regard to it. More than that, however, it was the result of a fairly widespread and none too flattering impression of the quality of Pakistan's contribution to the mujahideen's war-fighting abilities. This impression clearly had a grounding in fact: there is virtually no question, for example, that Islamabad, in seeking to frustrate Soviet designs in Afghanistan without stimulating an inordinate increase in Pakistan-Soviet enmity, discouraged unity among the mujahideen to ease its control of them and—much of the time—armed them lightly to avoid excessive provocation of the Soviets. In several fundamental respects, however, the impression ran quite contrary to fact. After all, no other outside power involved itself so long, so fully, and so directly in the resistance effort or took greater risks on its behalf as did Pakistan. By any fair reckoning, there was nothing in Pakistan's Afghan policy, overt or covert, that would merit a description of it as appeasement. Zia's policy was certainly restrained, in other words, but it wasn't cowardly.

Perhaps the supreme irony of Pakistan's dual—overt and covert—Afghan war policy is that it was declared by many observers to be nothing more than an extension of U.S. policy (that Zia, in other words, involved Pakistan in the war at the bidding of Washington, not by virtue of Pakistan's own calculation of its national interest), when in fact Pakistan was never an unwilling participant at all. For good reasons, Islamabad chose to downplay its military role in Afghanistan, leaving it to the Reagan administration, for quite dissimilar reasons, to publicize its own. Islamabad's inescapable duplicity in this regard naturally caused considerable awkwardness in the conduct of its Afghan policy. This had been apparent throughout the war. It was equally apparent in the process of negotiating a settlement.

VI. THE GENEVA SETTLEMENT

On 14 April 1988, representatives of four governments—Pakistan, Afghanistan, the Soviet Union and the United States—signed agreements in Geneva concluding just under 6 years of United Nations-sponsored negotiations aimed at bringing to an end the war in Afghanistan. The settlement consisted of four instruments. Two of these were bilateral agreements between Afghanistan and Pakistan, the one pledging them to noninterference and nonintervention in one another's internal affairs, the other establishing procedures for the voluntary and orderly return to their homeland of Afghan refugees. A third instrument was the declaration on international guarantees, signed by the United States and the Soviet Union, committing them to refrain from interference and intervention in the internal affairs of Pakistan and Afghanistan as well as to act as coguarantors of the entire settlement. The fourth instrument —the Agreement on the Interrelationships for the Settlement of the Situation Relating to Afghanistan—was signed by all four governments, the Soviet Union and the United States acting as witnesses. Apart from gaining the signatories' formal recognition of the interdependent and contingent nature of the agreements, this instrument provided for the withdrawal of Soviet armed forces from Afghanistan within a period of nine months beginning 15 May 1988.[94]

Crafted to a large extent by U.N. mediator Diego Cordovez through twelve rounds of often frustrating negotiations, the Geneva accords were undeniably a major victory for Pakistani foreign policy and diplomacy. For over 8 years, Pakistan had led the protest in the United Nations and other international forums against Soviet military intervention in Afghanistan. It had given generous support to the Afghan rebels in the face both of demoralizing international indifference to the fate of the Afghans and strong Soviet displeasure. It had borne the burden of millions of refugees and of relentless Soviet/Afghan retaliation. When Lieutenant General Boris V. Gromov, the last Soviet soldier to leave Afghanistan, crossed the Friendship Bridge to Termez in Soviet Uzbekistan right on schedule on 15 February 1989, any doubt that Pakistan had had a role in handing Moscow a stunning politico-strategic reversal was finally vanquished.

It was obvious even at the time, however, that Pakistan's victory was quite partial and in no small measure conditional. The accords contained no provision for a ceasefire. Neither did they address mujahideen demands for reconstitution of the government in Kabul. They were supposed to bring about the disengagement from Afghanistan of foreign powers (Pakistan, United States, Soviet Union); and the end of foreign interference, in turn, was expected to facilitate achievement of internal peace and conditions suited to the repatriation of refugees.[95] All they really accomplished, however, at least in the short term, was the withdrawal of Soviet forces.

The accords' painstakingly constructed fourth instrument on interrelationships, designed to weld the several parts of the settlement into a comprehensive whole, had begun to fall apart even before the signing in Geneva. At the last minute, in a move widely seen to have undercut the noninterference commitment of the agreement, Washington challenged Moscow's right to continue arms aid to Kabul. Arguing that Moscow's unrestricted supply of arms to its PDPA clients gave Kabul a military advantage in the face of the agreement's mandatory cutoff of arms to the Afghan resistance, Washington seems to have won Moscow's tacit consent to "positive symmetry," the right of both to continue arming their proxies.[96] At the same time, what Cordovez said was the essential "second track" of the peace process—involvement of the resistance in an intra-Afghan dialogue over the establishment of a future broad-based government in Kabul—never got off the ground. Instead, both sides continued to make heavy arms deliveries to their Afghan clients and the war went on as bitterly as before.

Absence from the negotiating agenda in Geneva of the issue of the Afghan government's future composition had all along loomed as a potential obstacle to settlement. It had been a particularly vexing matter for Pakistan, whose negotiators were compelled to maintain a public pose of noninterference in Afghanistan that had little resemblance to Pakistan's actual role in the war.

That role, as we have seen, had involved a strong military commitment to the rebels. The rebels' declared objective, unambiguously and consistently maintained, was the military defeat of Kabul's Soviet-backed forces and overthrow of the PDPA regime. That clearly differed from Islamabad's own more modest objective, at least for the larger part of the war, for so long as the Kabul regime was solidly protected by Soviet armed forces, its actual military overthrow, to all but the most ardent propagandists, seemed highly improbable. With the brightening of prospects for a negotiated Soviet military withdrawal, however, the opportunity naturally cropped up for Islamabad to move beyond a relatively modest strategy of defensive destabilization of the Afghan government to one encompassing active contemplation of its replacement. Understandably, therefore, Pakistan's public stand on the issue of the Afghan government's future composition, especially in the final stages of the Geneva negotiations, did not fully reflect its leaders' ambitions.

Faced with Kabul's implacable opposition, Islamabad had agreed in the preliminary stages of the talks to bar participation in them by the Afghan rebels. By way of compensation, it had then proposed inclusion on the agenda of Afghan "self-determination." This Moscow and Kabul had also emphatically opposed, however, and in April 1982, much to Washington's chagrin, it seems, Pakistan agreed to drop it.[97] According to Agha Shahi, Pakistan's Foreign Minister when the agenda for the talks was first being considered in 1981, insistence on any such proposal at that time, since it would have raised the prospect for the dissolution of one of the parties to the talks before they had even begun, was simply out of the question.[98] Pakistan did reject Kabul's demand for direct government-to-government talks, however, since these would have implied Islamabad's recognition of the communist regime. It insisted instead on U.N.-sponsored negotiations in which Afghanistan would be represented only by officials of the ruling PDPA. Ultimately, Pakistan settled for the indirect government-to-government negotiating format offered as a compromise by Cordovez.[99]

During the first two rounds of negotiation, Islamabad continued to raise the Afghan self-determination issue, but in muted form. It confined itself mainly to a demand for cosmetic change in Kabul—to Babrak Karmal's replacement, in other words, with someone less identified with the Soviet military intervention. Achieving more than that seemed to Pakistani policymakers, under the circumstances then prevailing, to be unrealistic. Pakistan's Foreign Minister at the time, Sahabzada Yakub Khan, was said to have conceded privately in late 1982, for instance, that Pakistan could "restore something like the situation that obtained before the Soviets came in—that is, a national communist setup. But we seriously doubt that we can turn the clock back before 1978."[100] Between the second and third rounds of negotiation, however, Yakub appeared to make a sudden break with this sentiment, demanding instead that a new, noncommunist government be installed in Kabul as the price of settlement. Yakub blamed the Soviets for undermining the negotiations. Selig Harrison, in his account of the talks, suggests that Pakistan probably bowed to American pressure, tacit or otherwise, and that failure to test ailing Soviet leader Yuri Andropov's intentions at that point may have been a serious miscalculation.[101] In any event, Andropov died not long thereafter and the issue of the Afghan regime's fate was temporarily set aside.

At the end of 1986, the problem of the postwar political succession in Kabul once again rose to the surface. Prompted by the Soviet Union, Kabul, for its part, launched a much-publicized effort to bring noncommunist Afghans into a coalition government with the PDPA. In November, it adopted a new constitution; and on 30 December, it announced plans to form a "government of national reconciliation." These efforts were dismissed by Washington as a tactic for perpetuating communist rule. By that time, both Pakistan and the United States had shifted to the position that the future of the Kabul regime should not be decided until after a firm date had been fixed for the withdrawal of Soviet forces. The Soviet Union and Kabul responded in spring 1987 with the demand that a broader-based regime be put in place as a precondition for the withdrawal of Soviet troops. Cordovez drafted a compromise proposal in July 1987 involving formation of a transitional or interim government that would include the PDPA but that would assure predominance to no party.[102] His proposal won no support. Islamabad at that time held fast to its demand for a shortened timetable for Soviet withdrawal. The negotiations appeared stalemated.

In the months between the September 1987 round of negotiations and 8 February 1988, when Gorbachev capitulated to Pakistan's demand for a much-shortened and date-specific timetable while at the same time formally dropping its own precondition that the pullout be linked to formation of a new coalition government, a dramatic softening occurred in the Soviet position. Most of the world rejoiced; but Pakistani policymakers, while undoubtedly welcoming the change, were clearly extremely upset by it. Not only did it expose the latent tension between the public and private strands of Islamabad's Afghan policy, but it also produced a major crisis within the Pakistan government over the issue of Afghanistan's future political order. Zia, on one hand, appears to have wanted Pakistan's negotiators to hold out for a change in government in Kabul; the civilian-led regime of Prime Minister Junejo, on the other hand, seemed strongly inclined to facilitate Soviet withdrawal. The result was a startling decision, revealed hardly more than a month before the final round of negotiations was scheduled to begin, that appeared to reverse Pakistan's entire position. On 24 January 1988, Zia announced in a press interview that Pakistan would not sign an agreement with officials of the Kabul regime then in power and that an interim coalition government excluding Najibullah and acceptable to the Afghan guerrilla forces had to be brought into being in advance of any settlement.[103]

Pakistan argued that the safe and assured return of the refugees lay at the heart of its concerns, that no agreement would work that did not have the support of the mujahideen leaders, and that Soviet departure alone did not supply credible assurance either that the fighting in Afghanistan would end or that conditions would change sufficiently to induce the bulk of the refugees to return to their homeland.[104] These arguments were valid enough, but they clearly failed to provide adequate explanation for Zia's eleventh-hour change of mind. Over the years, Pakistan itself had floated a number of proposals with far less severe terms in regard to the Kabul regime than what it was now advancing. In the months immediately preceding Zia's January announcement, moreover, the four instruments of the accords had been all but completed without serious objection from Pakistan. Indeed, only days in advance of Zia's announcement, he had said in another interview that only a compromise formula that provided representation in an interim government for all the warring factions in Afghanistan, including the pro-Moscow PDPA, could guarantee an end to the fighting.[105] Something else, it seemed, must have been at work to compel Zia to take a step that seriously embarrassed his government, alarmed his closest allies, and threatened to bring on the complete collapse of the Geneva talks.

Selig Harrison suggests that Zia's *volte-face* stemmed both from his frustration, not only with his Western allies but with the civilian government of Prime Minister Junejo, and from his confidence that Moscow had lost the will to defend its client in Kabul. Zia, he says,

> wanted to install a Kabul regime headed by its Islamic fundamentalist Afghan protégés, notably Gulbuddin Hekmatyar's Hizbe-Islami....Zia was pushed into going along with the accords by an assertive civilian cabinet and insistent allies. Confident that Moscow would eventually cave in, Zia wanted to hold out for a change of regime in Kabul even if it meant a collapse of the negotiations....After the signing, Zia favored a lightning military campaign to depose Najibullah and install a Kabul regime dominated by Islamabad-sponsored fundamentalist resistance factions.[106]

According to Harrison, Zia was terribly isolated in this period, his authority challenged from every side, and for all practical purposes had lost control over the negotiations. "On Junejo's instructions," he writes, "the foreign ministry had stopped clearing decisions with Zia during the last months of the U.N. negotiations. Cordovez recalled that Zia telephoned him in Geneva 'almost every night' during the final weeks to find out what Pakistani negotiators were doing and to vent his own views."[107]

Harrison's depiction of Zia as a man virtually stripped of power and reduced to making desperate phone calls to Geneva to keep abreast of his own negotiators strains credulity. No other evidence has come to light to lend it weight. Few, however, would contest Harrison's observation that Zia had grown increasingly isolated politically and that his authority was being gradually undermined by the elected civilian cabinet. Only days after the opening of the final round of negotiations in Geneva, for example, Junejo, in an obvious bid to mobilize opinion against Zia's hardened stand, called a 2-day meeting in Islamabad of leaders of 19 opposition political parties to confer on the question of signing the accords. The main thrust of the speeches, as expected, was that Pakistan should avoid taking an "extreme position" that might bring a halt to the negotiations.[108]

Much less in conformity with the facts, I think, is the other half of Harrison's argument, namely that Zia was motivated also by his confidence that Moscow would cave in sooner or later anyway and that by standing firm in regard to the demand for a change of regime in Kabul Pakistan could best assure the ultimate triumph of his fundamentalist clients. Harrison does not stand alone in this view. A retired Pakistani diplomat with intimate knowledge both of Zia's political outlook and his policy-making behavior explained Zia's policy reversal to the author in not dissimilar terms. Zia, he said, along with ISI chief General Akhtar, had come to the conclusion that Moscow's Afghan policy was in disarray and that Gorbachev would likely cave in if pressure were sustained. Urged on by Akhtar, he said, Zia may have thought that with his fundamentalist Afghan allies seated in Kabul, Pakistan would be able to carry out subversive activities even in Soviet Central Asia. Zia himself might then emerge as a hero of the Islamic world. It was very possible, he observed, that Zia's success in inflicting a political defeat on the Soviet Union had dulled his sense of reality and weakened his judgment. Zia, he thought, may at the time have been caught in the grip of megalomania.[109]

These are provocative suggestions. The trouble with them, however, is that they do not square very well with what is known publicly of Zia's character and temperament. Neither, as we discussed above, do they square very well with Zia's past policies. For me, it is very hard to believe that this quintessential pragmatist, despairing of domestic political trends and badgered internationally by both friend and foe, could still believe that the Afghan mujahideen were the vehicle of a renascent Islam and that they, together with Pakistan, could by themselves liberate Afghanistan (and, potentially, even Soviet Central Asia) by force of arms. These might have been the aspirations of Ayatollah Khomeini, but not of General Zia.

A more likely explanation, I think, is to be found in Zia's "second thoughts," as Agha Shahi put it, "about the correctness of Pakistan's long-held inarticulate premise of the inevitable collapse of the PDPA regime, once the Soviet troops bolstering it quit Afghanistan."[110] If the PDPA proved less fragile (or the mujahideen less mighty) than anticipated, Zia must have wondered, to whom could Pakistan turn for reliable assurances that Pakistani and mujahideen interests would not be neglected? These interests, after all, were only partially addressed in the accords and, apart from Soviet withdrawal, even in the accords only very weakly. Harrison, by the way, himself gives at least a hint that Zia's doubts may have played a role in his policy shift. In an interview in Islamabad a few months following the signing of the accords, Harrison claims that Zia complained to him that "Gorbachev pulled a fast one by leaving Najib behind. He threw the bait by agreeing to withdraw without a change of regime, and it was swallowed."[111] Not his confidence, in other words, much less his Islamic zeal, but Zia's fear of being duped may account for his maladroit last-minute maneuvers.

Be this as it may, Pakistan's efforts to force revision of the terms of settlement did not succeed. The momentum of the drive for a settlement and the high stakes of all participants in the negotiations overcame Pakistan's objections. Faced with strong pressure from both the United States and the Soviet Union, Islamabad quickly retreated from its demand for a change in regime, requiring only that Kabul make a vague commitment to separate negotiation of the issue of forming a broad-based interim government.[112] This helped pave the way to the final settlement; it left dangling, however, the matter of political succession in Kabul.

Pakistan's failure to build a strong link between the Geneva settlement and reconstitution of the government in Kabul was thus complete. The Soviets would leave Afghanistan, but the PDPA regime, for the time being at least, would not. The reasons for Pakistan's failure were fairly obvious.

One was that Pakistan's negotiators at Geneva were under strong pressure to reconcile their own desires with those of key allies. Washington, in particular, seemed keen to take Moscow at its word and to put no obstacle in the path of Soviet troop withdrawal. Secretary of State George Schultz was reported in late February 1988, for instance, following discussions in Moscow with Soviet Foreign Minister Eduard A. Shevardnadze, as having voiced strong confidence in the Soviet Union's decision to pull its troops out of Afghanistan and to have held back from endorsing Pakistan's demand that an interim government be formed prior to the signing of an accord.[113]

Another was the manifest impracticality of reaching agreement on an interim government under the circumstances then prevailing. The positions on the issue taken by the mujahideen and the PDPA leadership in Kabul seemed flatly irreconcilable. Nearly as contradictory, it seems, were the positions on the issue taken by rival groups *within* the Afghan resistance. Islamist elements in the resistance, for example, espoused reform of the Afghan government and society along more or less strict Islamic lines and declared themselves implacably opposed to any role in postwar Kabul for the exiled ex-King Zahir Shah. A purist Islamic state was wholly unappealing to the traditionalist elements, however, and a poll of refugee opinion taken in the first half of 1987 by the politically moderate Afghan Information Centre in Peshawar indicated that almost 72 percent of Afghan refugees favored a solution under Zahir Shah's leadership.[114]

A third was Pakistan's own strong interest in securing the withdrawal of Soviet forces from Afghanistan. The presence of these forces clearly posed a significant threat to the security of Pakistan. By relieving the pressure on Pakistan's northwestern border, the Soviet withdrawal promised to enable Islamabad to focus its defense more confidently on the eastern border with India, where the greatest threat to the country's security—at least in the view of the majority of Pakistanis—had always been felt to lie.

Finally, the fact that many Pakistanis were unquestionably weary with the war meant that the Soviet troop withdrawal also held promise of substantial domestic political dividends. The Geneva accords drew wide praise in Pakistan, and Junejo's Muslim League party naturally stood to gain from the popularity of its support of them.

Pakistan's choices, to be sure, were severely constrained. In retrospect, however, Zia's major mistake may not have been that he tried to hold out for regime change in Kabul but that he did not try hard (or early) enough. Skeptics' claims that fighting between the Afghan guerrillas and Kabul's forces would continue or even grow worse in the aftermath of the settlement proved valid. Notwithstanding agreements to the contrary, foreign interference mounted. Prospects for the safe and orderly repatriation of the refugees inevitably plummeted. The Geneva accords had little material impact on the situation, it seems, except for the Soviet troop withdrawal. Some observers argued that an incomplete settlement was the best that could be gotten under the circumstances, that the Soviet Union was simply not prepared to abandon its communist ally in Kabul, and that—in the absence of a U.N. agreement—Moscow might well have decided to extend the war into Pakistani territory.[115] This point of view granted Moscow considerable maneuverability. History will have to decide, but Zia's apparent belief that Moscow was in a tight corner and could be induced to jettison the PDPA regime may have been closer to the mark.

NOTES

1. Marek Sliwinski, "Afghanistan: The Decimation of a People," *Orbis* 33:1 (Winter 1989) 39-56. The study, based on a sample survey of nearly 2000 Afghan refugee families in Pakistan, was carried out by Gallup Pakistan in August 1987.
2. Other than Zia and Shahi, those present at the meeting included the Deputy Chief of Army Staff, Lt. General Mohammad Iqbal Khan; the Chief of Naval Staff, Admiral Karamat Rahman Niazi; Air Chief Marshal Mohammad Anwar Shamim; plus a number of senior bureaucrats, retired generals, and trusted politicians. Among these were Sahabzada Yakub Khan, Ghulam Ishak Khan, and Professor Khurshid Ahmad, Vice President of the Jama'at-i-Islami party.
3. Agha Shahi, *Pakistan's Security and Foreign Policy* (Lahore: Progressive Publishers, 1988) p. 50. The quotation is from an address given by Shahi in the United States in December 1984. Shahi recounted events leading up to Pakistan's decision on a response to the Soviet intervention in an interview with the author in Islamabad, September 1989.
4. Shahi, *Pakistan's Security and Foreign Policy*, pp. 50-1. Emphasis added.
5. For background on the border agreement, see Yaacov Y. I. Vertzberger, *China's Southwestern Strategy: Encirclement and Counterencirclement* (New York: Praeger, 1985) pp. 21-36; and Anwar H. Syed, *China and Pakistan: Diplomacy of an Entente Cordiale* (Amherst: University of Massachusetts Press, 1974) pp. 82-93.
6. See Mujtaba Razvi, *The Frontiers of Pakistan: A Study of Frontier Problems in Pakistan's Foreign Policy* (Karachi: National Publishing House, 1971); and Mahnaz Z. Ispahani, *Roads and Rivals: The Political Uses of Access in the Borderlands of Asia* (Ithaca: Cornell University Press, 1989).
7. See, for example, Latif Ahmed Sherwani, *The Partition of India and Mountbatten* (Karachi: Council for Pakistan Studies, 1986) pp. 140-51.
8. For background on the Pashtunistan issue, see Ispahani, *Roads and Rivals* pp. 83-144; Leon B. Poullada, "Pushtunistan: Afghan Domestic Politics and Relations with Pakistan," in Ainslie T. Embree (ed.), *Pakistan's Western Borderlands* (Durham: Carolina Academic Press, 1977) pp. 126-51; Louis Dupree, *Afghanistan* (Princeton: Princeton University Press, 1973) pp.

485-94, 538-54; S. M. M. Qureshi, "Pakhtunistan: The Frontier Dispute between Afghanistan and Pakistan," *Pacific Affairs* 39:1-2 (Spring/Summer 1966) 99-114; Khalid B. Sayeed, "Pathan Regionalism," *The South Atlantic Quarterly* 63:4 (Autumn 1964) 478-506; Razvi, *The Frontiers of Pakistan* pp. 143-65; Stephen Rittenberg, *Ethnicity, Nationalism and the Pakhtuns: The Independence Movement in India's North-West Frontier Province* (Durham: Carolina Academic Press, 1988); and S. M. Burke, *Pakistan's Foreign Policy: An Historical Analysis* (London: Oxford University Press, 1973) pp. 68-90.
9. Ibid., p. 73.
10. Ispahani, *Roads and Rivals,* pp. 106-8.
11. M. Nazif Shahrani, "State Building and Social Fragmentation in Afghanistan: A Historical Perspective," in Ali Banuazizi and Myron Weiner (eds.), *The State, Religion, and Ethnic Politics: Afghanistan, Iran, and Pakistan* (Syracuse: Syracuse University Press, 1986) p. 59; and Poullada, "Pushtunistan: Afghan Domestic Politics and Relations with Pakistan," pp. 133-4.
12. For an excellent exposition of the Pashtunistan issue's relationship to the problem of access, see Ispahani, *Roads and Rivals,* pp. 83-144.
13. Olaf Caroe, *The Pathans, 550 B.C.-A.D. 1957* (London: Macmillan, 1958) p. 437.
14. Interview with the author, Peshawar, March 1986. Babar reportedly stated in a press interview in April 1989 that the government of Zulfikar Ali Bhutto had taken the Afghan rebels under its cover in the early 1970s "because we knew that some day there would be trouble in Afghanistan. We wanted to build up a leadership to influence events." Henry Kamm, "Pakistanis Report Ordering Attacks by Afghan Rebels," *The New York Times,* 23 April 1989, p. A1. Babar was appointed Special Assistant to Prime Minister Benazir Bhutto in December 1988.
15. Author's interview with a guerrilla leader who participated in the uprising at Panjsher, Peshawar, March 1986; and Olivier Roy, *Islam and Resistance in Afghanistan* (Cambridge: Cambridge University Press, 1985) pp. 74-9. For Kabul's perspective on Bhutto's mujahideen force, see Abdul Samad Ghaus, *The Fall of Afghanistan: An Insider's Account* (Washington, D.C.: Pergamon-Brassey's International Defense Publishers, 1988) p. 120.
16. Interview with the author, Peshawar, March 1986.
17. Ghaus, *The Fall of Afghanistan* pp. 123-5. Bradsher suggests that a gradual cooling in Soviet support for Pashtunistan may also have had an impact on Kabul's calculations. Henry S. Bradsher, *Afghanistan and the Soviet Union* (Durham: Duke University Press, 1983) p. 63.
18. Ibid., p. 63.
19. Ghaus, *The Fall of Afghanistan,* p. 132.
20. Ghaus expresses the belief that "it is safe to say that in three to four years the Afghan-Pakistani dispute would have ceased to exist." Ibid., p. 147.

21. According to a senior Pakistani diplomat and advisor to Zia at the time, Zia brushed aside the Foreign Office view that his visit was premature and unlikely to succeed. Interview with the author, Islamabad, December 1987.
22. Bradsher, *Afghanistan and the Soviet Union*, pp. 100, 221.
23. Portions of this section borrow from my article, "Pakistan and the War in Afghanistan," *Asian Affairs* 14:2 (Summer 1987) 57-75.
24. For assessment of Pakistan-Soviet relations, see Robert G. Wirsing, "The Soviet Role in South Asia: Potential for Change," in Leo E. Rose and Kamal Matinuddin (eds.), *Beyond Afghanistan: The Emerging U.S.-Pakistan Relations* (Berkeley: Institute of East Asian Studies, University of California, 1989) pp. 283-301; Ali T. Sheikh, "Pakistan-Soviet Relations and the Afghan Crisis," in Noor A. Husain and Leo E. Rose (eds.), *Pakistan-U.S. Relations: Social, Political, and Economic Factors* (Berkeley: Institute of East Asian Studies, University of California, 1988) pp. 45-74; Syed Riffat Hussain, "Pak-Soviet Relations Since 1947: A Dissenting Appraisal," *Strategic Studies* (Islamabad) 10:3 (Spring 1987) 64-88; and Muhammad R. Azmi, "Pakistan's Soviet Policy: One Step Forward, Two Steps Back," *Asian Profile* 15:2 (April 1987) 167-78.
25. Bradsher, *Afghanistan and the Soviet Union*, p. 221.
26. Prime Minister Benazir Bhutto's Special Assistant Nasirullah Babar reportedly stated in a press interview in April 1989 that the United States had been financing Afghan dissidents since 1973 and that it had taken Hezb-i-Islami chieftan Gulbuddin Hekmatyar "under its umbrella" months prior to the Soviet military intervention. Kamm, "Pakistanis Report Ordering Attacks by Afghan Rebels."
27. Interview with the author, Peshawar, March 1986.
28. Bhutto had already withdrawn Pakistan's membership in the Southeast Asian Treaty Organization (SEATO) following the Bangladesh war.
29. Interview with the author, Islamabad, November 1985.
30. See, for example, Francis Fukuyama, *The Security of Pakistan: A Trip Report*, Rand Report N-1584-RC (Santa Monica: Rand Corporation, September 1980); and Lawrence Ziring, "Soviet Policy on the Rim of Asia: Scenarios and Projections," *Asian Affairs* 9:3 (January-February 1982) pp. 135-46.
31. For background on the 1981 agreement, see Herbert G. Hagerty, "United States Assistance to Pakistan," in Husain and Rose (eds.), *Pakistan-U.S. Relations*, pp. 237-51. See also Robert G. Wirsing and James M. Roherty, "The United States and Pakistan," *International Affairs* (London) 58:4 (Autumn 1982) 588-609.
32. David B. Ottaway, "Pakistan Is Said to Delay U.S. Aid to Afghan Rebels," *The Washington Post* 7 October 1986, p. A1b.
33. John Fullerton, *The Soviet Occupation of Afghanistan* (Hong Kong: Far Eastern Economic Review Ltd., 1983) pp. 181-2.

34. At an early stage of Gorbachev's peace offensive in Afghanistan, the U.S. ambassador to Pakistan, Deane Hinton, was reported to have conceded in an interview given to an English-language daily in Islamabad that differences existed between American and Pakistani officials in their assessments of peace overtures made by Kabul and Moscow. The Americans, he was reported to have said, were more skeptical than their Pakistani counterparts about how quickly a political settlement of the war could be reached. *The Muslim*, 29 January 1987. See also Selig S. Harrison, "A Breakthrough In Afghanistan?", *Foreign Policy* No. 51 (Summer 1983) 34.
35. Peter J. S. Duncan, *The Soviet Union and India* (New York: Council on Foreign Relations Press, 1989) p. 110.
36. On this point, see Robert G. Wirsing, "The Siachen Glacier Dispute—III: The Strategic Dimension," *Strategic Studies* 12:1 (Fall 1988) 38-54; and Ispahani, *Roads and Rivals*, pp. 145-213. See also Fahmida Ashraf, "The Strategic Wakhan," *Strategic Studies* 9:2 (Winter 1986) 48-67.
37. In December 1987, barely six weeks before Gorbachev's pullout proposal was made public, a top-level U.S. diplomat in Islamabad confidently told the author: "The Soviets will never leave Afghanistan."
38. Charles Dunbar, "Afghanistan in 1986: The Balance Endures," *Asian Survey* 27:2 (February 1987) 136-7.
39. See, for example, Sajjad Hyder, *Foreign Policy of Pakistan: Reflections of an Ambassador* (Lahore: Progressive Publishers, 1987) pp. 86-155.
40. See Nancy Hatch Dupree, "The VOLAG Explosion," *The Afghanistan Forum* 13:6 (November 1985) 23-28; Fazel Haq Saikal and William Maley, *Afghan Refugee Relief in Pakistan: Political Context and Practical Problems* (Canberra: Department of Politics, University College, The University of New South Wales, Australian Defence Force Academy, 1986); and John H. Lorentz, "Afghan Aid: The Role of Private Organizations," *Journal of South Asian and Middle Eastern Studies* 11:1 & 2 (Fall/Winter 1987) 101-11.
41. See, for example, *The Muslim*, 19 August 1987; Said Azhar, "Three Million Uprooted Afghans in Pakistan," *Pakistan Horizon* (Karachi) 38:1 (1985) 60-84; and Chief Commissioner for Afghan Refugees, Government of Pakistan, *Handbook on Management of Afghan Refugees in Pakistan*, revised edition (Islamabad: States & Frontier Regions Division, 1984) pp. 9-14.
42. The Chief Commissioner for Afghan Refugees of the Government of Pakistan, retired Brigadier Said Azhar, acknowledged to the author that the cash maintenance allowance was not paid regularly. He estimated that about 30 percent of it was being paid, but described the allowance as essentially an *objective* rather than a realization of the government's policy. Interview, Islamabad, May 1986. Cash payment allowance records checked by the author at one complex of camps in Peshawar district showed that the rupee payment had been distributed twice in the preceding twenty-three months (in June 1984 and in September 1985). An official of the United Nations High Commissioner for Refugees (UNHCR) in Peshawar stated flatly to

the author that the cash payment to refugees was simply not being made. He offered the comment that "once in a year" was an exaggeration. Interview, Peshawar, March 1986.
43. Interview with the author, Peshawar, October 1989.
44. The official estimate, which was certainly controversial and may well have been inflated, included 3.15 million refugees that were registered with the UNHCR plus an additional 300 000 unregistered refugees. Pakistan's population at the end of 1987 was officially estimated to be about 100 million. For background, see Nancy Hatch Dupree, "The Demography of Afghan Refugees in Pakistan," in Hafeez Malik (ed.), *Soviet-American Relations with Pakistan, Iran and Afghanistan* (New York: St. Martin's Press, 1987) pp. 366-94.
45. The total number of Afghan refugees in both Iran and Pakistan at about the time of the Soviet withdrawal was generally estimated to be in excess of 5 million—roughly one-third of Afghanistan's entire prewar population.
46. The following discussion draws heavily on my article, "Repatriation of Afghan Refugees," *Journal of South Asian and Middle Eastern Studies* 12:1 (Fall 1988) 20-41.
47. Deaths inside Pakistan from aerial attacks alone from December 1979 through August 1987 were estimated at 860. Goran Melander et al., *Report of the Independent Counsel on International Human Rights on the Human Rights Situation in Afghanistan,* typed copy, 18 November 1987, p. 28.
48. *The Muslim,* 13 March 1988. The NWFP's share of fatalities from terrorist bombings declined somewhat in 1987, but it still accounted for roughly two-thirds of the much larger nationwide total in 1987 of 263.
49. See, for example, John Fullerton, *The Soviet Occupation of Afghanistan* (Hong Kong: Far Eastern Economic Review Ltd., 1983) pp. 70-1, 148, 181. Fullerton claims that Abdullah used Commissionerate resources to boost the strength and numbers of "fundamentalist" guerrilla leader Gulbuddin Hekmatyar's organization, the Hezb-i-Islami, an ideological ally of the JIP. According to Fullerton, there was little doubt that under Abdullah "the best of international refugee relief aid [found] its way to refugee camps dominated by Hekmatyar's followers"[148]. In reply, Abdullah, a career civil servant, insists that he was never a member of the JIP and that it, in any event, had very little control over the Commissionerate's disbursal of resources to the refugees. According to Abdullah, he was the victim of a deep anti-Islamic prejudice that Fullerton and other Western journalists carried with them to Pakistan. Interview with the author, Peshawar, January 1986.
50. Fullerton, *The Soviet Occupation of Afghanistan,* p. 71.
51. *Gallup Political Weather Report* (Islamabad: Gallup Pakistan, 1987) p. 51. For the entire country, the corresponding figure was 38 percent.
52. See, for example, "Afghan Refugees Expulsion from Peshawar Demanded," *Dawn* (Karachi), 20 June 1986. In August 1987, it was reported that the government of Pakistan was preparing a comprehensive policy to

restrict refugees to their camps all over the country. *The Muslim,* 19 August 1987. No such policy was ever, in fact, announced.
53. Dr. Sayed Bahauddin Majrooh, Director, Afghan Information Centre, interview with the author, Peshawar, December 1987. Dr. Majrooh was the victim of assassination early in 1988.
54. Interview with the author, Islamabad, April 1986.
55. Interview with the author, NWFP, April 1986.
56. See, for example, Nancy Hatch Dupree, "'Allah Is Pleased . . .' in Baluchistan," *The Afghanistan Forum* (New York) 13:1 (January 1985) 23-25, and "Dateline: North & South Waziristan, August 1987," *The Afghanistan Forum* 15:6 (November 1987) 19-22. A report prepared around 1987 for an international agency operating in Peshawar included the following assessment of the refugees' economic impact:

> Afghans control a significant proportion of the merchant and service economy in Miranshah [the administrative and commercial center of North Waziristan Agency, one of the seven federally administered tribal agencies of NWFP] and outlying commercial areas. In Miranshah bazaar, Afghans operate hotels, restaurants, machine and appliance repair shops, fabric shops, and fruit and vegetable stands as well as providing local and long distance transport services. The residual effects of large scale refugee assistance and the financing of the Afghan resistance, combined with the remittance earnings of locals working in the Gulf, has been a remarkable stimulus to the local economy.

Contained in personal communication to the author from Nancy Hatch Dupree, April 1988.
57. Arbab Dost Mohammad Khan, interview with the author, Peshawar, March 1986. Some sources claimed that the discrepancy might have been due to the government's deliberate underreporting of refugee crimes.
58. Khan Abdul Wali Khan, interview with the author, Charsadda, April 1986.
59. Interview with the author, Peshawar, April 1986.
60. *Gallup Political Weather Report,* p. 51. Polling results showed 45% of Pashtu speakers favoring and 30% opposing continued Pakistani support for the Afghan guerrillas. Corresponding figures for the other language groups were: Hindko, 57-38%; Urdu, 47-39%; Punjabi, 43-38%; Siraiki, 32-35%; Baluchi, 22-55%; and Sindhi, 12-43%. For all of Pakistan, 37% favored continued support, 38% that support be withdrawn. The remainder expressed no (or other) opinion. The polling question was: After the bomb blasts in different cities of Pakistan, some people say that Pakistan should withdraw its support for the Afghan mujahideen. What is your view?
61. Ibid.
62. According to the 1981 census, the Baluch accounted for only 36 percent (if closely related Brahuis were included, 57 percent) of provincial households. See Government of Pakistan, Population Census Organisation, *1981 Census Report of Pakistan* (Islamabad: Statistics Division, December 1984) p.

186. Linguistic data in the 1981 census were recorded on a household rather than individual basis.

63. For additional comment on the province's ethnic problems, see Robert G. Wirsing, "Ethnicity and Political Reform in Pakistan," *Asian Affairs* 15:2 (Summer 1988) 67-83. See also Robert G. Wirsing, *The Baluchis and Pathans*, Report No. 48 (London: Minority Rights Group, 1987, revised edition).

64. For background on the insurgency and on the Baluch national movement, see Selig S. Harrison, *In Afghanistan's Shadow: Baluch Nationalism and Soviet Temptations* (Washington, D.C.: Carnegie Endowment for International Peace, 1981). See also Tahir Amin, *Ethno-National Movements of Pakistan: Domestic and International Factors* (Islamabad: Institute of Policy Studies, 1988); and A. B. Awan, *Baluchistan: Historical and Political Processes* (London: New Century Publishers, 1985).

65. The Baluch were barely represented in the heavily Pashtu-speaking districts of Quetta division in the northern part of the province, where only 9 percent of households reported Baluchi as mother tongue in 1981. See Government of Pakistan, Population Census Organisation, *1981 Census Report of Baluchistan Province* (Islamabad: Statistics Division, December 1984) p. 107; and Jonathan Addleton, "Language and Community in Pakistan," unpublished paper (Islamabad: U.S. Agency for International Development, 1985?) p. 14.

66. Selig S. Harrison, "Nightmare in Baluchistan," *Foreign Policy* No. 32 (Fall 1978) 136-60.

67. Azhar, interview with the author.

68. *The New York Times*, 16 December 1986, p. A2 and 17 December 1986, p.A6.

69. Azhar, interview with the author.

70. Interview with the author, Lahore, December 1987. The number of unregistered Afghan refugees in the Punjab was reported in 1986 to be 10 000. *Dawn*, 4 March 1986.

71. *The Muslim*, 25 July 1987; and author interviews in Lahore, December 1987.

72. Interview with the author, Lahore, December 1987.

73. *Gallup Political Weather Report*, p. 51.

74. See John G. Merriam, "Arms Shipments to the Afghan Resistance," in Grant M. Farr and John G. Merriam (eds.), *Afghan Resistance: The Politics of Survival* (Boulder: Westview, 1987) pp. 71-101.

75. According to a Pakistani source with extensive knowledge of SSG operations in Afghanistan, no SSG commandos were ever captured during these operations. Interview with the author, Rawalpindi, September 1989.

76. Sheikh, "Pakistan-Soviet Relations and the Afghan Crisis," pp. 59-60.

77. Bradsher, *Afghanistan and the Soviet Union*, pp. 221-2.

78. *Far Eastern Economic Review,* 10 November 1988, pp. 36-7. In the power reshuffle in Pakistan that followed Zia's death, control of the ISI was a major issue. See John Kifner, "Bhutto Shedding Army Holdovers," *The New York Times,* 1 June 1989, p. A6.
79. Lt. General Akhtar, in 1987 appointed Chairman of the Joint Chief of Staff Committee, was among those who were killed with Zia in the crash of the C-130 aircraft in August 1988.
80. Nancy Peabody Newell and Richard S. Newell, *The Struggle for Afghanistan* (Ithaca: Cornell University Press, 1981) pp. 187-8. In fairness to Western coverage of the war, we should note that reports depicting Pakistanis avidly confiscating rebel weapons at the border, patently absurd given the border's hundreds of unguarded crossing points and the Afghans' unmatched reputation for artful smuggling, cropped up very rarely within a year or so of the Soviet intervention.
81. Edward R. Girardet, *Afghanistan: The Soviet War* (London: Croom Helm, 1985) p. 67.
82. *Newsweek,* 23 March 1987, pp. 32-3. More difficult to believe is the estimate of one author that "somewhere between the authorizing of the money in Washington...and the delivery of arms to the freedom fighters inside Afghanistan, an estimated 70 percent disappears." Jan Goodwin, *Caught in the Crossfire* (London: Macdonald, 1987) pp. 45-6.
83. Interview, Peshawar, April 1986. In like manner, this source claimed that the chronic disunity of the mujahideen groups was deliberate, but justifiable, Pakistani policy.
84. Professor Khurshid Ahmad, Vice President, Jama'at-i-Islami party, interview with the author, Islamabad, October 1989. Ahmad was elected to the Pakistan Senate in 1985.
85. In conversation with the author, Islamabad, September 1989. Zia's pragmatism in matters Islamic was also apparent in his notably cautious approach to the implementation of Islamic jurisprudence in Pakistan. On this, see Charles H. Kennedy, "Islamization and Legal Reform in Pakistan, 1979-1989," *Pacific Affairs* 63:1 (Spring 1990) 62-77. Kennedy observes that

> President Zia was a consummate political strategist and consciously adopted policies which moved cautiously in Islamic matters....Zia's concerns throughout were to maintain stability in the state, and to curb the more zealous advocates of Islamic reform....He consistently stressed his administration's commitment to the Nizam-i-Mustapha [Islamic reforms] by engaging in calculated political hyperbole concerning his administration's accomplishments and initiatives. Simultaneously he quietly orchestrated and/or manipulated the political process to ensure that Islamic reform took place in an ordered and prudential manner. In sum, Zia's strategy paid lip service to the Islamic mandate, and helped to legitimize his government and to cement ties with the Islamic

world. Further, it did not challenge the vested interests of Pakistan's bureaucratic and military elites [73].

86. The fundamentalist groups were: (1) Jamiat-i-Islami Afghanistan (Afghanistan Islamic Society) (Rabbani); (2) Hezb-i-Islami Afghanistan (Afghanistan Islamic Party) (Khalis); (3) Hezb-i-Islami Afghanistan (Afghanistan Islamic Party) (Hekmatyar); and (4) Islamic Union for the Liberation of Afghanistan (Sayyaf). The traditionalist groups were (1) Harakat-i-Inqilab-i-Islami (Movement for the Islamic Revolution) (Mohammadi); (2) National Islamic Front for Afghanistan (NIFA) (Gailani); and (3) Afghanistan National Liberation Front (ANLF) (Mojadeddi).

87. Roy, *Islam and Resistance in Afghanistan,* pp. 209-10. At the time Roy was writing, the mujahideen were still organized into two rival alliances. Not until 1985 did they succeed in forming a reasonably stable coalition (the Islamic Unity of the Afghan Mujahideen) containing both fundamentalist and traditionalist groups. Roy's study was based on six field visits to Afghanistan made between 1980 and 1985.

88. See, for example, ibid., pp. 127-38; and Eden Naby, "The Afghan Resistance Movement," in Ralph H. Magnus (ed.), *Afghan Alternatives: Issues, Options, and Policies* (New Brunswick: Transaction Books, 1985) pp. 59-81.

89. Girardet, *Afghanistan: The Soviet War,* pp. 170-1. See also Fullerton, *The Soviet Occupation of Afghanistan,* pp. 68-71.

90. A Jama'at leader who often acted in a liaison capacity with the mujahideen groups in Peshawar conceded that internal fighting was extensive in the resistance, but that this had to be understood as an inevitable byproduct of the war, not of any particular leader's thirst for blood. After all, he said smiling, internal fighting in the Kabul regime was also extensive. "More of them, too," he added, "had probably died fighting each other as had died in fighting the enemy!" Interview with the author, Peshawar, October 1989.

91. Roy, *Islam and Resistance in Afghanistan,* p. 134. Emphasis added.

92. Ibid., pp. 210-11.

93. One Hezb media specialist in Peshawar reacted explosively to mention of Roy, describing him as the most biased of all foreign writers and calling him "a liar, staunch socialist, and hypocrite, who only pretends to be backing the mujahideen." Interview with the author, Peshawar, May 1986.

94. United States Department of State, Bureau of Public Affairs, *Agreements on Afghanistan,* Selected Documents No. 26 (Washington, D.C.: April 1988).

95. Barnett R. Rubin, "Afghanistan: The Next Round," *Orbis* 33:1 (Winter 1989) 57.

96. *The New York Times,* 8 April 1988, p. A1.

97. Selig S. Harrison, "Inside the Afghan Talks," *Foreign Policy* No. 72 (Fall 1988) 38.

98. Interview with the author, Islamabad, December 1987. Shahi resigned from the office of Foreign Minister in February 1982, several months prior to the first round of negotiations. According to Harrison, Shahi privately complained that American pressures lay behind his exit. Harrison, "Inside the Afghan Talks," 36.
99. Ibid., 36-7.
100. Quoted in ibid., 39.
101. Ibid., 46-7. See also Harrison's earlier essay, "A Breakthrough in Afghanistan?"
102. Rubin, "Afghanistan: The Next Round," 62-4; and Harrison, "Inside the Afghan Talks," 53-5.
103. *The New York Times*, 13 January 1988, p. A1.
104. *The New York Times*, 17 February 1988, p. A6.
105. *The New York Times*, 13 January 1988, p. A1.
106. Harrison, "Inside the Afghan Talks," pp. 54, 56-7.
107. Ibid., 57.
108. *The Muslim*, 7 March 1988.
109. Interview, Islamabad, September 1989.
110. Shahi, *Pakistan's Security and Foreign Policy*, pp. 104-5.
111. Quoted in Harrison, "Inside the Afghan Talks," 57.
112. *The New York Times*, 17 March 1988, p. A4.
113. *The New York Times*, 23 February 1988, p. A7 & 24 February 1988, p. A8.
114. See "What Do the Afghan Refugees Think? An Opinion Survey in the Camps," *Monthly Bulletin* No. 76 (Peshawar: Afghan Information Centre, July 1987). There was speculation in Peshawar that the assassination in February 1988 of the report's author, Professor Sayed Majrooh, may have been connected to the survey's results. *The New York Times*, 9 March 1988, p. A1.
115. Harrison, "Inside the Afghan Talks," p. 60.

3

THE ARMS RACE WITH INDIA: THE NUCLEAR IMPERATIVE

The military rivalry that had been emblematic of India-Pakistan relations ever since their establishment as separate states in 1947 continued to dominate their relationship in the Zia period. In this period, both sides continued to base military planning and arms acquisitions primarily on the prospect of war with one another. Both deployed by far the bulk of their forces along their common border; and skirmishes between these forces along the disputed portion of this border in Kashmir were a routine occurrence. In 1984, the worst fighting between India and Pakistan since 1971 broke out at the Siachen Glacier in the Karakoram Mountains near the Chinese border [see Chapter 4]. Each side regularly accused the other of aggressive intentions; and little existed between them of trade or cultural contact to temper the hard edge of their military hostility. To be sure, neither side appeared satisfied with the status quo; and apprehension was expressed in both countries that Indian and Pakistani threat perceptions, for long focused largely on one another, were perhaps dangerously outmoded. Nothing remained, however, of the conciliatory spirit that had been aroused between India and Pakistan at Simla in the wake of Pakistan's defeat in the Bangladesh war of 1971; and none of the steps taken by either government, including Zia's offer to India of a draft nonaggression pact in June 1982, were able to breathe much life into the near-moribund normalization process. For the most part, in fact, the traditional enmity between these two countries remained intact throughout the Zia period.

This enmity held obvious dangers for regional peace. India and Pakistan had already fought three wars with one another in less than the space of a quarter of a century. By Zia's time, moreover, India and Pakistan had both emerged as formidable military powers. Their forces were equipped with some of the most advanced air, ground, and naval weaponry available and were, without doubt, much stronger than those over which India and Pakistan had disposed when they last went to war with one another in 1971. The consensus among military professionals the world over was that these forces were well officered, well trained, and highly motivated. By Zia's time, no other state on the littoral of the Indian Ocean could match Indian military power, and very few could deploy anything to compare with Pakistan's.

It was not only the mounting capability of the Indian and Pakistani armed forces, however, that made their enmity appear increasingly dangerous in the Zia period. At least two additional factors were involved.

One was the sharp intensification of superpower confrontation that developed in the South Asian region in the wake of Soviet intervention in Afghanistan. By 1981, it had led to a situation in which the United States and the Soviet Union found themselves cast as direct competitors in the subcontinental arms race. This situation had very little precedent in the region. Washington's military assistance to Pakistan, launched in 1954 with the signing of the Mutual Defence Assistance Agreement, had antedated by a decade the appearance of a significant Soviet arms-supply relationship with India. And by the time the Soviet Union had become India's primary foreign arms supplier in the late 1960s, Washington's declining interest in South Asia and preoccupations elsewhere had led to a sharp reduction of its own arms-transfer programs in the region. In the 1980s, in contrast, the United States and the Soviet Union were engaged in massive, sustained, and directly competitive arms supply activity with their respective South Asian clients.

Insofar as the Indo-Soviet arms linkage was concerned, India's position of prominence in the hierarchy of Soviet arms customers was already well established at the beginning of the 1980s. Between 1976 and 1980, the Soviet Union supplied 82 percent of Indian arms imports ($2.3 of $2.8 billion), giving India the fourth largest share (after Libya, Syria, and Iraq) of total Soviet arms exports to noncommunist countries.[1] Washington's resumption of an arms-supply relationship with Pakistan in June 1981, on the other hand, enabled Pakistan to rise rapidly to an equally prominent position in the hierarchy of America's arms clients. For fiscal year 1985, the fourth installment of Washington's 6-year $3.2 billion military and economic assistance package came to $526 million, placing Pakistan fourth in the world (after Israel, Egypt, and Turkey) among nearly 100 recipients of U.S. security assistance.[2] The total U.S. security assistance program budgeted for India in this same year, one might note, was set at a modest $300 000 in International Military Education and Training (IMET) support funds. For well over a decade, there had been virtually no Soviet arms sales to Pakistan.[3] Thus, the emergent pattern of superpower engagement in the subcontinental arms race was juxtaposed against and appeared to reinforce the region's already intense military rivalry.

A second factor was the appearance in the Zia period for the first time of credible threats from both sides of significant progress toward nuclear weaponization. India, of course, had already established itself as a nuclear-capable state in 1974 by successfully detonating a nuclear device at its Pokharan test site in Rajasthan. Before the Bhutto era ended in 1977, Pakistan, in turn, had launched major efforts of its own to build the organizational infrastructure for a nuclear weapons research and development program, to acquire nuclear weapons-related technologies, and to gain mastery over the processes of manufacturing nuclear explosive materials. Not until the 1980s, however, did the actual fabrication and stockpiling of nuclear weapons by India and Pakistan—their simultaneous advance to "near-nuclear-weapon" or "threshold" status among the world's nuclear proliferators—seem imminent.[4] In a relationship as dominated by military considerations (and as vulnerable to escalatory pressures) as was that between India and Pakistan, the threatened addition of nuclear weapons to existing arms inventories was obviously not a trifling matter.

From the Indian perspective, responsibility for the arms race rested primarily in Pakistan's rejection of the territorial status quo resulting from partition and in its efforts to offset India's obvious advantage in size and potential by matching Indian military capabilities. Pakistan, said its Indian critics, pursued provocative arms-import policies, blocked progress toward regional cooperation, and deliberately drew the Cold War rivalry between the superpowers into the subcontinent. Regional stability, according to Indians, demanded that Pakistan come to terms not only with its own weakness but with India's "natural" regional dominance. Especially in regard to nuclear weapons, Pakistan was admonished to "face reality."

Pakistani policymakers, of course, viewed the rivalry with India from a rather different perspective. For them, reality was more complicated, India's regional objectives less innocuous, and Pakistan's policy choices more constricted than its critics generally allowed. Pakistanis held India responsible for the regional arms race, and insisted that the Indian military threat to Pakistan's territorial integrity and independence was no fiction. Pakistan's national survival was at stake, they said, and Indian military power had to be contained.

To many foreign observers, India and Pakistan seemed equally responsible for the arms race. Both were said to be the captives of historically rooted distrust and misperception; and both were accused of wasting resources on arms that would be better spent on the uplift of their impoverished societies. The criticism was particularly hard to withstand in Pakistan's case, however, not only because its far greater dependence on foreign aid made the complaints difficult to dismiss but because Pakistan alone was vulnerable to the charge that its arms policies had less to do with its legitimate defense requirements than with its army's bloated importance in the country's political system. As a result, deflecting such criticism and attempting to justify Pakistan's arms policies were major preoccupations of Pakistani policymakers throughout the Zia period.

The defiance of Indian military power was as fundamental to the foreign policy of the Zia government as it had been for all of its predecessors. It proved more difficult to implement in the Zia period, however, than ever in the past. The reasons for the difficulty and the alternative strategies pursued by the Zia government to overcome it are the focus of this chapter.

I. THE MILITARY THREAT FROM INDIA

We observed in the preceding chapter that Pakistan's leaders quickly recognized the scale of threat to Pakistan's security implicit in the Soviet occupation of Afghanistan. We observed also that their apprehensions in this regard were compounded to no small extent by realization of the increased potential for Indo-Soviet collusion inherent in the Soviet takeover of Afghanistan. Now we must contend with the fact that, notwithstanding the sudden appearance of a major Soviet threat on its western borders, there did not occur thereafter at any level of Pakistani society or in any branch of its government a radical revision in the long-standing national consensus on the preeminence of the threat from the east. This was apparent throughout the Zia period in public opinion polls[5] and in newspaper commentaries.[6] It was as apparent in the political opposition to Zia as within ruling circles. Indeed, alarmist language about India radiated from all points of the ideological compass. "The dilemma of the two-front situation notwithstanding," wrote the hard-line founder of a government-funded think tank in late 1985, "the greatest threat to Pakistan comes from India's national aim of achieving world power status and hegemony over the region, its armament programme, and its arm-twisting of its weaker neighbors."[7] A widely noted report published the same year by the anti-Zia and left-leaning Independent Planning Commission of Pakistan, based in Lahore, differed only in emphasis. It said that not only was the Indian threat to the independence and integrity of Pakistan increasing, but that "by any standard of future projection India qualifies as the most menacing of history's time bombs."[8] The commission's judgment that "the real danger [to Pakistan] lies in the militarization of Indian economy and polity, in the resurgence of religious and national chauvinism, and in superpower connivance of India's ambitions" contained little that the Pakistani right-wing would have found objectionable.

While the national consensus on the Indian threat thus seemed to yield little if any ground during the Zia period, it was paralleled by a number of developments that indicated a growing level of dissatisfaction in Pakistan with the traditional hostility between the two countries. There appeared to be widespread popular support in Pakistan, for instance, for the Zia regime's efforts to relieve pressures on Pakistan's eastern border by accelerating the normalization of relations with India.[9] In the popular media, at least, Pakistanis gave an almost uniformly positive response to formation of the South Asian Association of Regional Cooperation in Dhaka in December 1985; and there seemed to be genuine and widespread interest in furthering contacts of all kinds between the two countries. For the first time in Pakistan's history, the government routinely authorized the participation of leading Indian intellectuals and foreign-affairs specialists (K. Subrahmanyam, Bhabani Sen Gupta, Pran Chopra, Kuldip Nayar, among others) in public gatherings in Pakistan; and Indian journalists were occasionally featured in guest columns in leading Pakistani dailies. Most surprising of all, perhaps, was the growing frequency of public admissions in this period by eminent Pakistanis that Pakistan itself had to share some of the responsibility for its past wars with India.[10] These things seemed to imply that the climate of opinion in Pakistan under Zia contained a larger element of realism in regard to Pakistan's bilateral relations with India than had been characteristic even a decade earlier. They did not add up to a major breakthrough in the relations between India and Pakistan, however, and they certainly did little to change Pakistani minds about the magnitude of the Indian military threat.

A host of Indian writers strove doggedly to reassure the world that India was not expansionist, that its defense policy gave little cause for Pakistani apprehension, and that Pakistan—in league with its extraregional allies—was chiefly responsible for its own insecurity. No organization contributed more to this effort than the Institute for Defence Studies and Analyses in New Delhi. And no writer was more dedicated, prolific, or more influential in this organization than its director and leading light throughout the Zia period, Mr. K. Subrahmanyam. Equipped with an unusually capacious and inventive mind, Subrahmanyam tirelessly championed the Indian (conventional and nuclear) defense cause. His proposals were consistently hard-line and nearly always polemical in tone. Clearly, not all or even most of them had the stamp of approval of the official establishment. They reflected the views of far more than the "IDSA hawks," however, and were often echoed in official pronouncements.

Three fundamental themes appeared over and over again in Subrahmanyam's writings.[11] One was that India was the victim of distorted images projected abroad by its enemies (and accepted even by some Indians), and that Indian defense and security policy was, as a result, badly misunderstood and misperceived. One such image he pointed to was that of a large, militarily powerful, and "hegemonistic" India looming menacingly over its neighbors. This image, he argued, simply did not conform to the history of the last four decades. On the contrary, he wrote,

> India accepted a cease-fire in Kashmir on January 1, 1949, when the military situation was turning in its favour. After the wars of 1965 and 1971 India returned the occupied territories promptly to Pakistan without making them bargaining chips in the negotiations. The Indian Army vacated Bangladesh promptly. India supported Bhutan in its quest for full sovereign status and the membership of the United Nations. Though arms for Nagas and Mizos had been filtering into Indian territory via Burma, and hot pursuit would have been perfectly justifiable, India has scrupulously honoured the Burmese territorial integrity.[12]

Subrahmanyam suggested, moreover, that the South Asian region's aggressive image found equally little support in the record of defense expenditures and arms acquisitions in the subcontinent. There was a superpower-led arms race in the Indian Ocean, he said, but there was not one in South Asia. This region, he observed, although it held nearly 20 percent of the world's population, was responsible for only 1 percent of global military expenditures. On every side of the region, he pointed out, countries were spending much higher sums on defense, in relative and even in absolute terms, than was the case in the subcontinent. As far as modernization of conventional weaponry was concerned, the South Asian region had no choice but to follow suit behind the advanced countries, which had already gone through several generations of weapons recycling since World War II.[13]

A second theme in Subrahmanyam's writing was that Pakistan's security problems were largely self-inflicted, the product more of its leaders' mistaken choice of a postindependence path of development than of any external threat. Pakistan, he said, had followed the path of authoritarianism and religion-based statehood. India, in contrast, had chosen the path of democracy, federalism, and secularism, a path that rendered much easier the task of forging a stable and integrated polity. What Pakistan feared most was not a military or political hegemonic threat, he argued, but a "value-hegemonic threat"—the threat of contamination by these ideas. "When our neighbors use the terms hegemony and expansionism," he wrote, "they are in reality expressing their fears about the ideas of representative government, federal structure, linguistic autonomy and secularism spreading to their states."[14] He conceded that the Soviet presence in Afghanistan contributed to Pakistan's security problem. "The real security problem," however, was "the increasing alienation between the people of Pakistan and their present rulers....Most of Pakistan's security problems, and the haunting sense of insecurity of the country's rulers, are inherent in the nature of the Pakistani state and the relationship between rulers and ruled. India," he concluded, "can do nothing about it."[15]

A third theme was that Indian predominance in the South Asian region was natural and inevitable, that Pakistan, along with the other states in the region, ultimately had no choice but to accept this reality, and that once the region was set free of extraregional interference, a peaceful and cooperative regional political structure—with India as its core—was likely to develop. Efforts by the smaller states to preclude such development by enlisting the support of extraregional powers against India were to be expected, he cautioned, but they were

> bound to be a short-term phenomenon and in the longer run the imperatives of geography, cultural affinities, international politics at the level of major powers and the developing global economic stresses and strains will bring home to our neighbours the facts of life and of realpolitik among nations.[16]

There was clearly some merit in Subrahmanyam's observations. He was right to suggest, for instance, that the intensity of the arms race between India and Pakistan had often been exaggerated and that their enmity, in general, was far from unlimited. Their wars, after all, had all been exceptionally brief and, by twentieth-century standards, relatively light in casualties and material losses.[17] All had been concluded by formal treaty, and all of the treaty negotiations (even the Simla negotiations following Pakistan's out-and-out defeat in 1971) had shown a willingness to give and take on the part of both countries that was often lacking in other traditional rivalries.[18] Relative to the size of their populations, moreover, India and Pakistan, respectively the world's second and tenth most populous nations, did not seem to be unusually militarized or overarmed. A 1985 compilation of military-related data on 144 nations, for example, put India fourth, Pakistan ninth, in size of armed forces. This was about where they deserved to be, at least in terms of their global standing in population. In most other categories, however, their ranking was well beneath what might have seemed justified by the size of their populations. Moreover, in at least some categories (military expenditure

Table 3.1
World Ranking of Selected Countries, 1985
(by Military Indicators)

Indicators:

	POP	ME	AF	AI	AE	ME/GNP	ME/CGE	ME/POP	ME/AF	AF/POP
India	2	16	4	3	38	59	46	111	91	116
Pakistan	10	35	9	27	34	36	24	84	109	62
Iran	21	11	20	6	+	27	19	31	25	55
Iraq	46	8	7	1	+	2	4	7	39	1
Israel	96	27	33	12	18	12	47	8	40	2
Syria	58	25	18	8	+	5	10	16	52	3

+ Tied for last place with a zero value.

Explanation of abbreviations:

POP	Population	ME/CGE	Milex as % of Central Government Expenditures
ME	Military Expenditures (Milex)	ME/POP	Milex per capita
AF	Armed Forces	ME/AF	Milex per soldier
AI	Value of Arms Imports	AF/POP	Armed Forces per 1000 people
AE	Value of Arms Exports		
ME/GNP	Milex as % of Gross National Product		

Source: Adapted from tabulation in U.S. Arms Control and Disarmament Agency, *World Military Expenditures and Arms Transfers 1987* (Washington, D.C.: U.S. Government Printing Office, March 1988) pp. 38-9.

per capita, military expenditure per soldier, armed forces per 1000 people), they both stood among the less militarized countries in the world. Indeed, viewed against the background of other regional conflicts in Asia, as between Iran and Iraq, or between Israel and Syria, the military rivalry between India and Pakistan, as Subrahmanyam claimed, was in some ways remarkably restrained [see Table 3.1].

Where Subrahmanyam principally went astray was in his apparent assumption that the South Asian region was proceeding politically along a predetermined trajectory toward an Indian-managed security system—what Ashok Kapur, in his presentation of a similar argument, has called "an incremental development of an Indocentric power structure"[19]—and that the acquiescence of India's neighbors, including Pakistan, to this system was only a matter of time. While Subrahmanyam's postulated outcome was clearly well within the range of possibility, other outcomes—including some less favorable to India—were also possible. Moreover, even if his postulated outcome were in the end to materialize, the end might well lie in the distant future. The truth is that Subrahmanyam's invocation of a benign, historically inexorable, and Indian-orchestrated movement toward a reintegrated subcontinent ran afoul of his own emphatic insistence upon a power-oriented understanding of interstate relations. No matter how often he denied Indian hegemonism or derided the smaller states' fears of Indian power as "subliminal sibling rivalry,"[20] Subrahmanyam could not disguise the paramount importance attached to military force in the calculations of Indian policymakers or the rapidly growing discrepancy between the disposable force of India and that of its regional neighbors. He should have recognized that the smaller states were likely to calculate their chances in the same currency that India used and not according to an alleged centripetal impulse operating vaguely within Indian civilization. They were likely to be strongly tempted, moreover, to react to the discrepancy in regional military power by resisting rather than by appeasing India.

Among the smaller states in the region, only Pakistan, in fact, had ever had sufficient military capability to exercise fully the option of resisting India. All Pakistani governments, whether civilian or military, had chosen this option in the past; and the Zia government, upon taking power in 1977, gave no hint of a changed commitment in this regard. However, confronted in the 1980s with grave challenges to Pakistan's security on both its eastern and western borders, Pakistan's new leaders were forced to reconsider Pakistan's requirements for continuing to exercise the resistance option. This refocused the attention of military analysts on the scale of the discrepancy in military power that had arisen between Pakistan and India; and it led to renewed questioning of Pakistan's ability to overcome it.

India had always held a quantitative military advantage over Pakistan, and by the middle of the 1980s this advantage seemed to be overwhelming. By this time, India enjoyed a very comfortable lead, for example, in military manpower (2.1:1), in divisions (1.7:1), in main battle tanks (2:1), in major surface warships (4:1), and in total combat aircraft (2.9:1) [see Table 3.2]. Naturally, raw figures such as these, even if generally accepted, conveyed only a very rough indication of relative military strength.[21] In regard to the naval balance, for example, the situation seemed to give the Indian navy, with its rapidly expanding inventory numbering over 70 combatant ships, a spectacular advantage over Pakistan, the core of whose fleet still consisted of a handful of hand-me-down U.S. destroyers. Scrutinized more closely, however, the advantage was not so clear-cut. For one thing, Pakistan had prudently supplied its navy and air force with long-range, sea-skimming, and cost-effective antiship missiles (the Exocet and Harpoon) for which India's capital surface ships presented excellent targets. The sea-denial mission of

Table 3.2
Military Forces of India and Pakistan, 1984-85

	India	Pakistan
Population	743 300 000	92 450 000
Total armed forces	1 120 000	478 600
Estimated GDP 1983/4	$176.0 bn	$30.859 bn
Defense budget 1984/5	$6.326 bn	$1.957 bn
Army	**960 000**	**450 000**
Armored divisions	2	2
Mechanized divisions	1	–
Infantry divisions	18	16
Mountain divisions	10	–
Indep armored bdes	5	4
Indep infantry bdes	7	5
Paratroop bdes	1	–
Indep artillery bdes	17	7
AA artillery bdes	–	2
Aviation squadrons	–	5
Medium tanks	2900	1421
	(incl 300 T72s)	(incl 370 M47/48/48A5s)
Navy	**47 000 (incl air)**	**11 000**
Submarines	8 (Sov FClass)	11 (incl 5 midget)
Aircraft carriers	1 (18 attack ac)	–
Cruisers	2 (1 tng ship)	–
Destroyers	3 (Sov "Kashin" II)	8 (incl 6 US "Gearing")
Frigates	23	–
Corvettes	3	–
Fast attack craft	16	16
Large patrol craft	7	5
Minesweepers/hunters	16	–
Landing craft	10	–

(Table continues)

the Pakistan navy, moreover, was much more modest in its aims than that of the Indian navy, which had a nearly 5000-mile ocean coastline and distant archipelagic territorial possessions to protect and which sought increasingly to acquire power projection capabilities in the Indian Ocean. The Pakistan navy could conceivably accomplish its mission without measuring up to its adversary in any strictly quantitative sense. By the same token, Indian ships designed for a "blue ocean" mission might count for less in the subcontinent's naval rivalry.[22]

Table 3.2 (continued)
Military Forces of India and Pakistan, 1984-85

	India	Pakistan
Naval Air Force	2000	
	(37 combat ac, 23 combat hel)	3 combat ac, 6 combat hel
Attack sqns	1	—
ASW sqns	1	1
MR sqns	2	—
Comms sqns	1	—
ASW hel sqns	4	2
SAR/liaison hel sqns	1	
Air Force	113 000	17 600
	(920 combat ac, 60 armed hel)	(314 combat ac)
Lt bbr sqns	3	—
FGA sqns	15	9
Air defense sqns	21	—
Interceptor/FGA sqns	—	9
Recce sqns	2	1
Tpt sqns	9	2
HQ comms sqns	1	—
Tpt hel sqns	6	—
Utility hel sqns	—	1
Search/Res hel sqns	—	1
Liaison hel sqns	8	—
SAM sqns	30	—

Source: Adapted from International Institute for Strategic Studies, *The Military Balance 1984–1985* (London, 1984) pp. 98–100, 106–7.

The air balance presented a similar set of problems. If a count were made, for example, of *modern* combat aircraft, excluding from the Pakistani side all but the U.S.-supplied F-16s and late-model French Mirage IIIs and Vs, India's advantage came closer to a formidable 4 or 5 to 1 ratio over Pakistan. Moreover, given India's much greater size and depth of defense against an adversary, the Pakistan air force would have been hard pressed to match India's ability to threaten virtually every important military and industrial target in Pakistan. On the other hand, the combat effectiveness of the F-16 fighter-bomber had been rated by Indian officials in 1981 as 3 to 4 times greater than the nearest Indian equivalents—the MiG-21s and Jaguars.[23] And even the Chinese-supplied F-6 air-superiority fighter, albeit a copy of the unquestionably obsolete MiG-19, when numbered in the hundreds and equipped with modern air-to-air missiles, was assessed at the same time by the Pakistan air force itself "as equal to most of its opposition."[24]

The exact magnitude of the disparity in ground forces was equally disputable. While the Indian army was unquestionably larger and more mechanized, Pakistan's army conceivably gained from the fact that it was garrisoned much closer to the India-Pakistan border than was India's and, in theory, could be more swiftly mobilized for surprise attack. At least in a relatively short war, Pakistan could in this way achieve a semblance of numerical equality.[25] A closely related argument was that India's minimal airlift capacity and the problems arising from difficult topographical and climatic conditions, especially in mountain areas, would impede swift transfer of Indian forces in numbers sufficient to arrest a Pakistani advance, for example, in Kashmir. Also pointed to were the vulnerability of India's extraordinarily long land frontier and exposed ocean coastline; the requirement that India maintain large garrisons to protect its northern border with China and its eastern border with Bangladesh;[26] the availability to the Pakistani army of a large, well-equipped, and "disguised" ready reserve force in the form of contract personnel on loan to friendly Middle Eastern states (as many as 30,000, according to one estimate);[27] Pakistan's enhanced defensibility and compactness since the loss of its eastern wing; and, not least, the expansion of Pakistan's armed forces at a pace that had virtually doubled its divisional strength and military manpower assets in the decade since its defeat in the Bangladesh war.[28]

Obviously, these kinds of arguments served a useful purpose in helping to correct some of the distortion inherent in a purely quantitative presentation of the military balance between India and Pakistan. No amount of argument, however, could cause the glaring inequality between them to vanish. While India's military advantage over Pakistan in the Zia period obviously did not fall in the range of 8 to 1, as proposed by one analyst,[29] it was in no real danger of being overturned.

In all probability, Pakistan had from time to time over the course of the past 4 decades achieved temporary parity, perhaps even a marginal edge, in certain categories of arms. Even some Indian defense analysts conceded, however, that India always managed to close the gap and usually to resume the lead.[30] The fact of the matter was that India achieved a solid military advantage over Pakistan during the Zia era that was for all practical purposes insurmountable. This advantage lay not so much in the existing quantitative or qualitative gap between them as in the rapidly dwindling *potential* of Pakistan to even out the balance in the future. It was not the already wide gap itself, in other words, that posed the biggest problem for Pakistan, but Pakistan's mounting inability to arrest its steady enlargement. For this inability, several reasons presented themselves.

In the first place, Zia's rise to power in Pakistan appears to have coincided with a fundamental (from the Pakistani point of view, negative) shift in India's perception of its strategic environment. This shift, in the judgment of many observers, was responsible for a marked expansion in Indian defense capabilities in the 1980s and for a changed orientation in its defense posture vis-à-vis Pakistan. In one widely praised and sympathetic study of Indian security policy, for example, Raju Thomas has held that the Indian defense strategy up until the late 1970s had "been to maintain a slight edge in military capabilities against Pakistan and to maintain minimum border defense capabilities for a holding operation against China until some form of superpower intervention could be sought to forestall further advance."[31] This defense strategy, which had required India to do little more than match Pakistan militarily, he labeled one of "sufficient defense." However, alerted by potentially threatening developments in the Middle East, Central and Southeast Asia, and the Indian Ocean that seemed to indicate an extended strategic environment, India, said Thomas, had moved to a new defense strategy of "limited deterrence."[32] Underpinning this strategy were attempts to reduce Chinese and Pakistani incentives to resort to force both by striving to improve relations with them and by enhancing significantly Indian military capabilities. The latter moved India's military posture inevitably "to one of clear superiority over Pakistan."[33] Since India's defense programs were thus less than ever simply responses to Pakistani defense programs, and since India's strategic horizons now extended well beyond Pakistan's own strategic framework, Pakistan's ability to control the dynamic of the regional arms race was correspondingly reduced.

Secondly, Pakistan's ability to mobilize domestic resources to meet the accelerating costs of defense modernization programs fell well short of India's. Indians frequently (and correctly) pointed out that Pakistan had consistently earmarked a larger percentage of its GNP for military expenditures (at times nearly double) than had India [see Table 3.3]. Yet, while maintaining a defense allocation that ranked in the bottom quartile of all the world's states, India nonetheless vastly outspent Pakistan. India's military expenditures in the period 1971-80 exceeded Pakistan's by a ratio of well over 3 to 1 ($30.8 billion to $8.2 billion, or 3.8:1).[34] In the 11 years corresponding roughly to the Zia period (1977-1987), India outspent Pakistan by a ratio not far from 5 to 1 ($65.9 billion to $14.2 billion, or 4.65:1).[35] This India achieved in spite of the fact that Pakistan's annual military outlay

Table 3.3
Military Expenditures, India and Pakistan, as Percentage of Annual GNP, 1977–87

	1977	78	79	80	81	82	83	84	85	86	87
Pakistan	5.5	5.5	5.4	5.4	5.5	5.8	6.9	6.5	6.8	6.7	6.5
India	3.6	3.6	3.5	3.2	3.3	3.5	3.5	3.7	3.5	3.6	3.9

Source: Arms Control & Disarmament Agency, *World Military Expenditures and Arms Transfers 1988* (Washington, D.C.: U.S. Government Printing Office, June 1989) pp. 46, 56.

increased in this period by 415 percent (in current dollars), India's by only 282 percent.[36] Pakistan thus faced an ever-widening gap in absolute expenditures in spite of the fact that it sustained a higher rate of increase in defense spending. Moreover, having spent roughly twice as great a percentage of its GNP on defense, Pakistan had already traded away a far greater share of capital available for investment in development than had its neighbor. Domestic political pressures against increased military spending were strong in both countries, and neither India's nor Pakistan's economic situation had much slack available for sharp increases in military outlay. At least in theory, however, India alone retained "the facility to increase its defense expenditures over a wide margin if it wanted to match the percentage burdens of its commonly perceived adversaries or those of the major powers."[37]

Thirdly, Pakistan proved quite unable in the Zia period to close the arms gap with India by turning to foreign arms suppliers. Pakistan concluded a number of major arms deals in this period with the United States, China, and France; but these were vastly overshadowed by India's arms purchases in the same period from the Soviet Union, France, and the United Kingdom. In the 11 years from 1977 to 1987, India imported foreign arms with a value (in current dollars) over 4 times greater ($16,435 billion against $3815 billion) than Pakistan's own arms imports.[38] Moreover, India devoted a far higher percentage of its total import trade to the purchase of foreign arms in most of these years than did Pakistan [see Table 3.4]. Indeed, the scale of Indian arms imports in this period moved it entirely out of Pakistan's class. By 1985, India had risen to third place (after Iraq and Saudi Arabia) among the leading arms importers in the world.[39]

Table 3.4
Arms Imports, India and Pakistan, in Value and as Percentage of Total Imports, 1977-87 (in millions of current US$)

	1977	78	79	80	81	82	83	84	85	86	87
Pakistan											
Value $	230	210	240	420	300	480	370	575	470	370	150
%-age	9.4	6.4	5.9	7.9	5.3	8.8	6.9	9.8	8.0	6.9	2.6
India											
Value $	950	360	600	825	1100	1700	1300	1100	2300	3000	3200
%-age	14.3	4.6	6.1	5.6	7.1	11.5	9.5	7.7	14.3	19.5	19.1

Source: Arms Control & Disarmament Agency, *World Military Expenditures and Arms Transfers 1988* (Washington, D.C.: U.S. Government Printing Office, June 1989) pp. 88, 98.

Fourthly, Pakistan faced a mounting disparity between its own and Indian military capabilities in the area of weapons manufacture. By Zia's time, Pakistan had become, like India, relatively self-sufficient in meeting its army's requirements for light infantry weapons and ammunition. These it produced in a vast complex of ordnance factories located in and around Wah. Additionally, it had a Chinese-aided heavy-rebuild factory at Taxila for the country's large fleet of Chinese-supplied T-59 medium tanks. The manufacturing capacity of its largest defense works, the Pakistan Aeronautical Complex at Kamra, which was primarily a rebuild-and-repair facility for the Pakistan air force's Chinese-supplied F-6s and French-supplied Mirage IIIs and Vs, was said to be growing.[40] By the end of the Zia period, moreover, Pakistan was claiming success on a number of defense technological fronts, including short-range tactical missiles.[41] Nevertheless, insofar as the indigenization of weapons production was concerned, Pakistan was thoroughly outclassed by India.

By 1980, there were at least 33 ordnance factories and about the same number of major research and development units in India supporting its drive for military self-sufficiency. They turned out an extensive range of conventional weapons, including practically all of the country's requirements for small arms and ammunition, plus howitzers, mortars, armored tanks, light transport and high-performance fighter aircraft, helicopters, missiles, electronics and communications equipment, and a variety of naval warships.[42]

They took on increasingly formidable tasks. In 1980, for example, the last of six British-licensed Leander class frigates were delivered to the Indian navy by India's Mazagaon Dockyard at Bombay. In 1984, production began there under German license on six HDW 209 (Type 1500) attack submarines (the first two to be assembled from kits, the last four to be constructed locally from keel up). By 1985, two Indian-designed and -built Godavari class guided-missile frigates were completed at Mazagaon. And by 1988, planning for construction at the Cochin naval yard of an indigenously-produced aircraft carrier was under way. These accomplishments made a vivid contrast with Pakistan, whose navy was entirely foreign-supplied and which did not include one major surface combatant not considered obsolete by Western standards.

Most spectacular of all, perhaps, was the progress made by India during the Zia period in satellite, rocket, and missile technology. The goal of self-reliance in satellite technology had been set in 1970. In June 1979, India's first experimental satellite was ready for launching from a test site in the Soviet Union. Only one year later (July 1980), the Indian Space Research Organization (ISRO) successfully performed the first of several indigenous satellite launches that plunged India fully into the space age. At the time, New Delhi disclaimed any intent to translate its burgeoning space program into military capability. It was readily apparent, however, that in such areas as reconnaissance, command and control, weather forecasting, and ballistic missiles, India's gathering space accomplishments had direct military applicability.[43] Strong evidence of this surfaced in 1983 with founding of the Integrated Guided Missile Development Programme, the aim of which was the development of five different classes of missiles. Two of these (the Prithvi short-range ballistic missile and Trishul surface-to-air missile) were successfully test-fired in 1988. A third (the Agni medium-range surface-to-surface ballistic missile) was successfully tested at the Interim Test Range in Orissa in 1989, not long after Zia's death.[44] An Indian newsmagazine crowed that Agni was "only the precursor to larger intercontinental ballistic missile systems."[45] Even if India chose to stop short of an ICBM, however, its technological prowess and vast lead over Pakistan in the development of missiles had been clearly displayed.

Finally, Zia's Pakistan faced a seemingly insuperable Indian advantage in respect to availability of indigenous human resources for translating defense aspirations into concrete realities. India claimed the third largest pool of scientists and engineers in the world. Growth in the number and quality of its nuclear and space scientists and engineers, some of whom were said to be world class, had been "particularly spectacular."[46] A vast array of defense-related research and development organizations, supported by steadily increasing budgetary allocations, provided facilities and incentives for moving the country closer to its declared goal of defense self-reliance. Major central government units, such as the Defence Research and Development Organisation (DRDO), coordinated research efforts between the Ministry of Defence and both public- and private-sector industries, and maintained ties with major universities and research centers.[47] Pakistan, in contrast, could make no comparable claims. Against some 6000 formally trained scientists employed in India's government-run defense science organizations in the latter 1980s, Pakistan had no more than 50 of its own.[48] In Pakistan, there was little, if any, collaboration between government defense science organizations and private industry. There were few, if any, links, moreover, between universities and the government defense science organizations. Few, if any, university physicists were consultants for government defense industries or engaged in anything but teaching. In fact, only a tiny handful of institutions of higher learning were even capable of producing first-class science graduates. There had not been more than 25 or so Doctor of Philosophy degrees awarded in all of the natural sciences in all of Pakistan since independence. While India was awarding an estimated 3500 Doctor of Philosophy and Master of Science degrees per year by the late 1980s, Pakistan *in all fields* was producing only about 25.[49]

The Zia period was thus a major turning point in regard to Pakistan's prospects for preventing a steadily widening Indian lead in the subcontinental arms race. India, by then, was clearly setting the pace in the development, production, import, and deployment of modern conventional arms, and it was setting it in a manner that left Pakistan with receding ability to respond effectively. Pakistanis were far from inclined at this point to throw in the towel; but the fear was growing among them that Pakistan's capacity to maintain a credible conventional defense against Indian military power could not be assured with existing defense strategies. Proposals for modifying or even scrapping them thus surfaced regularly in both public and private discussion.

Dominating discussion of alternatives to Pakistan's existing defense strategies toward India were three possibilities—(1) arms control, (2) strategic alliance, and (3) nuclear weaponization.[50] The first depended on improved bilateral relations with India. The second required the sustained and strong commitment to Pakistan's security of its foreign allies, especially the United States. The third derived its inspiration mainly from development of autochthonous capabilities in the realm of nuclear science and technology. To many observers, these alternatives appeared contradictory. To some, they seemed dangerously illusory or even cynical. The Zia government actively pursued all three, though not with the same level of commitment, public acknowledgment, or success. We move now to consider the first two—nonnuclear—alternatives.

II. NONNUCLEAR ALTERNATIVES

Arms Control

Pre-Zia Pakistan had been relatively infertile soil for both regional and global arms-control initiatives. Indian proposals for bilateral no-war agreements between India and Pakistan, made first by Prime Minister Nehru in 1949 and then by Prime Minister Shastri in 1965, were turned down by Pakistan. Pakistan signed (without ratifying) the Partial Test Ban Treaty in August 1963;[51] but it declined, as did India, to sign the 1968 Non-Proliferation Treaty. Article 1 of the 1972 Simla Agreement committed both states "to refrain from the threat or use of force against the territorial integrity or political independence of each other." But India's successful detonation of a nuclear device in 1974, coupled with Pakistani bitterness over military defeat and enforced repartition in the Bangladesh war, stifled further progress toward more concrete bilateral arms control agreements. Pakistan sought relief instead from the United Nations. In 1974, in an obvious response to India's nuclear test, Pakistan pressed for international treaty guarantees against the threat to use nuclear weapons against nonnuclear weapon states as well as for United Nations endorsement of the concept of a South Asian nuclear-weapon-free zone (NWFZ).[52] Until Zia came to power in 1977, however, arms control as a major instrument of security policy was conspicuous mainly in its absence.

Soviet intervention in Afghanistan at the end of the 1970s and the almost simultaneous return to power in New Delhi of Islamabad's old adversary, Indira Gandhi, prompted Pakistan to give renewed attention to regional arms control. At a meeting with the Indian Foreign Minister in New Delhi in July 1981, Pakistan's Foreign Minister Agha Shahi formally proposed that the two countries engage in bilateral talks to reach agreement on a mutually acceptable ratio of conventional armed forces and armaments. That set in motion what Shahi has called Pakistan's "peace offensive," a lengthy string of proposals made to India over the next several years for agreement on bilateral and multilateral arms-control measures regarding both conventional and nuclear weapons. By the end of the Zia period, these proposals included:[53]

1. simultaneous mutual ratification of the Nuclear Non-Proliferation Treaty of 1968, calling for renunciation of nuclear weapons and submission to an international nuclear safeguards regime;
2. simultaneous mutual acceptance of International Atomic Energy Agency (IAEA) safeguards on all nuclear facilities;
3. establishment by treaty of a South Asian nuclear weapon-free zone (NWFZ);[54]
4. a No-War Pact;
5. comprehensive mutual inspection of each other's nuclear facilities;
6. a joint declaration renouncing the acquisition or manufacture of nuclear weapons; and
7. a South Asian Comprehensive Test-Ban Treaty.[55]

None of these proposals found favor with India. Indeed, the only arms-control measure that got the support of both states during the Zia period was proposed by the Indians themselves. At a meeting in New Delhi on 17 December 1985, Indian Prime Minister Rajiv Gandhi won President Zia's consent to negotiate a formal agreement not to attack each other's nuclear installations. Nothing came of this proposal, however, until after Zia's death.[56]

Pakistan's efforts to moderate the subcontinental arms race through arms control thus appeared to produce very meager results. One reason for this was that the Indians profoundly distrusted Pakistani motives. Zia's arms-control initiatives, seen from New Delhi, were little more than public relations gambits and artful political camouflage. Pakistan's offer, for example, of a No-War Pact to India in September 1981, at precisely the moment when Washington's renewed security ties with Islamabad were coming up for congressional inspection, seemed to Indians an all-too-convenient coincidence and an egregious instance of Pakistani duplicity. Distrust worked in both directions, of course. Conduct by the Indian army in the winter of 1986-87 of Operation Brass Tacks, for example, inevitably raised questions in Pakistan about India's real ambitions in the region. Held in the border state of Rajasthan in areas adjacent to Pakistan's politically troubled Sind province and involving as much as half the manpower of the Indian army, Brass Tacks was the largest military exercise in India's history. To many observers, it seemed clearly intended to intimidate Pakistan, perhaps "to remind Islamabad of India's regional primacy, to persuade Pakistan to terminate alleged support for Sikh terrorists, or simply to provide a foreign distraction for domestic political purposes."[57] Indeed, it was not an "exercise" at all, according to one well-known Indian defense analyst, but a calculated attempt to provoke Pakistan into war with India.[58] Whatever the truth, Brass Tacks most certainly did more to inspire Pakistan's reliance upon arms than upon arms control.

A second reason, rising in large measure from the region's starkly asymmetrical power configuration, was the seeming incommensurability of Indian and Pakistani security objectives. Indians almost invariably sensed in Pakistani arms control proposals a calculated effort to carve out a larger role for the international community in regional conflict management and/or to dilute India's natural advantages in size and power by inducing Indian acquiescence to the principle of arms parity. An arms agreement like the NPT, which would subordinate India (but not China) to an internationally supervised system of controls, was thus unlikely to generate much enthusiasm in New Delhi. By the same token, Pakistanis generally saw hidden in Indian arms-control proposals an effort to isolate Pakistan from its foreign allies and to compel Pakistani acceptance of subordinate status within the region. New Delhi's August 1982 offer of a Treaty of Peace and Friendship, for example, fell in this category. Made as a counter to Islamabad's earlier offer of a No-War Pact, New Delhi's treaty package seemed to Pakistanis to be less concerned with putting a lid on the arms race than with lending legitimacy to Indian regional dominance. Draft articles of the proposed treaty apparently called for strict adherence to the bilateral resolution of disputes along with a ban on the grant of military bases to any foreign power—both old favorites of India's. Pointedly omitted from them, however, were reaffirmations of such standard international principles as nonintervention and noninterference in internal affairs or the sovereign equality of states—both strongly favored by Pakistan.[59]

The arms-control initiatives undertaken by Pakistan during the Zia period clearly had some propaganda value. Conceivably, this was their only purpose. It is equally conceivable, of course, that they were made—or at least that some of them were made—in good faith. One close observer of arms-control developments in the subcontinent has suggested, for example, that Prime Minister Junejo's September 1987 proposal of a complete ban on nuclear tests, apart from providing Islamabad "the short-term political advantage of casting itself as the champion of nuclear restraint in the region," was also "a serious attempt to engage India in substantive nuclear talks that might eventually place a cap on the region's emerging nuclear arms race,..."[60] In general, however, Islamabad appears to have viewed arms control with the same heavy skepticism with which it was viewed in New Delhi and, as a consequence, to have placed very little reliance on it in managing its relationship with India.

Strategic Alliance

Alarmed by the potential strategic ramifications of the Soviet intervention in Afghanistan, the administration of President Jimmy Carter promptly took steps in the first months of 1980 to repair its badly strained relationship with Pakistan. These steps, which included a much-publicized visit to Khyber Pass on the Pakistan-Afghanistan border in early February by Carter's National Security Advisor, Zbigniew Brzezinski, culminated in Washington's formal offer to Pakistan later that same month of a $400 million 2-year package of economic and military aid. The offer clearly testified to the stunning reversal that the Soviet move had inspired in Washington's assessment of Pakistan's geopolitical importance. It apparently fell well short of President Zia's expectations, however, and he disdainfully dismissed it. As we know, his patience was later amply rewarded by the incoming Reagan administration, which reached agreement with Islamabad in June 1981 on a substantially larger $3.2 billion security assistance program. Spread over 6 years and aimed mainly at meeting some of Pakistan's more urgent arms requirements, this program lifted Pakistan by the middle of the decade to a position near the top of recipients worldwide of American security assistance. It was followed by a 5-year $4.02 billion program, negotiated in 1987, that was split in a ratio of roughly 57:43 between economic and military aid. Fated to outlast Zia by several years, this latter program held out for Pakistan the promise of continued preeminence among America's favored strategic clients at least into the 1990s.

The Reagan administration justified its offer of aid to Pakistan in large part in terms of the Soviet threat. In Senate hearings on the aid program and proposed sale of F-16 fighter aircraft to Pakistan held in November 1981, for example, James L. Buckley, the Under Secretary of State for Security Assistance, urged upon Congress the administration's view that

> a strong, stable and independent Pakistan is an essential anchor of the entire southwest Asian region....[U.S. military assistance is required] to give Pakistan the ability to handle with its own resources incursions and limited cross-border threats from Soviet backed Afghan forces and to keep the Soviets from thinking they can coerce or subvert Pakistan with impunity. We fully recognize that even with our proposed assistance Pakistan cannot acquire an independent capability to confront the full wave of a direct and massive Soviet attack. Our intention is

to raise the cost of potential aggression and to demonstrate that a strong security relationship exists between the United States and Pakistan which the Soviet Union must take into account in its calculations.[61]

Buckley acknowledged India's "expressed concerns" over the administration's assistance proposals. He contended, however,

> that the projected military assistance levels and provision of the F-16's to Pakistan will not upset the overwhelming qualitative and quantitative superiority which India enjoys in the region. The U.S. program for Pakistan will not inject a new element of instability into the South Asian sub-continent. It is the Soviets, by their aggression in Afghanistan, who have brought new instability to the region and our program is designed to offset that instability. Nor will U.S. policies fuel an arms race in South Asia.[62]

Buckley was clearly right in arguing that the Soviets, by virtue of their military occupation of Afghanistan, had injected a new element of instability into the South Asian region. His point that the contemplated level of U.S. arms assistance and sales to Pakistan might help to offset that instability without at the same time upsetting India's military superiority in the region, in view of our earlier discussion of trends in the military balance, would seem reasonable to most. His contention, on the other hand, that U.S. military aid would not itself be a destabilizing factor in the subcontinent or fuel an Indo-Pakistani arms race was much less convincing. The fact of the matter, as we have seen, was that the Indo-Pakistani arms race was already creating substantial tension in the region before the Soviet move into Afghanistan, and it was difficult to see how major new injections of American arms into the region were to be accomplished without adding measurably (and in somewhat unpredictable fashion) to this tension. Pakistan's motives were obviously complex, more so it seems than suited the legislative strategy of the Reagan administration. Tailored to the need for building bipartisan congressional support for a firm U.S. response to the Soviet move into Afghanistan, this strategy precluded the administration's frank admission that a policy designed to stabilize one of Pakistan's borders could not be guaranteed to stabilize the other.

The substantial convergence in the outlooks of Islamabad and Washington in regard to Afghanistan thus cloaked but could not eradicate the fact that these two allies had separate and in some ways contradictory priorities in the region. Pakistan's leaders were bound to seek renewal of security ties with the United States not only to counter the Soviet threat but to a considerable extent, perhaps even primarily, to offset Pakistan's weakness relative to India. They were quite likely, moreover, to seek not so much a stable relationship with India as one that placed the two countries on a more equal military footing.[63] American leaders, on the other hand, while not unmindful of the steady growth of Indian military power and of the potential threat to Pakistan that it represented, had long ago made it plain that the American commitment to Pakistan did not extend to contingencies arising from Pakistan's rivalry with India. For them, the trend toward Indian military dominance in the region was far less a development to reverse than one to manipulate for American strategic purposes.

The region's military rivalry had severely undermined Pakistan's security relationship with the United States on two earlier occasions, first in 1965 and then again in 1971, when the outbreak of war between India and Pakistan had precipitated American arms embargos against both belligerents. At those times, the anger Pakistanis felt over what seemed to them America's betrayal of an ally was matched only by the frustration Americans felt over what seemed just as clearly to them Pakistan's reckless provocation of its more powerful neighbor. The Soviet military takeover of Afghanistan restored the grounds for renewed cooperation between the United States and Pakistan. It did nothing, however, to reward the faith of those observers who, like Rodney Jones, expected the Soviet threat in Afghanistan to help promote Indo-Pakistan reconciliation.[64] That project could not be accomplished by Pakistan alone and, as Thomas Thornton suggested, India was little likely to take the lead.[65] There could be no more certainty in the 1980s than there had been in earlier decades, therefore, that Pakistani perceptions of the Indian threat would be much appreciated in Washington, or that the policies adopted in response to it would get American endorsement. No less than in those earlier periods, however, Pakistanis were drawn to strategic alliance with America as the only practical way to counter the challenge of India's growing military might.

To be sure, Pakistani support for the revived U.S. connection was far from universal. Pakistan's affiliation with the Non-Aligned Movement at the end of the 1970s had been a popular decision, and to some elements of the population the restoration of a military relationship with Washington threatened to reverse it. The dangers of dependency on Washington were a staple feature of newspaper commentary throughout the 1980s. Zia's civilian political opponents, especially those on the ideological left, routinely accused him of sacrificing Pakistani interests on the altar of the West's Cold War against the Soviet Union. Right-wing Islamist groups, fearful of the long-term consequences for Islam of the Soviet takeover in Afghanistan, were generally supportive of Zia's pro-West policies. Nevertheless, they too questioned the depth and durability of Washington's commitment to the

Islamic jehad. When in his public speeches and writings, ex-Foreign Minister Agha Shahi warned of America's habit of deferring to "regional influentials" such as Israel and India, and urged Pakistan, therefore, to move toward what he termed "positive neutrality" in global politics, numerous Pakistanis, in and out of government, must have felt at least some sympathy with him.[66] Pakistanis unquestionably had lower expectations in the 1980s in regard to American support than they had had in the 1950s. On the whole, however, Zia's decision to restore Pakistan's connection with Washington met with very little resistance from Pakistanis. If the pictures of F-16s painted on the sides of thousands of Pakistani busses and trucks were any indication, it was, in fact, very popular.

The same could not be said about American reaction to the renewal of security ties with Pakistan. Memory of the mob attack on the American Embassy in Islamabad in November 1979 was still very fresh when the Carter administration moved to restore ties with Islamabad in the early months of 1980; and by the time the Reagan administration announced its security assistance program for Pakistan the following year, the military government's various transgressions against American sensibilities had already made Zia's Pakistan an easy target for its critics. The warmest support for the U.S. aid program for Pakistan came from conservatives worried about Soviet adventurism in Southwest Asia. Indeed, popular support in the United States for Pakistan was mainly derivative of Pakistani support for the Afghan resistance. There were no significant pro-Pakistani public lobbies operating in the United States during the Zia period. Of anti-Pakistani lobbies, on the other hand, there were many. Practical grounds for U.S.-Pakistan cooperation clearly existed; and, so long as Soviet troops remained in Afghanistan, Islamabad's ties with Washington seemed reasonably secure. Resistance to the relationship was strong all along, however, and there was never the slightest chance either that Pakistan's security predicament would arouse mass sympathy among Americans, much less that the generals who had seized power in the 1977 coup would win American affection. In short, Pakistani doubts in regard to the long-term durability of the American connection were far from misplaced.

The pronounced reticence in American support for the renewed security relationship with Pakistan stemmed in part from the revulsion many Americans felt toward the government of Pakistan itself. Its leader, after all, had been inexplicably slow to respond effectively to desperate American pleas for assistance when Pakistani mobs attacked the American Embassy in Islamabad on 21 November 1979.[67] Only months before, he had ignored presidential and congressional pleas for clemency toward the fallen Prime

Minister Zulfikar Ali Bhutto, whose death sentence had been awarded following court proceedings of extremely doubtful legality. He had seized power by force from an elected leader, and, once having gotten control of government, refused to give it up. Instead, he clamped down on the press, banned political parties, jailed his political opponents, and crippled the courts.[68] On top of that, he launched a multifaceted and far-reaching program of Islamization, whose most publicized aspects—public lashings and draconian penalities for sexual misconduct—ran directly counter to American liberal values.

Some American observers familiar with Pakistan strove to explain that Pakistan's unstable polity was not uncharacteristic of third world countries, furthermore, that the human rights record of the Zia regime was no worse than that of its elected predecessor (or of its democratic neighbor, India).[69]

More common, however, was the view that Pakistan had never been a viable state, that brute force was all that held it together, and that the United States, in supplying its government with the arms to repress dissent, was exposing itself to considerable risk of guilt by association. No one more tirelessly advanced these themes than the Carnegie Endowment's long-time South Asia-watcher, Selig Harrison. "As the Bengalis still bitterly recall," Harrison reminded his listeners in congressional hearings on the Reagan administration's proposed aid package in September 1981, "it was American weaponry that the Pakistan army used against them. Similarly, when the Baluch [tribesmen of Pakistan's southwestern province of Baluchistan] staged an insurgency of their own in 1973, Islamabad once again turned its U.S. equipment not against invading Communist forces, but against its own people. It took 80,000 Pakistani troops four years to subdue the Baluch, despite repeated strafing attacks on the Baluch villages by U.S. fighter planes received under the military aid program and by Huey-Cobra helicopters borrowed from the Shah of Iran."[70] In an article published in 1978, Harrison had written that "at the height of the fighting in late 1974, American-supplied Iranian combat helicopters, some of them manned by Iranian pilots, joined the Pakistani air force in raids on Baluch guerrilla camps. These AH-IJ Huey-Cobra helicopters provided the key to victory in a crucial battle at Chamalang in early September when a force of some 17,000 guerrillas of the Marri tribe, one of the 27 major Baluch subdivisions, was decimated."[71]

Harrison's claim was factually inaccurate and highly misleading. By 1970, Chinese-supplied aircraft made up "33 percent of the Pakistan Air Force's 270 planes, 65 percent of all the interceptor-bombers, and 90 percent of the first-line modern fighter planes at its disposal."[72] These percentages rose even higher in the first few years of the 1970s (prior to the outbreak of the Baluch insurgency) with additional large Chinese transfers to Pakistan of the Shanyang F-6 (MiG-19). The sinification of PAF's aircraft inventory was clearly in an advanced stage when the insurgency broke out in Baluchistan in 1973. To the extent that the air force was involved at all in the fighting in Baluchistan, the probability was slight that it would have used its Korean War vintage F-86 Sabre jets and not its newer and far more numerous Chinese aircraft. As for the Huey-Cobra helicopter gunships, no armed helicopters of any kind were used by the Pakistan army against the Baluch insurgents. Pakistan had none of its own at that time, and the Shah loaned Pakistan only a small number (most sources say ten, but estimates range as high as thirty) of unarmed, Iranian-piloted Chinook transport helicopters. These, according to well-informed sources, played an extremely minor role in the fighting and were returned to Iran in May 1974 after only eight months or so in Baluchistan.[73] They played absolutely no role, incidentally, in the battle at Chamalang, which took place months after the Iranian helicopters had been withdrawn.

Though its authenticity was questionable at best, Harrison's evocative tale of the gunship helicopters was picked up and repeated for years thereafter by a wide variety of commentators on Pakistan.[74] The picture he painted of the dread American killer Cobras raining death upon the practically defenseless Baluch insurgents inevitably made a powerful impression in a population that had only a few years earlier forced its own government to abandon a much bloodier counterinsurgency war in Vietnam. Doubtless, Pakistan's repression of the Baluch insurgency was brutal. But the responsibility for it of U.S. arms transfer policy was a great deal less than Harrison implied.

A second element contributing to American reticence to form a close relationship with Pakistan was the widespread belief that American buttressment of Pakistan's armed forces, unless strictly limited, would do more harm than good for the stability of the region. Underpinning this belief was the existence of a school of thought favoring closer ties with India and the development of a regional policy that deemphasized military weapons.[75] Also underpinning it was the fact that American arms had been employed by Pakistan in two wars against the Indians—never against a communist adversary. To this the Reagan administration responded that the situation had changed enough so that Pakistan could now be militarily strengthened against the Soviet threat without adding to tensions with India. This argument, as we observed earlier, lacked credibility.

Not the least reason for its lack of credibility was that several of the major weapons systems that were being sought from Washington by Pakistan, including medium tanks, heavy artillery, the F-16 strike aircraft, helicopter gunships, and antiship missiles, seemed better suited for a conflict with India than with Afghanistan. They seemed equally well suited, moreover, for either defensive or offensive warfare. Such anomalies prompted demands by Reagan administration critics that U.S. arms transfers to Pakistan be strictly limited to defensive weapons, that they be tailored primarily for defense of Pakistan's border with Afghanistan, and that they not be made without taking Indian interests into account.[76]

To Pakistanis, of course, acquiescence to these demands would have amounted to a concession to India of a tacit veto over Pakistan's arms acquisitions from abroad. This Islamabad wanted desperately to avoid. Its opposition to any such concession undoubtedly strengthened its determination to hold out for the F-16 aircraft in negotiations with Washington over the initial arms package in 1981. Far better configured than any other aircraft in the Pakistan air force to stop advancing columns of Indian tanks on the flat Punjabi plains, the F-16 served better than any other weapon system to give a symbolic lift to Pakistan's overt standing in Washington's hierarchy of security commitments.

Such symbolism was a very pale substitute, however, for an American guarantee of Pakistan's eastern border against India or, indeed, for a formal strategic alliance with Pakistan. While that type of commitment had never appealed to Washington, it had almost always appealed to Islamabad, in the Zia period as much as before. No matter how often Pakistan's leaders in this period paraded their fidelity to the cause of nonalignment, the evidence suggests that they wanted an alliance and not just a limited "security relationship" with the United States. In negotiations with the Carter administration in 1980, Zia apparently pressed for a formal treaty, ratified by Congress. Carter, however, offered only to reaffirm the executive agreement forged between Ayub Khan and the Eisenhower administration in 1959.[77] According to Agha Shahi, who negotiated the 1981 security-assistance agreement with the United States, the government of Pakistan, recognizing that there was little likelihood of congressional acceptance of a formal defense treaty, did not even raise the matter with the Reagan administration.[78] Instead, Shahi maintains that he held out in the negotiations for conditions that conformed to international commitments he had already made to the Non-Aligned Movement in order to gain Pakistan's acceptance in it, namely: (1) that Pakistan should not be expected to join in any "strategic consensus" on the Middle East; (2) that Pakistan should not be required to make military bases available to the U.S. military; and (3) that Pakistan should not be expected to serve as a conduit of Western arms aid to the Afghan resistance.[79] These conditions, according to Shahi, were accepted by the United States at the time the agreement was signed. To Shahi's amazement and disappointment, however, they were not held to by Pakistan's own leaders. Zia, says Shahi, asked the American negotiators at the conclusion of the discussions: "Why are you being shy? Why don't you ask for bases?" In one stroke, says Shahi, Zia, who had offered the Americans what they themselves had not demanded, had overturned the nonaligned basis of Pakistan's foreign policy! He undermined it further, according to Shahi, by gradually "giving away" Shahi's condition that Pakistan not be made to serve as a conduit of Western arms to the Afghan rebels. In Shahi's view, President Zia did not share Shahi's confidence in nonalignment, often commenting instead that there were, after all, only two genuinely nonaligned countries in the world—the United States and the Soviet Union. It does not appear that many others in charge of affairs in Islamabad at the time shared it, either.[80] Ironically, Shahi's preference for a nonaligned Pakistan may have been better appreciated—albeit in somewhat reduced form—in Washington than in Islamabad!

A third element contributing to the reticence in American support for Pakistan was the fear in some quarters that Washington's commitment to nuclear nonproliferation objectives would inevitably be diluted if it moved to create a close military relationship with Pakistan. The Carter administration, which had given particularly high priority to nonproliferation objectives, had carried them in Pakistan's case to the point of precipitating a nearly complete break in U.S.-Pakistan relations by the end of the 1970s. The Reagan administration declared itself equally committed to these objectives; but it was never in doubt that countering the Soviet threat would be given precedence over nonproliferation by the Reagan White House. Pakistan's stubborn refusal to give more than token assurances of its own commitment to nonproliferation gave its critics, in and out of Congress, perhaps their most powerful ammunition against the U.S.-Pakistan security relationship. It was a major stimulus, moreover, for frequent congressional hearings on the nuclear proliferation problem as well as for a string of legislative enactments aimed at forcing would-be proliferators to toe the American nuclear line. It exposed major contradictions in American foreign-policy priorities and dramatically underscored the fragility of the U.S.-Pakistan security relationship.

When this relationship was renewed in 1981, the Reagan administration advanced the argument that bolstering Pakistan's conventional forces against the Soviet threat might also deter it from acquiring nuclear weapons. The administration drew a distinction at the time between the *development* and the *utilization* of a nuclear explosives capability, that is, between the maintenance of a nuclear option and actual construction of nuclear weapons. In the face of accumulating evidence of Islamabad's clandestine nuclear weapons program, it conceded that Pakistan was engaged in nuclear weapons development; but it insisted that Pakistan had given convincing assurances of its willingness to forgo making nuclear weapons.[81] Congress accepted the distinction and consented to a temporary (6-year) waiver of the antiproliferation Section 669 (Symington amendment) of the Foreign Assistance Act. It compensated for this, however, by tightening the requirement (the Glenn amendment) for termination of U.S. assistance in the event Pakistan was found to have received, transferred, or exploded a nuclear device. In return for U.S. help in modernizing its conventional armed forces, Pakistan was thus advised to limit its exercise of the nuclear weapons option to the development of capabilities. A nuclear test, it was cautioned, would very likely result in the cutoff of American aid.

In this way, U.S. nonproliferation policy became entangled in its containment policy, congressional approval of the Reagan administration's stiffening of the latter having been gained on condition of Pakistan's willingness to observe reasonable restraint in regard to the former. Once having consented to the scheme, the White House was poorly placed to control its consequences. U.S. aid could not be effectively channeled to the Afghan resistance forces except via Pakistan; and so long as Washington attached importance to the struggle for Afghanistan, Pakistan, because of its pivotal brokerage role in the war, could afford a certain indifference to U.S. antiproliferation policies. This angered congressional nonproliferation supporters, however, who demanded that Pakistan be pressed to observe nuclear celibacy at home even while running risks for Washington in Afghanistan. As things turned out, linking both anti-Soviet and antiproliferation policies to the aid package required considerably more leverage with Pakistan than the aid package itself supplied. It was asking quite a lot of Pakistan, in other words, to adhere to equally high standards in regard both to conduct of the war and control over the spread of nuclear weapons—given the risks to Pakistan implicit in both—in return for a relatively short-term, annually reviewed security-assistance agreement.

It was not surprising, therefore, that the arrangement showed little success in slowing Pakistan's nuclear weaponization program or even in preventing Pakistan from an occasional show of brazen disregard for American nonproliferation laws. In fact, accusations that Pakistan was forging ahead with the development of nuclear weapons surfaced even before Congress had given final approval to the administration's aid package for Pakistan in 1981, and they were still being made when Zia died. Pakistan's nuclear scorecard of real or alleged developments for the years 1981-88 included the following:[82]

1981: report that Pakistan was constructing a nuclear test site in the Baluchistan mountains;

1981: report that Pakistan was secretly diverting plutonium-bearing spent fuel from the safeguarded KANUPP reactor in Karachi;

1981: arrest of a retired Pakistani army colonel while he was allegedly attempting to smuggle a shipment of zirconium metal, considered an essential component in the nuclear fuel fabrication process, to Pakistan through New York's Kennedy Airport;

1983: report that China had given Pakistan information relating to the design of nuclear weapons;

1984: report that China had given Pakistan technical advice on the uranium enrichment process and possibly the design for the weapon used in China's fourth nuclear test;

1984: arrest and indictment of three Pakistanis in Houston, Texas, for allegedly attempting to ship 50 high-speed electronic switches (krytrons), used to trigger nuclear weapons, out of the United States;

1984: report that Dr. Abdul Qadir Khan, head of Pakistan's uranium enrichment program, had stated in an interview that Pakistani scientists had managed for the first time to produce low-enriched uranium and that, if ordered to do so, they could make a nuclear bomb;

1984: report that Dr. Abdul Qadir Khan had stated in an interview that Pakistan could achieve nuclear-weapons capability without a test;

1985: report that Pakistan had conducted a successful test of the non-nuclear triggering package for a nuclear weapon;

1985: report that Pakistan army had been attempting to purchase a U.S.-manufactured flash X-ray machine used in nuclear weapons development programs;

1986: report that Pakistan had masterminded an operation to smuggle almost 2000 pounds of specially hardened maraging steel, a uranium-centrifuge component, out of West Germany to Pakistan;

1986: report that Pakistan had attempted to purchase several hundred tons of pure graphite, used in production of plutonium for weapons, in the United States, Britain, France, and West Germany;

1986: report that Pakistan had purchased six flash X-ray machines from a Swedish firm;

1986: report that U.S. intelligence sources had concluded that Pakistan had produced weapons-grade uranium and might be able to produce nuclear weapons in as little as 2 weeks;

1987: report that Dr. Abdul Qadir Khan had stated in an interview in Islamabad with Indian journalist Kuldip Nayar that Pakistan had succeeded in producing weapons-grade uranium and that it had built nuclear arms;

1987: report that President Zia had stated in an interview with a *Time* magazine correspondent that Pakistan had the ability to fabricate nuclear weapons whenever it wished;

1987: report of a Swiss-West German investigation into an allegedly Pakistan-directed operation to smuggle out of Europe specially manufactured equipment—including large precision furnaces called autoclaves—and blueprints allegedly for a second uranium enrichment plant at Golra;

1987: arrest in Philadelphia of Arshad Pervez, a Pakistani-born Canadian businessman, for allegedly attempting in concert with retired Pakistani Brigadier Inam Ul-Haq to export illegally to Pakistan the controlled metals beryllium and maraging 350 steel.

1988: report in *The New York Times Magazine* by Hedrick Smith that Pakistan had accumulated enough highly enriched uranium for four to six nuclear weapons, that Pakistan had fabricated virtually all essential components for these weapons, and that it could rapidly deploy them in any future conflict.

Congress struck back at Pakistan's seeming disregard for American nuclear sensitivities by supplementing existing nonproliferation laws with additional enactments threatening termination of U.S. economic and military assistance if Pakistan failed to mend its ways. In March 1984, Senators John Glenn and Alan Cranston proposed an amendment to the Foreign Assistance Act which, had it been enacted, would have compelled the President to certify as a condition of aid that Pakistan did not possess a nuclear explosive device, was not developing such a device, and was not acquiring, overtly or covertly, the technology, material, or equipment intended for the manufacture or detonation of such a device. Responding to the Reagan administration's contention that such legislation would effectively prohibit further security assistance to Pakistan, the Senate adopted a less severely worded amendment, proposed by Senators Pressler, Mathias, and Percy, obliging the President to certify only that Pakistan did not possess a nuclear explosive device and that the proposed U.S. assistance program would reduce significantly the risk that Pakistan would come into possession of any such device. In addition to the certification requirement, Congress in 1985 adopted the Solarz amendment barring aid to nonnuclear-weapon countries that illegally exported nuclear commodities from the United States for use in nuclear explosives.[83]

Waiver provisions in this legislation enabled the Reagan administration to carry on with its aid program for Pakistan in spite of mounting evidence that Pakistan stood in gross violation of U.S. nonproliferation laws. Congress was evidently unwilling to precipitate a policy crisis over the issue so long as Pakistan continued to play a vital role in promoting U.S. interests in Southwest Asia. Consequently, the demand by such groups as the Carnegie Task Force on Non-Proliferation and South Asian Security that American resolve be stiffened and that the President act to compel Pakistani acquiescence to American nonproliferation objectives by withholding at least a portion of the aid authorized by Congress, received little support.[84] In fact, such proposals struck most observers, including some members of the Task Force itself, as impractical and counterproductive.[85]

The distinction drawn by the Reagan administration between the development and utilization of nuclear explosives capability, sustainable perhaps in 1981, appeared much less tenable by the end of the Zia period. But the tension between the competing policy priorities of containment and nonproliferation had produced confusion and disarray among the proponents of a strengthened nonproliferation policy. Nowhere was this more apparent than on the editorial page of *The New York Times*. During congressional hearings in March 1987 on the proliferation problem, the *Times*, in an editorial entitled "Stop Pakistan's Nuclear Bomb," pleaded for Congress to gamble on Pakistan's need for U.S. military and economic assistance and to threaten to end aid entirely if Islamabad failed to stop its nuclear program where it stood. The editorial conceded that an aid cutoff might endanger the anti-Soviet resistance in Afghanistan, but argued that the risk had to be taken.[86] Perhaps having reflected on the wider implications of these remarks, the *Times* soon softened its stance. In an editorial entitled "Arm Afghans, balance the rest," it conceded only a few weeks later that it was "far better for Washington to sustain the military pressure in Afghanistan, balancing this as far as possible with the search for an Afghan peace, nuclear restraint and detente on the subcontinent." Though continuing to insist that Washington sustain "maximum pressure on Islamabad to stop its nuclear weapons program," it agreed that "the United States must balance its anti-Soviet goals in Afghanistan with its global nuclear nonproliferation policy."[87]

So long as Zia lived, the contradictions in American policy worked to Pakistan's advantage. It was clear, however, that American concerns over Pakistan's nuclear weaponization program hung like Damocles' sword over the future of the U.S.-Pakistan aid relationship.

III. THE NUCLEAR ALTERNATIVE

Pakistan's nuclear program survived the overthrow of Zulfikar Ali Bhutto in 1977 without suffering any apparent major change in personnel. Munir Ahmad Khan continued under Zia to direct the Pakistan Atomic Energy Commission, a post to which Bhutto had appointed him in 1972; and Dr. Abdul Qadir Khan continued to direct the uranium enrichment facility at Kahuta, a task to which he had been assigned by Bhutto upon Dr. Khan's return from the Netherlands in 1975. Both of these men were still at the helm of these organizations at Zia's death in 1988. Bhutto's fall seems not to have resulted in any major change in the pace and direction of the program, either. As we have already seen, the evidence is persuasive, in fact, that Pakistan's nuclear scientists labored throughout the Zia period as industriously as ever to acquire enhanced nuclear weapons capability. No doubt, the country's *declared* policy, now that its government was visibly under greater pressure not to antagonize its allies, had shifted away from Bhutto's occasionally explicit endorsement of military nuclearization. Actual policy, however, displayed no change in the country's level of commitment to the bomb.[88]

Earlier sections of this chapter have already provided part of the explanation for Pakistan's unwavering commitment under Zia, in spite of considerable opposition from abroad, to nuclear weaponization. The development of an increasingly unfavorable conventional military balance in the subcontinent, as we have seen, went hand in hand with gathering anxiety in Pakistan that this trend was becoming increasingly irreversible. In these circumstances, nuclear weapons were almost inevitably seized upon as an equalizer and the best insurance against growing Indian military power. We have seen, too, that Pakistani threat perceptions overlapped only partially (and somewhat intermittently) with those of Pakistan's primary ally, the United States, and that Pakistan's security decision-making elite, therefore, had gradually been driven to adopt what Haass called a "go-it-alone mentality" in regard to its basic defense priorities.[89]

Perhaps part of the explanation for Pakistan's determined drive for nuclear weapons capability, as various writers have suggested, should also be sought in Pakistan's efforts since its humiliating defeat in the 1971 war to enhance its standing, influence, and prestige among its fellow Muslim nations by being the first among them to master the esoteric technology of nuclear weapons. Entirely apart from the extremely contentious (and not infrequently propagandized) matter of whether Pakistan ever intended to sponsor a literal Islamic Bomb, Pakistan clearly stood to gain from the symbolic sharing with the rest of the Islamic world of its acquisition of nuclear capability. Such an accomplishment, according to Rodney Jones, would unquestionably

> be perceived with greater interest by Islamic countries than by most of the non-Islamic world. It would excite curiosity. It would invite open-ended speculation. It would put Pakistan more in the limelight. Arguably, it would enhance Pakistan's status. It would be unnatural if Pakistani leaders were unconscious of this or studiously brushed aside whatever new elements of influence flew their direction spontaneously from other states.[90]

Obviously the most direct—and probably the most powerful—incentive for Pakistan's nuclear weapons program, however, was the existence of a rival and much more advanced nuclear program in India. India's nuclear research activities had been launched even before independence; and with the formation in 1948 of the Indian Atomic Energy Commission, India gained a considerable head start over Pakistan.[91] India commissioned its first research reactor (Apsara, at the Trombay Atomic Research Center near Bombay) in 1956, the same year in which Pakistan took its first significant nuclear step by creating the Pakistan Atomic Energy Commission. Thereafter, India moved swiftly to master the entire nuclear fuel cycle. In 1960, it commissioned a much larger 40-megawatt research reactor from Canada (CIRUS, in Rajasthan). In 1962, it began operating a West German-built heavy water plant at Nangal. And in 1966, it began full-scale operation of an American- and French-assisted pilot plant at Trombay for the extraction of plutonium from spent reactor fuel. None of these facilities was covered by any international safeguards agreement. In May 1974, barely 2 years from the date when Bhutto is generally believed to have launched Pakistan on an active program of nuclear weapons research, India detonated a Hiroshima-sized, plutonium-fueled nuclear device at its Rajasthan desert test site. Though characterized by New Delhi as a "peaceful nuclear explosion," this unambiguous display of Indian nuclear prowess sent political shockwaves through Pakistan and gave powerful impetus to Islamabad's fledgling nuclear weapons program. Still smarting from India's rout of the Pakistani army in Bangladesh and the country's humiliating dismemberment, Pakistan simply could not "accept the prospect of an Indian nuclear monopoly."[92]

The Arms Race with India: The Nuclear Imperative 115

Zia took power from Bhutto 6 years after the Bangladesh debacle, 5 years after Bhutto is said to have unveiled his plans for a nuclear weapons program to a secret conclave of top scientific advisors at Multan in January 1972, and scarcely more than 3 years after India's nuclear detonation. Whatever may have been his private musings on the subject of nuclear weapons, retreat from the path layed down by his predecessor would have required extraordinary boldness. True, India made no overt moves to follow up its successful nuclear detonation with a program of weaponization. Indeed, the Janata government that replaced the Congress government of Mrs. Gandhi in December 1977 not only pledged itself to reconciliation with Pakistan but was led by an aging ex-Congressman, Morarji Desai, who publicly professed opposition to India's development of nuclear weapons. Well into the 1980s, many foreign observers held that it was not India but Pakistan, with its relentless effort to challenge India's manifest nuclear superiority, that was threatening to precipitate a nuclear arms race in the subcontinent. In a widely noted book published in 1984, for instance, Leonard Spector argued that India had actually exercised restraint in the face of Pakistani provocations, that the Pakistani nuclear challenge might necessitate "reactivation of India's nuclear explosives program," and that Mrs. Gandhi had, up to that time, "apparently been unwilling to pursue" the development of nuclear weapons. "Judging from the Indian reaction to reports of Pakistan's emerging nuclear capabilities," he observed,

> ...it seems evident that the pace and direction of any Indian nuclear weapons program will depend in significant part on developments in Pakistan. Were Pakistan, for example, to conduct a nuclear test, an Indian test series would seem an almost inevitable response, and some observers have suggested that India might "trump Pakistan's ace by detonating a hydrogen bomb."...Whether India will respond to Pakistan's progress toward acquiring a "bomb in the basement" by revitalizing the Indian nuclear explosives program or by accepting a de facto nuclear-armed neighbor remains uncertain.[93]

To Pakistanis, of course, nothing seemed less uncertain than that India would never, under any circumstances, practice nuclear celibacy in the face of a nuclear-armed Pakistan. New Delhi's security planners had long since insisted upon a substantial margin of superiority over Pakistan in *conventional* weaponry; and, given the vast size of India's nuclear establishment and the considerable potential for political trouble-making of its probomb lobby, there seemed little reason to question the Pakistani conviction that New Delhi would seek to retain its existing superiority in *nuclear* weaponry, too. Too often overlooked was the relative ease with which India avoided premature tipping of its nuclear hand by pursuing an enormous array of nuclear-related dual-use technologies. Raju Thomas pointed out in 1986, for example, that

> India's civilian nuclear energy and space programs, whether intended or not, provide the country with nuclear weapons and strategic nuclear delivery vehicles. In this respect, the nuclear and space programs are not different from several other developmental projects that have military implications. Development in the aeronautical, shipbuilding, automotive, electronics, metallurgical, mechanical, and civil engineering industries automatically carries indirect military benefits. The central point, therefore, is not whether India's motives are developmental *or* strategic. The rationale for India's nuclear and space programs is provided by the future combination of energy, telecommunications, and other development requirements in the civilian sector, and strategic necessities in the defense sector. The development sector provides the technological capability; the defense sector can utilize the latter if it demonstrates the need.[94]

Contrary to the widespread assumption that, in matters nuclear, there existed a relatively simple action-reaction sequence in South Asia (Pakistan acting, India largely reacting), the actual sequence was a lot more complex—and a lot less Pakistan-directed.[95] With gathering force as the 1980s progressed, India unquestionably posed a nuclear threat to Pakistan. "Whereas it is believed in the West that India has not 'weaponized' its nuclear capability or stockpiled nuclear weapons as such," Rodney Jones observed in a 1987 publication, "Pakistani planners would have to assume that India could make the transition to weapons production and deployment with delivery systems in a matter of one or two years, or perhaps just a few months."[96] In June 1985, in fact, Indian Prime Minister Rajiv Gandhi was reported to have said in an interview in Paris that nuclear arming would take India only "a few weeks or a few months."[97] By the time of Zia's death, even some of those Western observers who had most consistently held India to be a reluctant nuclear weaponizer had begun to change their tune.[98]

The Domestic Nuclear Consensus

There can be little doubt that Pakistan's nuclear policy, to the extent that anything was known of it outside the highly secretive nuclear establishment, had strong popular support throughout the Zia period. Admittedly, polling data that would provide clear evidence of this proposition, especially in regard to support of a nuclear *weapons* program, did not exist. And the government's relentless dissembling on the matter and meager public disclosure of its nuclear activities obviously did little to elevate the quality of discussion about these activities in the public media. Nevertheless, at least rudimentary public discussion of the nuclear issue was quite common in Pakistan, especially after martial law was lifted at the end of 1984, and unequivocal statements of dissent from the government's apparent, even if undeclared, policy of acquiring nuclear weapons capability were rarely to be encountered in the media,[99] in public seminars and conferences focused on regional security, or in the public pronouncements of major opposition political leaders.[100] There was, in fact, a broad consensus that seemed to stretch across most of the political spectrum that Pakistan should have an independent nuclear policy, that it should maintain the nuclear weapons option, and that it should not knuckle under to foreign pressures.

We may note a few examples. At a public meeting in November 1985, the Tehrik-i-Istiqlal party leader (and former Air Chief Marshall) Asghar Khan stated that it was not in Pakistan's interest to develop nuclear weapons. Earlier, he had told me privately that such a step by Pakistan would be "stupid." But on both occasions he was careful to indicate that there should be no compromise on Pakistan's "peaceful" nuclear program—an oblique endorsement, I think, of Zia's policy.[101] At that same public meeting, Mian Tufail Mohammad, the former leader of the right-wing Jama'at-i-Islami Pakistan party, surprised (and pleased) the audience with a forceful statement criticizing what he called Zia's "apologetic" stand on the nuclear question and demanding that Pakistan make full use of its nuclear research capabilities to manufacture nuclear weapons. This was not much of a rebuke for the government, however, since Mian Tufail had been a close ally of Zia and his demand, in any event, was for an acceleration in, not the reversal of, Zia's policy. In a speech on "The Atomic Priorities of Pakistan" given in November 1985 to the Pakistan Philosophical Congress in Lahore, the former Federal Finance Minister Dr Mubashir Hasan—an extremely vocal left-wing critic of the Zia regime—excused Pakistan's nuclear program on grounds strongly reminiscent of the discredited arguments India had marshaled on behalf of its "peaceful nuclear explosion." He was reported to have drawn a distinction between atomic bombs and atomic technology, pointing out that Pakistan's development of the latter, including atomic explosive devices for the removal of mountains in order to raise dams, was a desirable step to take.[102] People's Party leader Benazir Bhutto, the regime's most formidable opponent, had said nothing on the issue in public to distinguish her position from that of President Zia. Since it had been her father who let Pakistan's nuclear genie out of the bottle in the first place, it was unlikely anyway that she would take the lead in trying to put it back in.

Ideological opposition to nuclear weapons was confined largely to left-regionalist groupings in the political opposition. They were hardly united on the subject, however, and none of them commanded a popular majority in any of the country's three ethnic minority provinces—Sind, Baluchistan, and the North West Frontier Province. The tiny nuclear disarmament movement in Pakistan, quite in contrast to its ideological bedfellows in the West, was of no political consequence. Some Pakistani political commentators expressed strong reservations about the benefits to Pakistan's security of nuclear weapons capability;[103] and in one of the most sober and knowledgeable studies of the nuclear issue written by a Pakistani in the entire Zia period, the author recommended Pakistan's conditional accession to the Non-Proliferation Treaty.[104] Nevertheless, the Swedish alternative to nuclearization (unilateral renunciation) had very few advocates. On the need for Pakistan to continue on the nuclear path, President Zia and most of the political opposition appeared to be essentially of one mind.

What accounted for this nuclear consensus in Zia's Pakistan? For one thing, the government's nuclear policy, from the perspective of most Pakistanis, looked altogether reasonable. They believed it to be *reactive* to India's own already demonstrated and (to Pakistanis) much more formidable and threatening nuclear weapons program, *peacefully intended* as a deterrent to an Indian conventional or nuclear attack, and *essential* to the nation's defense, in part because Pakistan was obviously weaker than India in conventional weaponry, in part because Pakistan had no allies to whom it could safely entrust its security. Publicly (and so far as I could judge, privately as well), Pakistanis expressed overwhelming preference for a denuclearized subcontinent.[105] No doubt, Pakistan had its Dr. Strangeloves. But its nuclear consensus drew nourishment largely not from an irrational fascination with the bomb but from the almost universal assumption that Pakistan's security requirements—pending a change of heart in New Delhi—simply allowed it no other choice.

A second source of Pakistan's nuclear consensus was national pride in what the whole world reckoned to have been Pakistan's spectacular nuclear achievement. Each new revelation by Western intelligence of Pakistan's clandestine march toward nuclear weapons capability was understood in Pakistan as a grudging admission of respect for Pakistan's national prowess.[106] Pakistan's nuclear-components "smugglers," though they were more likely to be considered thieves abroad, were national heroes at home. Pakistanis decried as propaganda the charge that Islamabad was making an

Islamic Bomb. They could hardly be blamed, however, for thinking it a compliment.

A third source of Pakistan's nuclear consensus was the belief that Pakistan had been the victim of highly selective and discriminatory international nonproliferation standards, that the international nonproliferation regime itself was ineffective and unreliable, and that Pakistan thus could not entrust its security to it. This aspect of the problem deserves a closer look.

Deficiencies in the Global Nonproliferation Regime

India was seen by Pakistanis as having escaped the same level of punishment for its nuclear infractions by the international community not because New Delhi was less guilty of offending international nuclear sensibilities, but because it was both less feared and less vulnerable to punitive sanctions. The lesser vulnerability was an obvious consequence of India's size, strength, and self-sufficiency. As for the lesser fear, a great many Pakistanis, at every level of society and including those who held the highest offices in government, seemed utterly convinced that Washington's apparent deference to Israel and the Israeli lobby, with its antipathy for anything approximating an Islamic Bomb, accounted in very large measure for what seemed to them a consistent pattern of discrimination in U.S. nuclear policy toward South Asia—for American laxity, in other words, when it came to India's 1974 nuclear detonation and for its extraordinary attentiveness in regard to every last detail of Pakistan's nuclear program.[107] Apart from the Indian threat, in fact, there was nothing in Pakistan's politics more certain to produce an emotional and positive response to Pakistan's nuclear program than invocation of the Israeli influence on Washington's policy.

Whether or not Israel actually deserved credit for all the attention given to Pakistan's nuclear program, there clearly were some grounds for Pakistani suspicion that the proponents of nonproliferation, as Pakistan's Minister of Foreign Affairs put it in a public address in 1985, had displayed "an obvious proclivity to accept a nuclear monopoly in South Asia."[108] At least the rudiments of a double standard seemed already in place, in fact, when India detonated a nuclear explosive in 1974. The test provoked Canada, chagrined over India's apparent violation of assurances that material from the Canadian-supplied CIRUS reactor would be used purely for peaceful purposes, to suspend and ultimately to terminate entirely all nuclear cooperation with India. The response of the rest of the world, however, including the United States, was a great deal more lenient. Washington issued a mild rebuke and moved to tighten up its own existing safeguards arrangements with India covering U.S.-supplied nuclear fuel for India's Tarapur nuclear reactors near Bombay. But in most other respects, it seemed prepared to carry on with business as usual. "The Nixon administration," according to Peter Clausen, a nuclear nonproliferation specialist with the U.S. Department of Energy from 1978 to 1981, "deliberately chose to play down the significance of the test and not to impose sanctions, nuclear or otherwise."[109] Indeed, barely a month after India's nuclear test, Washington went along with the decision of the Aid India Consortium to raise economic assistance to India by $200 million.[110]

Many of the key nonproliferation laws enacted in the United States in the 1970s and 1980s, including the 1976 Symington amendment and the 1977 Glenn amendment, were clearly reactions primarily to Pakistani nuclear activities. And some of them, such as the 1985 presidential certification requirement, were explicitly and solely directed against Pakistan.[111] While the Carter administration did not hesitate to slap harsh sanctions against Pakistan in 1978 and again in 1979 in an effort to deter it from acquiring access to nuclear explosive materials, it displayed no such firmness of will in the same period when it came to deterring India from the same thing.

Passage by Congress in 1978 of the Nuclear Nonproliferation Act, which required cutoff within two years of U.S. nuclear exports to nonnuclear-weapon states that had not accepted full-scope international safeguards, precipitated a crisis in Indo-U.S. relations. The legislation had been framed with India in mind; and it was generally understood, since India was expected to reject the safeguards provision, that it would mean termination of U.S. shipments of low-enriched uranium to fuel the Tarapur reactors. Since Washington had undertaken in the 1963 Tarapur agreement with India to supply the fuel for 30 years (until 1993), its threat to stop the supply naturally was "seen by India as a kind of blackmail and a default on the 1963 agreement to which it would be politically difficult to submit."[112] Unwilling to run the risk of snapping ties with India, the Carter administration finally, and against considerable political opposition in Congress, moved to overrule the Nuclear Regulatory Commission's May 1980 decision to bar further licensing of Tarapur fuel shipments. Nonproliferation advocates suffered another blow when the Reagan administration, equally concerned not to force a break with India, reached an agreement with Delhi in July 1982 permitting France to assume the role of substitute supplier.[113]

Pakistan's claim that it was held to higher nonproliferation standards by the West during the Zia period than was India thus had some plausibility during the Carter administration, at least the first few years of it. It would be difficult to sustain Pakistan's claim when judged against the 8 years of the Reagan administration, however, since Washington during that period held Islamabad to nonproliferation standards that were scarcely more rigorous than were being applied to India. While it was unquestionably true that nonproliferation was forced to take a back seat to other foreign policy priorities in the American relationship with India in this period, it was no less true in the relationship with Pakistan. The Carter administration's handling of Islamabad's nuclear program, in other words, was not an adequate yardstick for measuring America's long-term commitment to nuclear nonproliferation. On the contrary, it represented a significant deviation from American nonproliferation norms.

For Pakistan, the real lesson gained in the Zia period from its own and India's successful defiance of the international nonproliferation regime was that that regime was in the last analysis relatively toothless, that the problem was not really one of double standards but of no (effective) standards. Few, if any, nations were willing to give nonproliferation objectives top priority in regard either to India or Pakistan. Nonproliferation advocates continued throughout the Zia period to demand strengthening of nonproliferation enforcement measures in South Asia; but their arguments often seemed impractical—sometimes, even to themselves.[114] By the end of the Zia period, at least some analysts seemed about ready to bury nonproliferation—although their logic too, at least in some cases, seemed contorted by doubt and equivocation. "The trouble is," said Richard Haass, then Lecturer in Public Policy at Harvard University's JFK School of Government,

> American actions cannot solve either the Afghanistan or proliferation problem. Soviet withdrawal and peace in Afghanistan remain distant, while Pakistani leaders seem intent not to foreclose the nuclear option.... Should the United States stop trying so hard to prevent the acquisition of nuclear weapons and instead try to prevent the use of such weapons by those who have acquired them? The answer is no....Given the uncertainties and risks, the United States government is right to try to prevent a nuclear South Asia. An active non-proliferation policy mixing technical denial and security assistance, with warnings that the latter cannot be sustained if Pakistan violates certain nuclear norms, is a must....Yet despite the best efforts of the United States and other advanced industrial countries, this policy may not prevail....No amount of American activism is likely to prevent the nuclearization of South Asia; indeed, to a significant extent it is already a fact. If and when it becomes an undeniable one, the United States may well want to shift directions and replace a policy of prevention with one of management. This would entail continuing to provide a non-nuclear security option, namely security assistance, once Pakistan had

nuclear weapons. A Pakistan facing defeat with conventional weapons or resorting to nuclear arms...should scare Washington. In such circumstances, the United States would want to work with both Pakistan and India to promote arms control and to enhance their command and control systems to lessen the likelihood of accidental war. It could even selectively enhance nuclear capabilities to strengthen retaliatory potential and, thus, reinforce mutual deterrence.[115]

One presumes that Pakistan's leaders noticed the West's fading confidence in the nonproliferation regime, also that they lowered their own expectations to correspond with it. After all, if a regional nuclear deterrent strategy and even the selective enhancement of nuclear capabilities were beginning to sound reasonable in Washington, then pressure not only on Pakistan but on India to conform to the nonproliferation regime ultimately would surely lift. Pakistan's solo adherence to nonproliferation, under these circumstances, would seem not merely hazardous, but downright foolish, to most. Absent relentless Western pressure to secure India's equal and simultaneous adherence, Pakistan would be at high risk of being left holding the nuclear nonproliferation bag.[116]

Zia's Nuclear Legacy: An Assessment

From all that we have considered thus far, one may safely conclude that the Zia period ended, as it had begun, with Pakistan strongly, probably irrevocably, committed to the acquisition of nuclear weapons capability. The frailty of its allies' commitments, the worsening conventional military balance, the prestige of nuclear weapons, and deficiencies in the international nuclear nonproliferation regime all had conspired to move Pakistani decision-makers in this direction. But how far in this direction had Pakistan actually gone? Relative to India, where did it stand on the "proliferation ladder" by 1988? And, in terms of its future security, how much had really been gained?

We have noted that considerable controversy raged in the global nuclear community throughout the Zia period in regard to the amount of responsibility each of the two rivals, India and Pakistan, should bear for the pace of the nuclear arms race in the region. Inevitably, there was also controversy about the magnitude of the *product* of this race, that is, about the true nature and scale of the nuclear capabilities acquired. The Carnegie Task Force on Non-Proliferation and South Asian Security, convened in Washington, D.C., in July 1986, identified four principal rungs relevant to South Asia on a hypothetical proliferation ladder:[117]

1. The manufacture of atomic (fission) weapons, including production of fissile material (plutonium or highly enriched uranium), design and fabrication of weapons (whether or not fully assembled), and (possibly) testing.
2. The militarization of a basic nuclear weapons capability (aircraft delivery, military strategy and operations, and procedures for political control).
3. Steps toward more advanced proliferation, including expansion and qualitative improvements to the arsenal, the development (possibly) of fusion bombs, the development of ballistic missiles, and work on tactical nuclear weapons.
4. The development and deployment of secure retaliatory nuclear forces, such as the development and deployment of sea- or land-based nuclear missile systems.

According to the Task Force report, India and Pakistan both appeared to have reached the first rung, with India undoubtedly in the lead but with neither necessarily having actually assembled complete nuclear devices. Clearly, neither had made it to the fourth; but, insofar as the intermediate rungs were concerned, uncertainty prevailed. The Task Force estimated that India may have accumulated enough plutonium from wholly unsafeguarded reactors by mid-1987 to have manufactured anywhere from 12 to 40 nuclear weapons, and to have achieved sufficient plutonium-producing capacity by that time to make from 15 to 30 weapons annually.[118] Pakistan, it said, arming its weapons from highly enriched uranium produced at its centrifuge enrichment plant at Kahuta, might have stockpiled enough of the material by mid-1987 for one or two weapons, and might by the same time have achieved the capacity to make from one to four weapons annually.[119]

Both governments, of course, denied making any nuclear bombs. Both made it clear, however, that they had the ability to produce them on short order if required. The director of Pakistan's uranium enrichment program, Dr. Abdul Qadir Khan, reportedly declared in a controversial press interview published in March 1987 that "what the CIA has been saying about our possessing the bomb is correct and so is the speculation of some foreign newspapers. They told us that Pakistan could never produce the bomb and they doubted my capabilities, but they know we have done it."[120] A key figure in Pakistan's nuclear establishment was said to have confided to some Pakistanis some months before this that Pakistan possessed twelve nuclear bombs (at whatever state of assembly or disassembly was not disclosed).[121] Coming at a time when the Indian army was conducting Operation Brass Tacks, a massive military exercise in Rajasthan close to the Pakistan border, his revelations may have been intended to warn New Delhi of Pakistan's retaliatory potential.[122] They may well have been a bluff. Domestic political compulsions mixed with the potential deterrent value of an existing stockpile undoubtedly fostered a certain amount of exaggeration, especially in Pakistan. When it came to nuclear weapons, where rhetoric ended and reality began was practically impossible to say. No wonder, then, that when President Reagan certified in December 1988 that Pakistan did not possess a nuclear explosive device, he confessed to strong reservations.[123]

Overshadowing the rather perplexing efforts at nuclear bean-counting in South Asia was the important fact that an even worse asymmetry than that governing the conventional military balance between India and Pakistan appeared to govern the emerging nuclear balance between them. The speculative ratios of existing stockpiles and annual weapons manufacturing capacity cited above, whatever they might say about the audacity and resourcefulness of the Pakistani nuclear program, clearly had to excite despair among Pakistan's top decision-makers. Authors might write that by the time the Soviets departed Afghanistan, Pakistan's nuclear program "had achieved mature technical status."[124] They might point to evidence "that both countries have even more extensive nuclear weapons research, development, and production programs than previously thought."[125] And they might describe Pakistan's worldwide clandestine network of nuclear smugglers as having been "phenomenally successful" in acquiring nuclear materials and equipment.[126] But they could not sweep aside the stark fact, almost universally conceded, that India was far ahead on the road to nuclear weapons capability, that it had mastered a far greater range of nuclear weapons-related technologies, that it commanded a vastly larger nuclear infrastructure, and that it had achieved, in fact, an insuperable nuclear lead.[127]

Pakistan's nuclear program displayed astonishing enterprise, no doubt, but its inherent limitations were glaringly apparent to anyone taking the trouble to look. There was a marked tendency (probably welcomed in Pakistan) among some outside observers to overstate Pakistan's nuclear progress and to minimize the technical and other difficulties which its nuclear weapons program faced.[128] Too much attention was paid to the cunning of its nuclear smugglers, too little to their greed, the mounting restrictions on their enterprise, and their near-certain inability, even under the best of circumstances, to keep pace with the requirements of a mushrooming nuclear weapons program in an industrially backward society. At the same time, there was an equally pronounced tendency in some quarters to understate India's nuclear attainments, to pay too little attention to the cunning—and accomplishments—of its own traffickers in illicit nuclear imports,[129] and to exaggerate its leaders' reluctance to move ahead with nuclear weaponization.

Observe S.P. Seth's statement—"The very fact that for 14 years (since India exploded its first atomic device in 1974) New Delhi has not made any move to acquire a nuclear arsenal is indicative of India's nuclear allergy or confusion, or both."[130] By 1988, when it was made, this statement was barely conceivable, and then only if we attached the most literal and restrictive meaning to the acquisition of a nuclear arsenal. The fact is that a very large gap existed between India and Pakistan with respect to nuclear weapons capability at the time of Zia's death; and Pakistan's chances for narrowing that gap seemed to be inexorably diminishing.

Notwithstanding the shortcomings of Pakistan's covert nuclear weapons program, one can certainly imagine some benefits that Pakistan derived from it during the Zia period. The threat of bomb-making, as Ashok Kapur argued even before Pakistan secured handsome security assistance from the United States in 1981, probably gave Islamabad some leverage with Washington, apart from Afghanistan, in its quest to overcome international isolation and to increase its access to more conventional arms.[131] As we have already seen, restraining Pakistan's nuclear quest was a key argument made by Washington at the time. A number of authors, moreover, have suggested that Pakistan's nuclear program, whatever its material limitations, had already achieved some deterrent value in relation to India. John Schulz argued, for example, that Pakistan, India, and a few other states (the "maybe states" whose potential nuclear arsenals remained uncertain) were pioneering a new type of deterrence—"deterrence by bluff"—a conscious policy of ambiguity that "may be a highly effective alternative to the other two types of deterrence—punishment and denial—and could represent the most likely form of proliferation in the future."[132] This form, he suggested, was probably cheaper, less dangerous if managed wisely, and yet effective.[133] Zia himself was said to have owned up to a deterrent strategy shortly prior to his death. In a conversation with Stephen Cohen in July 1988, he is said to have described South Asia "as having achieved 'stable nuclear deterrence based upon ambiguity as to whether either India or Pakistan had nuclear weapons, and if they did, how many they possessed.' He felt that South Asia would now be 'crisis stable' and that the nuclear deterrent would also prevent large-scale conventional war between the two states."[134]

No doubt Pakistan's ability to wield a nuclear threat of sorts added to its diplomatic leverage with the United States and helped to hold its critics at bay. But, as Rodney Jones has pointed out, proliferation threats were a two-edged sword, as likely to impair the ability of the United States to maintain a security relationship with Pakistan as to bolster it.[135] It was extremely doubtful, furthermore, that Pakistan's "bomb in the basement" held any bargains for Pakistan's hard-pressed public exchequer. On the contrary, "not only [was] the price of entry high, the cost of staying in a nuclear military contest tend[ed] to be staggering."[136]

One should not make too much, either, of the deterrent value of the nuclear capabilities acquired by Pakistan during the Zia period. Eleven years of effort clearly did not produce anything resembling a force equalizer—or more than the most slender prospects for ever doing so. The process of proliferation in South Asia had certainly brought closer the threat of terrible catastrophe;[137] it had brought no "nuclear revolution" to the region, however, with the promise of liberating Pakistan from the customary vulnerability and dependency of its security situation. Some temporary stabilization in the Indo-Pakistan equation it may have purchased; but not more than that. As for Zia's remarks on Pakistan's supposed achievement of a nuclear deterrent posture, they were every bit as likely to have been the product of the rather tenuous "deterrence by bluff" as of the more muscular "deterrence by possession."

In a book published in 1984, Professor Cohen suggested that "the most effective approach [for dealing with the proliferation problem] would be one that assists regional states in isolating South Asia...from superpower conflict and simultaneously settles major regional disputes....The states involved can move toward their own version of a regional peace agreement and devote their resources to their only permanent enemy: domestic disorder, poverty, and low growth rates. Pakistani arms," he advised,

> can be left at a level sufficient to deter the unlikely straight-on Soviet or Indian attack but not so large that it would enable Pakistan to carry out a successful attack on India. There is an upper limit of arms which Pakistan need not cross, for to do so would be threatening to India; but there is an important lower limit. Below this mix of numbers, quality, and tactical disposition Pakistan cannot fall; India and Pakistan must jointly determine these upper and lower limits....Pakistanis may have to reconcile themselves to second-rank regional status,....[138]

What would motivate Pakistanis to want to join with their adversaries in joint determination of the upper and lower limits of Pakistan's (but apparently not India's) arms and thereby to fix Pakistan's second-rank regional status Cohen didn't say. His proposal, in any event, was likely to get a far better reception in New Delhi than in Islamabad. Zia's nuclear legacy to Pakistan was far from attractive; yet, acquisition of nuclear weapons capability was, and remains, an imperative of Pakistan's security policy, not really because Pakistan's leaders were enamored of its long-range prospects but because the alternatives proposed were so utterly unpalatable.

NOTES

1. U.S. Arms Control and Disarmament Agency (ACDA), *World Military Expenditures and Arms Transfers, 1971-1980* (Washington, D.C.: U.S. Government Printing Office, March 1983) pp. 117-20.
2. U.S. Department of State, *Congressional Presentation FY 1985: Security Assistance Programs* (Washington, D.C., 1984) pp. 13-14.
3. In spite of strong Indian opposition, Moscow concluded a $30 million arms supply agreement with Pakistan in 1968. For background, see Stockholm International Peace Research Institute (SIPRI), *The Arms Trade with the Third World* (New York: Humanities Press, 1971) pp. 498-9. See also Zulfikar A. Khalid, "What Went Wrong with Pak-Soviet Relations?", *Asian Defence Journal* (January 1983) 70-6.
4. See Leonard S. Spector, *Going Nuclear* (Cambridge, Mass.: Ballinger Publishing Company, 1987).
5. According to a national poll of Pakistani opinion published in July 1985, for example, India ranked first in untrustworthiness among fourteen nations. Of those polled, 59 percent put India first, 50 percent the USSR. Ijaz S. Gilani, *Gallup Political Weather Report* (Islamabad: Institute of Public Opinion, July 1985) pp. 18-19.
6. Two of Pakistan's leading independent English dailies—*The Muslim* (Islamabad) and *Dawn* (Karachi)—often pleaded for greater openness to India, and both gave editorial support to Zia's efforts to normalize relations with India. But an estimated 97 percent of the country's newspaper readers read the Urdu press, whose leading representatives—*Jang* and *Nawai Waqt*, both Lahore-based—generally took a hard line on India. Husain Haqqani, "Press Freedom Debated by Officials, Muslims, Secularists," *Far Eastern Economic Review* (19 September 1985) 28-31.
7. Lt. General (Retd.) A. I. Akram, *The New Order in Delhi* (Islamabad: Institute of Regional Studies, October 1985) p. 36.
8. Independent Planning Commission of Pakistan, *Federal and Sovereign: A Policy Framework for the Economic Development of Pakistan*, Draft report (Lahore, August 1985) p. 54.
9. National survey data collected over a four-year span (1981-84) by the Gallup Pakistan organization revealed, for example, that approximately 50 percent of respondents in each of those years supported government efforts to promote a no-war pact with India. Ijaz S. Gilani, *The Four 'R's of Afghanistan* (Islamabad: Institute of Public Opinion, 1985) p. 35.
10. In a book published in 1983, the late General Mohammad Musa, who led the Pakistan army for eight years (1958-66) and who more recently served as Governor of Baluchistan province, wrote that Pakistan bore a major share of the responsibility for the outbreak of war in 1965. *My Version: India-Pakistan War 1965* (Lahore: Wajidalis, 1983). On the floor of the National Assembly and in public meetings, Noor Khan, the retired chief of the

Pakistan air force (and its commander during the 1965 war), unequivocally held Pakistan responsible for that war. His public statements were confirmed in interview with the author, Islamabad, November 1986.

11. For this section, I have relied chiefly on the following works by K. Subrahmanyam: "India and Its Neighbours: A Conceptual Framework of Peaceful Co-existence," in U. S. Bajpai (ed.), *India and Its Neighbourhood* (New Delhi: Lancer International, 1986) pp. 109-39; and *Indian Security Perspectives* (New Delhi: ABC Publishing House, 1982). Among numerous additional works published in India in the 1980s and reflecting similar perspectives on India-Pakistan relations are U. S. Bajpai, *India's Security* (New Delhi: Lancers Publishers, 1983); R. G. Sawhney, *Zia's Pakistan: Implications for India's Security* (New Delhi: ABC Publishing House, 1985); Surendra Chopra, *Post-Simla Indo-Pak Relations: Confrontation to Deescalation* (New Delhi: Deep & Deep Publications, 1988); Ratna Tikoo, *Indo-Pak Relations: Politics of Divergence and Convergence* (New Delhi: National Publishing House, 1987); and S. P. Shukla, *India and Pakistan: The Origins of Armed Conflict* (New Delhi: Deep & Deep Publications, 1984).
12. Subrahmanyam, "India and Its Neighbours," pp. 123-4.
13. Ibid., pp. 128-9.
14. Subrahmanyam, *Indian Security Perspectives*, p. 213.
15. Ibid., pp. 176, 178.
16. Subrahmanyam, "India and Its Neighbours," p. 137.
17. See Sumit Ganguly, *The Origins of War in South Asia: Indo-Pakistani Conflicts Since 1947* (Boulder: Westview Press, 1986) pp. 18, 59, 100.
18. India had an obvious advantage, of course, in the negotiations following the 1971 war. However, it did not press this advantage to any great extent. On this, see Imtiaz H. Bokhari and Thomas Perry Thornton, *The 1972 Simla Agreement: An Asymmetrical Negotiation,* Foreign Policy Institute Case Studies Number 11 (Washington, D.C.: The Johns Hopkins Foreign Policy Institute, 1988).
19. Ashok Kapur, "The Indian Subcontinent: The Contemporary Structure of Power and the Development of Power Relations," *Asian Survey* 28:7 (July 1988) 693.
20. Subrahmanyam, "India and Its Neighbours," p. 125.
21. This section draws upon my article, "The Arms Race in South Asia: Implications for the United States," *Asian Survey* 25:3 (March 1985) 265-91.
22. On the naval balance in South Asia, see Ashley J. Tellis, "The Naval Balance in the Indian Subcontinent: Demanding Missions for the Indian Navy," *Asian Survey* 25:12 (December 1985) 1186-1213; G. Jacobs, "The Pakistan Navy," *Asian Defence Journal* (September 1981) 43-52; Gary L. Sojka, "The Missions of the Indian Navy," *Naval War College Review* 36:1 (January-February 1983) 2-15; Michael Vlahos, "Middle Eastern, North African, and South Asian Navies," U.S. Naval Institute *Proceedings* 114:3

(March 1988) 58-66; Lieutenant Mark Montgomery, "The U.S.-Pakistani Connection," U.S. Naval Institute *Proceedings* 115:7 (July 1989) 67-73; and Maqsudul Hasan Nuri, "Indian Navy in the 1980s," *Regional Studies* (Islamabad) 7:3 (Summer 1989) 3-43.
23. Raju G. C. Thomas, *Indian Security Policy* (Princeton: Princeton University Press, 1986) p. 170.
24. John E. Fricker, "Chinese FT-6s Enhance Pakistan Fleet," *Aviation Week & Space Technology* (13 April 1981) 49.
25. Bajpai, *India's Security*, p. 74.
26. Lt. General M. L. Chibber, *Paramilitary Forces* (New Delhi: United Services Institution of India, 1979) pp. 2-4, cited in Thomas, *Indian Security Policy*, p. 142.
27. International Institute of Strategic Studies (IISS), *The Military Balance 1983-1984* (London, 1983) p. 97.
28. These arguments are reviewed briefly in Mohammed Ayoob, "India, Pakistan and Super-Power Rivalry," *The World Today* 38:5 (May 1982) 194-202. For additional commentary on the military balance in South Asia, see Wirsing, "The Arms Race in South Asia"; Jerrold F. Elkin and W. Andrew Ritezel, "The Indo-Pakistani Military Balance," *Asian Survey* 26:5 (May 1986) 518-538; and Abdus Samad Khan, "The Indo-Pakistan Rivalry and the Sub-Continental Security Calculus," *Strategic Studies* (Islamabad) 9:1 (Autumn 1985) 15-45.
29. Shirin Tahir-Kheli, *The United States and Pakistan* (New York: Praeger, 1982) p. 137.
30. The prominent Indian journalist and author Ravi Rikhye, for instance, has labeled the suggestion that Pakistan had achieved virtual parity with India in deployable forces as sheer propaganda. "The lies are obvious," he says; "there is *no* area in which there is virtual parity,...It passes imagination as to how a 1.5 times advantage in divisions and armor, a 3 times advantage in total fighter aircraft and a 4 times advantage in first-line fighters, and an approximate 5 times superiority in naval forces can be construed as virtual parity by even the most paranoid of analysts." *The War That Never Was: The Story of India's Strategic Failures* (Delhi: Chanakya Publications, 1988) p. 158. See also Rikhye's newer and equally provocative book, *The Militarization of Mother India* (Delhi: Chanakya Publications, 1990).
31. Thomas, *Indian Security Policy*, p. 17.
32. "India's growing economic ties with the oil-exporting Islamic nations in the Middle East," wrote Thomas, "and the concurrent growth of Pakistani military links with these states have tended to bring about the strategic interdependence of the South Asian and Middle Eastern regions. The prospect that a Sino-American quasi-military alliance may develop in the future in response to the growth of Soviet military power, the continuation of Soviet-American naval rivalry in the Indian Ocean and accompanying efforts to seek military bases among the littoral states, and the potential U.S.-assisted rearmament of Pakistan and China in response to the Soviet invasion of Afghanistan suggest the need to monitor developments beyond

33. Ibid., p. 22.
34. ACDA, *World Military Expenditures and Arms Transfers, 1971-1980*, pp. 52, 62.
35. ACDA, *World Military Expenditures and Arms Transfers 1988* (Washington, D.C.: U.S. Government Printing Office, June 1989) pp. 46, 56.
36. Ibid., pp. 46, 56.
37. Onkar Marwah, "India's Military Power and Policy," in Onkar Marwah and Jonathan D. Pollack (eds.), *Military Power and Policy in Asian States: China, India, Japan* (Boulder: Westview, 1980) pp. 128-9.
38. ACDA, *World Military Expenditures and Arms Transfers 1988*, pp. 88, 98.
39. Ibid., p. 8.
40. John E. Fricker, "Chinese Assisting Pakistani Industry," *Aviation Week & Space Technology* (30 March 1981) 58-9. For a brief profile of Pakistan's defense industry, see Tariq A. Husain, *Defence Production in the Muslim World*, Islamabad Papers No. 11 (Islamabad: Institute of Strategic Studies, 1986) pp. 69-82.
41. Pakistan was reported to have launched an atomic-capable missile at a test range in southern Pakistan on 25 April 1988. There were indications that it had been produced with Chinese assistance. Bernard E. Trainor, "Pakistan Accused of a Nuclear Move," *The New York Times*, 24 May 1988, p. A1.
42. For an excellent discussion of the growth of India's defense industry and technological strategy in the 1980s, see Thomas, *Indian Security Policy*, pp. 234-74. For additional commentary, see Onkar Marwah, "India's Military Power and Policy," pp. 101-46; and Sarbjit Johal, *Conflict and Integration in Indo-Pakistan Relations*, Monograph No. 30 (Berkeley: Centers for South and Southeast Asia Studies, University of California at Berkeley, 1989) esp. pp. 186-7, 214-15.
43. See Jerrold F. Elkin and Brian Fredericks, "Military Implications of India's Space Program," *Air University Review* 34:4 (May-June 1983) 56-63; Anita Bhatia, "India's Space Program: Cause for Concern?", *Asian Survey* 25:10 (October 1985) 1013-30; and Raju G. C. Thomas, "India's Nuclear and Space Programs: Defense or Development?", *World Politics* 30:2 (January 1986) 315-42.
44. The 7.5-ton Agni missile, with a reported range of 1500 miles, was fired from India's test site on the Bay of Bengal on 22 May 1989. Barbara Crossette, "India Reports Successful Test of Mid-Range Missile," *The New York Times*, 23 May 1989, p. A28.
45. Sarada P. Nanda and Mukundan C. Menon, "Fire in the Sky," *Sunday* (Calcutta), 4 June 1989.
46. Thomas, *Indian Security Policy*, p. 238.
47. Ibid., pp. 234-74.

48. This figure was suggested to me in fall 1989 by one of Pakistan's leading physicists with many years experience in Pakistan's defense science establishment.
49. This statistic was reported in a government-paid advertisement by the Ministry of Science and Technology in *The Muslim,* 4 December 1989.
50. A small but vocal group of Pakistanis advocated Pakistan's neutralization, on the Finnish, Swedish, or Austrian model, as the best course of action under the circumstances prevailing in the 1980s. For example, see Sajjad Hyder, *Foreign Policy of Pakistan* (Lahore: Progressive Publishers, 1987) esp. pp. 146-7. Hyder, at one time Pakistan's ambassador to the Soviet Union, coupled his plea for a neutralized Pakistan with an unequivocal endorsement of Pakistan's acquisition of a credible nuclear deterrent. In any event, the government appeared never to have given the neutralist solution serious consideration, and significant public support for it never developed.
51. Pakistan finally ratified the Partial Test Ban Treaty in December 1987, a step India had taken earlier.
52. These proposals were repeatedly endorsed by the General Assembly with overwhelming majorities.
53. See Agha Shahi, *Pakistan's Security and Foreign Policy* (Lahore: Progressive Publishers, 1988) pp. 184-6; Fahmida Ashraf, "Pakistan's Relations with India and South Asia," in Noor A. Husain and Leo E. Rose (eds.), *Pakistan-U.S. Relations: Social, Political, and Economic Factors* (Berkeley: Institute of East Asian Studies, University of California, 1988) pp. 154-5; and Leonard S. Spector, *The Undeclared Bomb* (Cambridge: Ballinger Publishing Co., 1988) pp. 96-8.
54. As pointed out earlier, Pakistan's original proposal for a South Asian NWFZ was made in 1974.
55. The test ban offer was made by Prime Minister Mohammad Khan Junejo in September 1987 in a speech to the United Nations General Assembly. Junejo indicated in the speech that his government would also accept a test ban treaty restricted to India and Pakistan. "Pakistan Proposes Nuclear Test Ban in South Asia," *The New York Times,* 25 September 1987, p. A5.
56. The nonattack agreement was not formally signed until the end of 1988 during Rajiv Gandhi's three-day visit to Islamabad. By that time, Zia had been replaced by Benazir Bhutto. Barbara Crossette, "Gandhi Ends 3-Day Visit to Pakistan," *The New York Times,* 1 January 1989, p. A3.
57. Richard N. Haass, "South Asia: Too Late to Remove the Bomb?", *Orbis* 32:1 (Winter 1988) 112.
58. Rikhye, *The War That Never Was,* p. 19. For a Pakistani point of view on Brass Tacks, see Samina Yasmeen, "India and Pakistan: Why the Latest Exercise in Brinkmanship?", *Australian Journal of Politics and History* 34:1 (1988) 64-71.
59. Shahi, *Pakistan's Security and Foreign Policy,* pp. 183-93.
60. Spector, *The Undeclared Bomb,* p. 140.

61. Committee on Foreign Relations, U.S. Senate, *Aid and the Proposed Arms Sales of F-16's to Pakistan* (Washington, D.C.: U.S. Government Printing Office, 1982) p. 7.
62. Ibid., p. 8.
63. The centrality of India in Pakistani defense calculations was pointedly illustrated in an unusually candid address given at the Institute of Strategic Studies in Islamabad on 16 December 1985 by retired Air Chief Marshal Muhammad Anwar Shamim. Shamim, who headed Pakistan's air force from 1978 to 1985, and who thus presided over the selection and induction of the F-16 into the air force, spoke on "The Role of the F-16 in the Defence of Pakistan." In his talk, which the author attended, Shamim hardly mentioned the Soviet Union or Afghanistan. In describing the process of threat-assessment that had preceded the selection of the F-16, Shamim focused exclusively on the Indian air force. He made it very clear that Pakistan had insisted upon the F-16 over other aircraft because of its superior strike capability against India. A major bonus of the acquisition, he said, was that it had "saved Kahuta"—a reference to Pakistan's secret nuclear facility near Islamabad. Kahuta, he said, had been sited far too near the Indian border and was virtually impossible to defend. With its ability to penetrate Indian defenses and to strike at India's own highly vulnerable nuclear installations, the F-16, said Shamim, enabled Pakistan to retaliate in kind. The Pakistan air force could now strike, for instance, at India's Bhabha Atomic Research Center at Trombay. This would result in a huge catastrophe for India, he said, "and they know it." The F-16, he said, was "Pakistan's nuclear option minus the nuclear bomb." Shamim remarked to the author after the talk that in early rounds of negotiations over the sale of the F-16, the American negotiators had sought to build the Soviet threat into the discussion. The Pakistanis, he said with a grin, eventually succeeded in turning discussion to the east. Shamim's talk was reported in *The Muslim*, 17 December 1985.
64. Jones, a widely noted analyst of South Asian defense matters, wrote in 1986 that Pakistan's existence since 1971 on only one side of the subcontinent, the diminishing appeal of Pakistani irredentism in Kashmir, and a gradual thaw in Sino-Indian relations had already made the promotion of Indo-Pakistan reconciliation a live alternative for India. The same option, he said, "is more feasible today for Pakistan because of the Soviet threat in Afghanistan. *This is a situation far more promising for diminished rivalry than any since India and Pakistan became independent.*" Rodney W. Jones, "India: Defense Policy, Modern Weapons, and Regional Power," in Rodney W. Jones and Steven A. Hildreth (eds.), *Emerging Powers: Defense and Security in the Third World* (New York: Praeger, 1986) pp. 208-9. Emphasis added. Jones's assertion of a "diminishing appeal of Pakistani irredentism in Kashmir" might itself be difficult to sustain in the light of recent developments in that Indian state.

65. Thornton, a retired career diplomat, argued that the primacy of Soviet friendship in Indian security calculations plus the incompatibility of Pakistan's security policy with Indian regional aspirations created little stimulus for a constructive regional approach to Afghanistan. "India's chances of guiding a regional approach to a successful solution are small," he observed, "in part because of Indian shortcomings, but even more because of the sheer intractability of the issues involved." Thomas Perry Thornton, "India and Afghanistan," in Theodore L. Eliot, Jr., and Robert L. Pfaltzgraff, Jr., (eds.), *The Red Army on Pakistan's Border: Policy Implications for the United States* (Washington, D.C.: Pergamon-Brassey's, 1986) pp. 63-70.
66. Shahi, *Pakistan's Security and Foreign Policy,* pp. 209-26.
67. Lt. General Faiz Ali Chisti, who held various high posts in Zia's martial law regime until his retirement in 1980 and who was the man whom Zia ultimately delegated to direct the rescue effort at the embassy, has written that Zia himself may have contributed directly to the disaster. Chisti says that Zia, who spent the morning of 21 November on a much-publicized cycling tour of Rawalpindi city and cantonment, inflammed the crowds who gathered to hear him speak with incautious references to rumors of American involvement in an attack upon the Holy Kaaba of the Grand Mosque in Mecca. Chisti, *Betrayals of Another Kind: Islam, Democracy and the Army in Pakistan* (Cincinnati: Asia Publishing House, 1990) pp. 101-7.
68. For an illuminating discussion of Zia's policies, see Mohammad Waseem, *Politics and the State in Pakistan* (Lahore: Progressive Publishers, 1989) pp. 362-433.
69. See, for example, the statements of Robert LaPorte, Jr., and Craig Baxter, South Asia specialists at, respectively, Pennsylvania State University and Juniata College, given in testimony on 22 September 1982, in Hearings, House of Representatives, Committee on Foreign Affairs, Subcommittees on Asian and Pacific Affairs and on Human Rights and International Organization, *Reconciling Human Rights and U.S. Security Interests in Asia,* 97th Cong., 2d Sess., 1982 (Y.E. F76/1: H88/22) pp. 167-88, 208-15.
70. Statement of Selig S. Harrison, Senior Associate, Carnegie Endowment for International Peace, on 22 September 1981, in Hearings, House of Representatives, Committee on Foreign Affairs, Subcommittees on International Security and Scientific Affairs, on International Economic Policy and Trade, and on Asian and Pacific Affairs, *Security and Economic Assistance to Pakistan,* 97th Cong., 1st Sess., 1981 (Y.4. F.76/1/P 17/8) p. 151.
71. Selig S. Harrison, "Nightmare in Baluchistan," *Foreign Policy* 32 (Fall 1978) 139.
72. Yaacov Vertzberger, *The Enduring Entente: Sino-Pakistani Relations 1960-1980* (New York: Praeger, for the Center for Strategic and International Studies, 1983) p. 88.
73. These comments are based on extensive interviews by the author with a wide range of Pakistanis directly knowledgeable of events in Baluchistan during the insurgency, including retired Air Chief Marshal Zulfikar Ali

Khan, the Chief of Air Staff from 1974 to 1978; a senior bureaucrat and advisor to the Baluchistan government in the initial phase of the insurgency; and a senior officer in Pakistan's Special Services Group who was posted in Baluchistan for one year during the insurgency. Khan, interviewed in Islamabad in September 1985, said that Iran supplied only U.S.-made Chinook troop transport helicopters. There were no Huey-Cobra gunships (or any other sort of gunship) in Baluchistan at any time during the insurgency. In general, he observed, "the fighting that went on in Baluchistan was greatly exaggerated." According to the SSG officer,

> Pakistan did not employ a single armed helicopter in any way during the insurgency. Not a single shot was ever fired from a helicopter during the insurgency. In fact, there were hardly any heliborne operations of any kind in the Baluchistan fighting. Pakistan then had not a single Huey-Cobra gunship of its own. It did have a few MI-8 (Soviet Hind) and French-made Alouettes plus a handful of U.S.-made Chinooks loaned (with pilots) by the Shah of Iran. None of these were armed attack helicopters. The Iranian-supplied Chinooks were unarmed troop-carrying assault copters. No helicopters of any kind were deployed in the fighting at Chamalang. The Chinooks were eventually returned to the Shah as they proved of little use. The Baluchistan conflict was very largely a ground war, and it was fought by the infantry.

74. One writer, citing Harrison, informed her readers that Iranian pilots were still flying the Huey-Cobra helicopters against Baluch guerrilla camps in Pakistan *in 1977*—years after the Iranian pilots and their unarmed helicopters had been returned to the Shah. Tahir-Kheli, *The United States and Pakistan,* p. 88.

75. See, for example, Francine Frankel, "Play the India Card," *Foreign Policy* No. 62 (Spring 1986) 148-66; Robert L. Hardgrave, Jr., "Why India Matters: The Challenge to American Policy in South Asia," *Asian Affairs* 11:1 (Spring 1984) 45-56; and Lloyd I. Rudolph and Susanne H. Rudolph, "The United States, India and South Asia," in John P. Lewis and Valeriana Kallab (eds.), *U.S. Foreign Policy and the Third World: Agenda 1983* (New York: Praeger, 1983) pp. 86-113. See also Teresa L. Shanahan, *The United States and India: Strategy for the 1990s,* unpublished MA thesis, Naval Postgraduate School (Monterey), June 1989.

76. See, for example, the testimony of William L. Richter, Ainslee Embree, Stephen P. Cohen, and Selig S. Harrison on 21 September 1981, in Hearings, *Security and Economic Assistance to Pakistan,* pp. 93-208. All four of these witnesses urged downscaling of the administration's proposed military assistance program to Pakistan. All four expressed specific opposition to the sale of the F-16 to Pakistan. Cohen said he didn't think India was alienated by U.S. arms sales to Pakistan. What he found distressing, he said, was "our lack of consultation or involvement of the Indians in assisting Pakistan in reaching that level of force which enables it to defend itself yet not threaten India. I think this process should begin now [187]." See also

the Staff Report prepared for the Committee on Foreign Relations, Senate, 98th Cong., 2nd Sess., April 1984, *United States Security Interests in South Asia (Pakistan-India)* (Washington, D.C.: U.S. Government Printing Office, 1984). Written by staffer Peter W. Galbraith, the report recommends that the United States consult with India on arms sales in the region.

77. "Carter," according to one author,

    tried to allay Zia's fears by reaffirming the 1959 Agreement of Cooperation with Pakistan in his speech before Congress. It was symbolism, but it was nonetheless important because Pakistan had raised questions of a congressional (as opposed to an executive) understanding. The reasoning behind such a move was the realization that Pakistan had suffered from the personalized nature of its relationship with Washington and that congressional commitment would provide much-needed continuity. Zia wanted a formal treaty, ratified by Congress. The State Department, however, from the Office of the Secretary all the way down to the Pakistan Office..., all felt it to be a totally inappropriate request on Zia's part.

    Tahir-Kheli, *The United States and Pakistan,* p. 101.
78. Interviews with the author, Islamabad, June 1986 and December 1987.
79. In addition to these three conditions, Shahi says that he informally made it clear to the American negotiating team that Pakistan could not supply an absolute guarantee that it would not detonate a nuclear explosive. In this connection, he says, the American negotiators agreed not to make the nuclear issue a pivotal element in the aid negotiations. Interview with the author, Islamabad, December 1987. See Agha Shahi, "Pakistan's Relations with the United States," *Pakistan Journal of American Studies* (Islamabad) 3:1 (March 1985) 9-11.
80. While the 1981 negotiations with the United States were under way, Shahi says that he gave a talk to a group of Pakistani army generals on the objectives of Pakistan's policy toward the United States. According to Shahi, he stressed the importance of nonalignment and the need to avoid overdependence on a superpower. Only a few days later, one of the generals, who later rose to a position in the army second only to Zia, met Shahi and in the course of conversation commented that he had been very impressed by Shahi's presentation but that, of course, the Americans should be given bases in return for the aid! Interview with the author, Islamabad, December 1987.
81. Testimony of Under Secretary of State James L. Buckley to the Senate Subcommittee on Energy, Nuclear Proliferation, and Government Processes of the Committee on Governmental Affairs, *Hearing on Nuclear Non-Proliferation Policy,* 97th Cong., 1st Sess., 24 June 1981 (Washington, D.C.: U.S. Government Printing Office, 1981) pp. 16-19.
82. The following were compiled from the series of studies done during the 1980s for the Carnegie Endowment for International Peace by Leonard S. Spector, *Nuclear Proliferation Today* (New York: Vintage Books, 1984) pp. 70-110; *The New Nuclear Nations* (New York: Vintage Books, 1985)

pp. 113-30; *Going Nuclear* (1987) pp. 101-24; and *The Undeclared Bomb* (1988) pp. 120-53.
83. Antiproliferation laws adopted in the last half of the 1970s included the 1976 Symington amendment barring aid to nonnuclear-weapon countries that import uranium enrichment technology; the 1977 Glenn amendment barring aid to countries that import reprocessing (plutonium extraction) technology; and the 1977 ban (enacted as a modification of the Glenn amendment) on aid to nonnuclear-weapon countries that receive, detonate, or transfer nuclear explosives. For details of this legislation, see Carnegie Task Force on Non-Proliferation and South Asian Security, *Nuclear Weapons and South Asian Security* (Washington, D.C.: Carnegie Endowment for International Peace, 1988) pp. 129-33.
84. Ibid., p. 114. See also the testimony of Leonard Spector, chairman of the Carnegie Task Force, in hearings before the Subcommittees on Asian and Pacific Affairs and on International Economic Policy and Trade of the Committee on Foreign Affairs, House of Representatives, 100th Cong., 2nd Sess., 17 February 1988, *The Implications of the Arshad Pervez Case for U.S. Policy Toward Pakistan* (Washington, D.C.: U.S. Government Printing Office, 1989) pp. 46-66.
85. The author was a member of the Task Force and was among those who submitted separate dissenting statements. See Carnegie Task Force on Non-Proliferation and South Asian Security, *Nuclear Weapons and South Asian Security*, pp. 126-8.
86. *The New York Times*, 13 March 1987, p. A30.
87. *The New York Times*, 30 March 1987, p. A18. The *Times* admitted, at least, that accomplishing all this would be quite a trick.
88. Among earlier efforts to assess nuclear incentives in the subcontinent are Richard K. Betts, "Incentives for Nuclear Weapons," in Joseph A. Yager (ed.), *Nonproliferation and U.S. Foreign Policy* (Washington, D.C.: The Brookings Institution, 1980) pp. 116-44; and Neil Joeck, "Pakistani Security and Nuclear Proliferation in South Asia," in Neil Joeck (ed.), *Strategic Consequences of Nuclear Proliferation in South Asia* (London: Frank Cass, 1986) pp. 80-98.
89. Richard N. Haass, "South Asia: Too Late to Remove the Bomb?", *Orbis* 32:1 (Winter 1988) 114. See also Stephen P. Cohen, *The Pakistan Army* (Berkeley: University of California Press, 1984) pp. 154-5.
90. Rodney W. Jones, "Pakistan's Nuclear Options," in Hafeez Malik (ed.), *Soviet-American Relations with Pakistan, Iran and Afghanistan* (New York: St. Martin's Press, 1987) pp. 212-13. In an earlier discussion of this subject, Jones observed that

> it would not be unnatural for Pakistan to view the development of nuclear technology as a comparative advantage or novel source of bargaining power in foreign relations. Pakistan's interests in expanding its export earning power, assuring an oil supply, and promoting a network of security relationships with its natural allies in the Persian Gulf area presumably all could be advanced by

> building a sophisticated national cadre of physical scientists, engineers, and nuclear technicians capable of contracting technical services to wealthier but technically less advanced neighbors.
>
> Cooperation specifically in nuclear weapons development need not be a part of nuclear cooperative relationships to make them attractive, but the very possibility of transfer of weapons technology or fissionable materials would arouse added interest. Moreover, the proliferation potential would increase the incentives for the United States and other Western states to accord greater importance and offer more substantial assistance to Pakistan in order to encourage its restraint.

Rodney W. Jones, *Nuclear Proliferation: Islam, the Bomb, and South Asia* (Beverly Hills: Sage Publications, 1981) p. 51. See also Richard P. Cronin, "Prospects for Nuclear Proliferation in South Asia," *The Middle East Journal* 37:4 (Autumn 1983) 612; and S. P. Seth, "The Indo-Pak Nuclear Duet and the United States," *Asian Survey* 28:7 (July 1988) 715-16.

91. For a detailed account of the development of the Indian and Pakistani nuclear programs, see Spector, *Nuclear Proliferation Today*, pp. 23-110.

92. Cronin, "Prospects for Nuclear Proliferation in South Asia," 610. S. P. Seth, formerly Senior Research Officer, Ministry of Defence in Delhi, suggests that "Pakistan's overriding compulsion in its nuclear quest" was "its enhanced insecurity vis-à-vis India after Pakistan's dismemberment and the creation of Bangladesh in 1971. The Simla Agreement," he said,

> which India conceived as a vehicle for amicable bilateral relations, was certainly a reminder to Pakistan of its defeat and humiliation. With Pakistan cut in half, the old approach of rough conventional military parity (with a possible edge over India) seemed not only impractical but outmoded. A nuclear deterrent, on the other hand, seemed an effective alternative—possibly a permanent answer to Pakistan's perennial security problem with India.

"The Indo-Pak Nuclear Duet and the United States," p. 712.

93. Spector, *Nuclear Proliferation Today*, pp. 59, 63.

94. Thomas, "India's Nuclear and Space Programs: Defense or Development?", 341. See also Bhatia, "India's Space Program: Cause for Concern?", 1013-30; Elkin and Fredericks, "Military Implications of India's Space Program," 56-63; and Onkar Marwah, "India's Nuclear and Space Programs: Intent and Policy," *International Security* 2:2 (Fall 1977) 96-121.

95. For an interesting comment by a maverick Indian defense analyst on the action-reaction sequence in regard to induction of advanced *conventional* weapons systems in the subcontinent, see Rikhye, *The Militarization of Mother India*, pp. 34-9.

96. Jones, "Pakistan's Nuclear Options," p. 207.

97. Spector, *The Undeclared Bomb*, p. 85.

98. Leonard Spector's fourth volume in the Carnegie Endowment series on the spread of nuclear weapons, published in 1988, achieved greater balance than had the earlier works on the question of Indian and Pakistani responsibility for the nuclear arms race. Among other things, Spector noted in the latest volume reports that India may in fact have manufactured a number of nuclear devices in the three-year period between the 1974 test and Mrs. Gandhi's fall from power in 1977. Echoing Rodney Jones's view, quoted in the text, he also noted that "whether or not India in fact possesses a number of nuclear weapons at this time [1988], it clearly has the capability to manufacture them quickly and,...Pakistani strategists would have to assume that Pakistan would confront a nuclear-armed adversary in any future conflict." Ibid., p. 106.
99. For one exception to the rule, see Rabia Ali, "Counterpoint: Against Pakistan Going Nuclear," *The Muslim*, 7 February 1987.
100. As reported in *The Muslim*, 5 November 1985, the President of the National Democratic Party (Punjab Province) did flatly oppose Pakistan's acquisition of nuclear weapons capability. The same position was reported to have been taken by Khurshid Hasan Meer, former Central Minister and now President of the fringe Pakistan Awami Jamhoori Party. *The Muslim*, 19 February 1987.
101. *The Muslim*, 30 November-1 December 1985; and interview with the author, Abbottabad, August 1985.
102. *Dawn*, 7 November 1985.
103. See, for example, Rasul B. Rais, "Pakistan's Nuclear Program: Prospects for Proliferation," *Asian Survey* 25:4 (April 1985) 458-72; and Akhtar Ali, *Pakistan's Nuclear Dilemma: Energy & Security Dimensions* (New Delhi: ABC Publishing House, 1984) esp. pp. 61-85.
104. Ibid., pp. 132-5.
105. See, for example, the various Pakistani contributions to "Nuclear Non-Proliferation in South Asia," a Special Issue of *Strategic Studies* 10:4 and 11:1 (Summer and Autumn 1987). This issue contains presentations made to an International Conference on Nuclear Non-Proliferation in South Asia held in Islamabad in September 1987.
106. About Pakistan's Kahuta nuclear enrichment project, for example, one prominent Pakistani commented:
> The result was Kahuta, which rose from the ashes of Chashma [Pakistan's foiled effort at acquiring a reprocessing plant] to assert the national will and determination to have what the nation needed. Pakistan's efforts were belittled by hostile powers which treated the country like an insolent upstart who would never make it. But the jibes were silenced and Kahuta proved to be a fantastic success story. Within a few years, unhampered and unaided by anybody, in a project directed and run by its own dedicated and patriotic scientists and engineers, Pakistan had achieved uranium enrichment. It was one of the very few countries in the world which could do that. It was away ahead of India in uranium enrichment, just as

India was ahead in the field of reprocessing, where we had not even got started, thanks to our friends.

Lt. General (Retd.) A. I. Akram, *South Asia and the Bomb*, Regional Perspective No. 12 (Islamabad: Institute of Regional Studies, December 1985), pp. 7-8.

107. Retired Lt. General A. I. Akram, the late president of the government-financed Institute of Regional Studies in Islamabad and a confidant of Zia's, commented in late 1985, for example, that Pakistan's success at Kahuta in mastering the uranium enrichment process had been

achieved in the teeth of opposition from friend and foe alike. For many years we had witnessed a campaign in the West against Pakistan's nuclear programme, a well-orchestrated campaign designed to give the image of a rising nuclear peril from Pakistan which would have a devastating effect on the peace of the world. Its organisers were the Jewish lobby in the West, which more or less controls the American media and exercises considerable influence over the media of Western Europe....The bomb allegedly being fabricated by Pakistan was happily flaunted as the *Islamic Bomb*. This created a disturbing picture in the minds of the Christians, and later also of the Hindus, of a great nuclear onslaught to be launched by Islamic fundamentalists against the rest of the world with obviously shattering results.

Ibid., p. 8. Agha Shahi, Foreign Minister of Pakistan until 1982, wrote in 1985 that

Pakistan has been greatly concerned over the propaganda about the Islamic Bomb depicting Pakistan as the villain and inciting Israel and India to acts of aggression aimed at the destruction of the Kahuta facility. For nearly a decade, US pressure on Pakistan to forego plutonium reprocessing or uranium enrichment has been intense and unrelenting....One cannot but ask the question why is Pakistan being singled out for this treatment when a more or less permissive attitude is indulged towards Israel, South Africa, and India? The characterisation of the Bomb as Islamic suggests it is because Pakistan is a Muslim country.

"Pakistan's Relations with the United States," 13-14.

108. Sahabzada Yaqub Khan, "Nuclear Non-Proliferation in South Asia," *Strategic Studies*, Special Issue on Nuclear Non-Proliferation in South Asia, p. 16.
109. Peter A. Clausen, "Nonproliferation Illusions: Tarapur in Retrospect," *Orbis* 27:3 (Fall 1983) 748.
110. Spector, *Nuclear Proliferation Today*, p. 36.
111. The major nonproliferation laws are described in Carnegie Task Force on Non-Proliferation and South Asian Security, *Nuclear Weapons and South Asian Security*, pp. 129-34.
112. Clausen, "Nonproliferation Illusions," p. 750.
113. Ibid., 755.

114. After arguing forcefully for renewed and strenuous efforts to compel Indian acceptance of international controls "in perpetuity" over nuclear materials produced at India's Tarapur plant, the University of Wisconsin's nonproliferation specialist Gary Milhollin asked the question: "What are the chances that this will be done?" His rather mournful reply was: "They are not very great." "Stopping the Indian Bomb," *The American Journal of International Law* 81:3 (July 1987) 609.

115. Haass, "South Asia: Too Late to Remove the Bomb?", 116-17. Haass was appointed Senior Director of Near East and South Asian affairs at the National Security Council by the Bush administration in January 1989.

116. See Mahnaz Ispahani, "Showing Sensitivity to Pakistan," *The New York Times*, 20 March 1987, p. A31.

117. Carnegie Task Force on Non-Proliferation and South Asian Security, *Nuclear Weapons and South Asian Security*, pp. 7-8.

118. Ibid., p. 9.

119. Ibid., p. 15.

120. Kuldip Nayyar, "India Forcing Us to Go Nuclear: A. Q. Khan," *The Muslim*, 3 March 1987. See Spector, *The Undeclared Bomb*, pp. 133-4.

121. Interview with the author, Islamabad, November 1986.

122. Hedrick Smith, "A Bomb Ticks in Pakistan," *The New York Times Magazine*, 6 March 1988, p. 95.

123. David Albright and Tom Zamora, "India, Pakistan's Nuclear Weapons: All the Pieces in Place," *Bulletin of the Atomic Scientists* 45:5 (June 1989) 20.

124. Stephen P. Cohen, *The Nuclear Futures of South Asia*, Occasional Paper 89-2, Program in Arms Control, Disarmament, and International Security, University of Illinois at Urbana-Champaign, April 1989, p. 6.

125. Ibid., p. 20.

126. K. Subrahmanyam, "The Nuclear Issue," unpublished paper prepared for the Indo-Pak Dialogue, a conference sponsored jointly by the Institute for Defence Studies and Analyses (New Delhi) and the Institute of Strategic Studies (Islamabad). The conference, scheduled to have been convened in New Delhi from 17-19 April 1990, was finally canceled.

127. For an excellent status report on the Indian and Pakistani nuclear programs as of 1988, see Spector, *The Undeclared Bomb*, pp. 80-153. See also Albright and Zamora, "India, Pakistan's Nuclear Weapons: All the Pieces in Place," pp. 20-6.

128. A notable exception in this regard was the view of Pakistan's nuclear capabilities taken by the Indian defense analyst Ravi Rikhye. See, for example, the discussion of his background paper on Pakistan in Bhabani Sen Gupta, *Nuclear Weapons? Policy Options for India* (New Delhi: Sage, 1983) pp. 53-62.

129. Gary Milhollin, a professor of law at the University of Wisconsin, was an outstanding exception in this regard. See, for example, his articles "Dateline New Delhi: India's Nuclear Cover-Up," *Foreign Policy* No. 64 (Fall 1986) 161-75; "Stopping the Indian Bomb," *The American Journal of International Law* 81:3 (July 1987) 593-609; and "India's Missiles—With a Little Help From Our Friends," *The Bulletin of the Atomic Scientists* 45:9 (November 1989) 31-5. See also Rodney Jones, "India's Nuclear Strategy: A Threat to World Peace?", *NBC Defense & Technology International* 1:2 (May 1986) 66-72.
130. Seth, "The Indo-Pak Nuclear Duet and the United States," p. 721.
131. Ashok Kapur, "A Nuclearizing Pakistan: Some Hypotheses," *Asian Survey* 20:5 (May 1980) 507, 513.
132. John J. Schulz, "Bluff and Uncertainty: Deterrence and the 'Maybe States,'" *SAIS Review* 7:2 (Summer-Fall 1987) 182.
133. Ibid., 190.
134. Cohen, *The Nuclear Futures of South Asia*, p. 5. In the same month, Zia made roughly the same admission to a member of a Carnegie Endowment delegation in Pakistan to examine the regional nuclear proliferation problem. Spector, *The Undeclared Bomb*, pp. 144-5.
135. Rodney Jones, "Nuclear Non-Proliferation Issues: The South Asian Context," *Strategic Studies*, Special Issue on Nuclear Non-Proliferation in South Asia, 68; and "Pakistan's Nuclear Options," pp. 213-14.
136. Jones, "Nuclear Non-Proliferation Issues: The South Asian Context," p. 70.
137. For an estimate of the likely damage from a nuclear exchange between India and Pakistan, see S. Rashid Naim, "Asia's Day After: Nuclear War Between India and Pakistan?", in Stephen P. Cohen (ed.), *The Security of South Asia: American and Asian Perspectives* (Urbana: University of Illinois Press, 1987) pp. 251-82.
138. Cohen, *The Pakistan Army*, pp. 157-8.

4

THE SIACHEN GLACIER TERRITORIAL DISPUTE WITH INDIA: THE IRREDENTIST IMPERATIVE

The Siachen Glacier is located in the Karakoram Mountains at the extreme northern edge of the Indian subcontinent immediately south of China's Xinjiang province.[1] One of the world's largest and longest nonpolar glaciers, it is a prominent feature in a wedge-shaped piece of territory situated between the Chinese border and the Saltoro Range. Until June 1984, few people outside of mountaineering circles had ever heard of it. In that month, Indian and Pakistani military forces battled one another in the Saltoro Range for control of access routes to the glacier, inaugurating a high-altitude struggle that was continuing unabated when Zia died in August 1988.[2] Reports of fierce fighting quickly earned the glacier a reputation as the world's loftiest battleground. Facing each other in some areas at elevations over 20 000 feet above sea level, the two armies were contesting for possession of about 1000 square miles of spectacular and heavily glaciated terrain claimed by both India and Pakistan but never before effectively controlled by either. The Siachen dispute was the most severe armed conflict between these two traditional rivals since the Bangladesh war of 1971. It was an offshoot of the long-smoldering Kashmir dispute, which had triggered two earlier wars between them. Precisely why it had erupted was not fully apparent. Its outcome, however, was certain to affect the long-term geopolitical fortunes of India and Pakistan, possibly even of other powerful states in the neighborhood, namely the Soviet Union and China.

India was the first to move its forces onto the glacier (in April 1984); and these forces rapidly gained and managed to retain the upper hand. They controlled practically all of the forty-six-mile long glacier, from where it begins at Indira Col to Dzingrulma at its mouth, and clearly held the high ground in two of the three principal passes (Sia La and Bilafond La, also called Saltoro Pass) that led onto the glacier's southern rim through the Saltoro Range. Pakistani troops occupied advantageous positions in the Gyong La Pass, overlooking supply trails leading to Indian outposts in the vicinity of the pass; but this gave Pakistani commanders small comfort in the face of India's apparent success in gaining control of a large wedge of uninhabited mountain territory that Pakistanis insisted belonged to them.

By twentieth-century standards, the scale of fighting over the glacier and adjacent mountain territory was relatively modest. Early press reports of combat casualties mounting into the thousands and describing pitched battles spread over many days and involving heavy armor and air strikes were clearly exaggerated.[3] The few massed assaults that Pakistan attempted (in 1985 and 1987) had failed to dislodge the Indians. For the most part, the Siachen "war" consisted of fairly routine artillery exchanges and infrequent skirmishes. It was a brutal and punishing contest. Plainly, however, it was more a test of endurance, courage, and ingenuity in matters of transport, equipment, and protection against a harsh environment than of anything else. The high altitude, numbing cold, and treacherous terrain made any movement hazardous and fighting, in a conventional sense, barely conceivable. Nevertheless, both armies had inducted substantial forces into the area and both appeared determined to remain in spite of the forbidding climate and the extraordinary hardships borne by their troops.

Coming at a time when Pakistan's policymakers were preoccupied with the Afghanistan war and when the country's eastern border was already severely threatened, the Siachen dispute confronted Islamabad with a major set of problems. Most obvious of these was its damaging impact on India-Pakistan relations. Military confrontation on the Siachen threatened to block the much-delayed process of normalization between Pakistan and India; and, more ominously, it significantly enlarged the prospects for a serious escalation of military conflict between them. The dispute, moreover, was unquestionably costly. Although both sides reported relatively light casualties, as often climate- as battle-related, there was no doubt that by the time of Zia's death there had been hundreds of deaths and thousands of injuries on both sides from combat, weather, accidents, and various hazards of altitude and terrain.[4] The dispute was also costly in material terms. Both sides had committed four battalions (between 5000 to 6000 men, including special units and support elements) directly to the Siachen front. India probably deployed about 3000 men in the Saltoro Range and its immediate vicinity, Pakistan somewhat less than that, perhaps about 2000 men. In both countries, headquarters and supply operations occupied far larger numbers than these.

Logistical support of these troops, made under conditions virtually without precedent anywhere in the world, was a constant nightmare for both countries.[5]

Islamabad also had to cope with the fact that while some of its allies, including the United States, did not consider the Siachen Glacier a particularly valuable piece of territory, not valuable enough, in any event, to risk jeopardizing Pakistan's overall relations with India, Pakistanis themselves generally drew different conclusions. For most of them, there was little to distinguish between the Siachen and Kashmir disputes, and over the latter Pakistan had already fought two wars. The Siachen dispute drew far less public attention in Pakistan than did the Afghanistan war, no doubt, but the Siachen dispute was also a significant—and potentially volatile—domestic political issue.

In this chapter, we examine Pakistan's policy in regard to territorial conflict with India. We focus on an offshoot of the Kashmir conflict—the Siachen Glacier dispute—that led to a major military confrontation between India and Pakistan during the Zia period. We assess the military and strategic importance of the Siachen, taking account both of its regional (India-Pakistan) and extraregional (Soviet-Chinese) dimensions. We pay particular attention to the relationship between the Siachen dispute and its Kashmir parent, for it is in the undiminished importance of the territorial conflict over Kashmir, I think, that much of the explanation for the continuing hostility between India and Pakistan is to be discovered.

I. THE TERRITORIAL ISSUES

The Siachen dispute has its origins in the armed conflict over possession of the former princely state of Jammu and Kashmir that erupted between India and Pakistan in 1947 at the time of independence. That conflict ended inconclusively in January 1949 with both sides occupying parts of the disputed territory. The area controlled by Pakistan fell broadly into two administrative categories: the Northern Areas (at the time of independence called Gilgit Agency) and Azad (Free) Jammu and Kashmir (hereinafter referred to as Azad Kashmir), a technically autonomous but Pakistan-administered strip of territory along the western edge of Jammu and Kashmir state. India retained about 62 percent of the total disputed territory, including Kashmir Valley, Jammu, and Ladakh. Following successful mediation efforts by the UN Commission on India and Pakistan (UNCIP), military representatives of India and Pakistan, meeting in Karachi in July 1949, agreed to establish a cease-fire line (CFL) in Jammu and Kashmir. Drawn between the positions of the two armies held at the time hostilities ended, the CFL extended from a point near Chhamb in Jammu in a rough arc running a bit under 500 miles north and then northeastward to a point (map reference point NJ 9842) about 12 miles north of the Shyok River in the Chulung Group (mountains) of the Saltoro Range. Since neither side had ever deployed any troops in the territory north of the line's northeasternmost extremity, and since it was considered an inaccessible no-man's-land anyway, no attempt was made to delineate the CFL as far as the Chinese border. That left undelineated a distance (due north) of about 40 miles. Controversy would later erupt over the wording of the Karachi Agreement, specifically over the nebulous statement that the CFL, from the last-named location (Khor) given in the summary verbal description of it, moved "thence north to the glaciers."[6] Many Indians claimed that the agreement's authors meant by this that the undelimited portion of the CFL (the portion beyond NJ 9842) ran northward through glacial terrain all the way to the Chinese border, a reading that would put most of the Siachen Glacier legally in Indian hands.[7] The Indian contention was rejected by Pakistanis, who insisted that the 1949 delimitation agreement contained no reference at all to the CFL beyond NJ 9842.[8]

The CFL's failure to reach the border with China was not corrected by either of the two subsequent wars which India and Pakistan fought against each other. The Soviet-supervised Tashkent negotiation that followed the 1965 conflict resulted in an agreement by the two sides to withdraw all armed forces essentially to the positions they held before the outbreak of hostilities, thus reaffirming the CFL without attempting to extend it. The July 1972 Simla Agreement following the 1971 conflict, on the other hand, did not reaffirm the 1949 CFL. New Delhi insisted that the old line be scrapped and that a new line be drawn under a new agreement acknowledging the actual line of control resulting from the cease-fire of 17 December 1971. Accordingly, a new Line of Control (LOC) was drawn up on a series of nineteen maps, final versions of which were initialed and exchanged by senior military representatives of the two countries on 11 December 1972. Since there were again no troops in contact in the vicinity of the Siachen Glacier, this line too did not cover the territory beyond grid point NJ 9842. Further confusing the matter was the description of the new line given the next day to the Indian Lok Sabha by then Foreign Minister Sardar Swaran Singh. Adding contradiction to existing problems relating to the line's northernmost extremity, it said that from Chorbatla in the Turtok sector, "the line of control runs northeastwards to Thang (inclusive to India) thence eastwards joining the glaciers."[9]

Further complicating the boundary question was the fact that the southern border of China's Xinjiang province, where a northward extension of the present LOC would terminate, was itself in dispute. The border agreement signed by Islamabad and Beijing in March 1963 did not fully resolve this dispute. That agreement covered a stretch of China's common border with Pakistan's Northern Areas extending over 200 miles from the trijunction of Afghanistan, Pakistan, and China's Xinjiang province eastward to the Karakoram Pass. Under terms of the agreement, the government of Pakistan relinquished claims to over 1500 square miles of territory, no part of which was under its actual control, in return for China's cession to Pakistan of about 750 square miles of territory actually administered by China. The agreement was clearly advantageous to Pakistan and undoubtedly gave a boost to Sino-Pakistani relations. Nevertheless, it fell well short of a definitive boundary settlement. It dealt only with a relatively small segment of China's southern boundary, leaving unaddressed the signatories' overlapping and vastly more complicated border disputes with India. Indeed, the joint declaration published at the time the Sino-Pakistan agreement was concluded conceded its provisional status pending Pakistan's final settlement of the Kashmir dispute with India. The agreement's preamble described the territory lying south of the agreed boundary as "the contiguous areas the defence of which is under the actual control of Pakistan," not as *Pakistani* territory.[10] In admitting the possibility that the "sovereign authority" empowered to reach a final settlement—hence, in possession of the territory south of the border with China—might be India,[11] the agreement left the door ajar in respect to permanent sovereignty over the area in which the Siachen Glacier is found. As things transpired, the agreement was promptly rejected by India, which argued that Pakistan had no right to barter away territory belonging to India.[12] Pakistani spokesmen, we might take note here, would later contend that India, while rejecting Pakistan's right to cede the territory to China, all along had given tacit acceptance to Pakistan's de facto control over it.[13]

The obviously provisional wording of the 1963 Sino-Pakistani border treaty, together with the Indian reaction to it, revealed a very substantial difference in the way the Indian and Pakistani governments conceived the territorial question. India has always claimed outright all the territories ruled by Maharaja Hari Singh, the last Hindu ruler of the state of Jammu and Kashmir, by virtue of his accession to India upon the lapse of British paramountcy over the Indian princely states in 1947. These territories, according to India, included not only the state of Jammu and Kashmir proper, but all the trans-Indus territories (including Ladakh, Baltistan, Gilgit, and, in some formulations, even Chitral district in Pakistan's North West Frontier province) lying to the south of Chinese Turkestan.[14] In spite of the fact that China successfully defended its claim to the Aksai Chin region of Ladakh against India in the short war of 1962 and, furthermore, that Pakistan had been in continuous control of the Northern Areas and Azad Kashmir since late 1947, all of these territories were always depicted on Indian maps as belonging to India. Perhaps this was simply a tactical maneuver meant to buffer India's claim to the area actually under its control. Or it may have been a device for pressuring Pakistan to accept the cease-fire line as the legal boundary. Some evidence clearly points in this direction. In July 1950, for example, the Indian Prime Minister apparently informed the UN Representative for India and Pakistan, Sir Owen Dixon, that India was ready to accept the immediate partitioning of the state of Jammu and Kashmir and to concede to Pakistan the bulk of the territories then under Pakistani control.[15] Indian proposals in the abortive India-Pakistan ministerial-level talks on Kashmir from December 1962 to May 1963 seemed to have had basically the same objectives.[16] Some observers, moreover, have interpreted India's voluntary restoration to Pakistan of territory captured in the western region in the 1965 and 1971 conflicts as strong signs of India's continued willingness to settle for the present LOC in Kashmir as its permanent international boundary with Pakistan.[17] Nevertheless, India has never relented from its *formal* claim to the whole.

There have been, of course, contradictions in the Indian position. At an early stage in the Kashmir crisis, in late 1947, the then Prime Minister Jawaharlal Nehru committed India to a plan for a UN-sponsored plebiscite over the future status of Kashmir that clearly conceded a provisional element in the Indian claim.[18] And in a gesture reflecting India's initially more ambivalent stand on the issue, Article 370 of the Indian constitution, adopted in 1951, conferred on Kashmir a degree of autonomy unique among Indian states.[19] The idea of a plebiscite never had New Delhi's unqualified support, however, and, in fact, has been effectively ruled out by India at least since 1954.[20] Moreover, there have been recurring efforts in India, led by right-wing Hindu nationalist groups, to eliminate whatever traces of Kashmiri autonomy yet remained by abrogating Article 370.[21] Indeed, for most of the last 4 decades of struggle over Kashmir there has been very little wavering in the Indian position: India's right to *Indian-administered* Kashmir, at least, has been considered final, its standing as an integral component of the Indian union irrevocable and nonnegotiable. On this, the Indian stand over the years has, if anything, hardened. What this portends in regard to the Siachen Glacier, which appears to have figured in neither government's territorial calculations until rather recently, we will come to later in the discussion. Insofar as the glacier is concerned, however, India is presumably free, like Pakistan, to interpret ownership of the undelimited territory north of the present terminus of the LOC in a way most advantageous to itself. Perhaps most revealing about the Indian stand on the Kashmir territorial issue, in fact, is the contrast it offers with the Pakistani stand which, in a curious reversal of the Indian pattern, has shown a greater inclination to change with the passage of time.

Pakistan's claim to Kashmir has always, in fact, been couched in a certain amount of calculated ambiguity. Since Pakistan was the weaker side in a contest wherein the stronger had successfully clamped its control over the larger and more heavily populated part of the disputed territory, such an approach—at least in the early phases of the dispute—made considerable sense. Had it simply annexed the areas it administered to the west and north of the CFL, Pakistan's case for a plebiscite in *Indian-controlled* areas would almost certainly have lost legitimacy. Since international support for its claim weighed heavily with Pakistan, it chose instead to designate the whole of the state of Jammu and Kashmir—including Azad Kashmir and all of the Northern Areas (Baltistan and Gilgit)—as "disputed territory."[22] This inevitably implied that the fate of these areas was to be settled, if not by plebiscite, at least by negotiation. As a consequence, the state of Azad Kashmir did not appear on any published Pakistani map, in spite of the fact that it had its own constitution, its own capital city (Muzaffarabad), a full-fledged government (including its own President), a national flag, and the warm support (albeit not formal recognition) of Pakistan. Publicly sold Pakistani maps were, in fact, less clear on the matter of Azad Kashmir in recent years than they once had been. Past practice allowed at least for the display of the CFL.[23] Recent maps avoided showing the location of the CFL's successor, the LOC, leaving in doubt where Azad Kashmir left off and the Northern Areas began or, for that matter, whether there *was* any boundary between them.

Aware of the tangled anomalies in Pakistan's territorial claim, successive Pakistani governments attempted various measures to unravel them. Ayub Khan's principal effort in this direction culminated in the Sino-Pakistani border agreement of 1963. That agreement, as we have seen, did not claim Pakistani sovereignty over any part of the Northern Areas. On the contrary, it settled for a clearly provisional status for those territories. That fact must have been known to Zulfikar Ali Bhutto, who was an outspoken supporter of the pact and headed Pakistan's Foreign Office under Ayub from 1963 to 1966. Having himself come to power in 1971 in the wake of the Bangladesh debacle, moreover, Bhutto had obvious and powerful motivation to reduce remaining territorial vulnerabilities by seeking to clarify the status of the Pakistan-administered areas of the old Jammu and Kashmir state.

By Bhutto's time, Azad Kashmir was in most respects, and certainly economically, already an integral part of Pakistan. To further the process of unification, Bhutto ordered in 1971 the full absorption of its armed forces into the Pakistan army. Apparently, in public addresses at Muzaffarabad and Mirpur (in Azad Kashmir) in autumn 1973, he even floated a proposal for absorbing Azad Kashmir as a fifth province of Pakistan.[24] That proposal was strenuously objected to by Kashmiri leaders in Pakistan, on grounds that it would imply recognition of the LOC as a permanent international boundary, and the idea was quickly dropped. Instead, in 1974 Bhutto amended the Azad Kashmir constitution, incorporating immensely popular provisions giving it its own supreme court, prime minister, and chief election commissioner, and thus, on the surface at least, reinforced the *political* separateness essential to the credibility of Pakistan's case for Kashmiri self-determination. However, creation at the same time of the quasi-federal Kashmir Council, chaired by the Prime Minister of Pakistan and consisting of elected representatives of the Azad Kashmir Assembly, the Pakistan National Assembly, and members of both the Azad Kashmir and central cabinets, made explicit the *federal* presence in the governance of Azad Kashmir and, in the opinion of a senior minister in Bhutto's cabinet at the time, clearly was a step toward the integration into Pakistan of Azad Kashmir.[25] Moreover, in organizing a unit of the Pakistan People's Party in Azad Kashmir toward the end of his rule, Bhutto departed from the convention that Azad Kashmir was for Kashmiri parties only, thus further diluting the proposition that Azad Kashmir was a separate political entity.

In regard to the Northern Areas, Bhutto apparently resisted the pleas of Azad Kashmir leaders that these areas be understood to be a part of Jammu and Kashmir state, holding instead that the Northern Areas lay in a separate jurisdiction and were for all practical purposes a part of Pakistan.[26] Early in his rule, he introduced a number of administrative changes in these areas, including the establishment of district-level representative councils. In September 1974, he announced the abolition of princely rule of the state of Hunza and its full merger with Gilgit, a step which India duly claimed was taken without any legal right.[27] As it turned out, however, Bhutto fell from power well before implementing any sort of a final territorial solution.

It was thus left to Bhutto's successor, President Zia ul-Haq, upon coming to power in 1977, to attempt the resolution of Pakistan's territorial dilemma. Evidence is plentiful that he did not shrink from the task. In fact, measures adopted since 1977 unquestionably blurred more than ever the jurisdictional boundaries between the Northern Areas and Pakistan proper, enough anyway to convince most observers, including the first President of Azad Kashmir, Sardar Mohammad Ibrahim Khan, and virtually every other Kashmiri leader interviewed by the author, that the government of Pakistan's ultimate objective was the full annexation of the Northern Areas into Pakistan.[28]

Some hint of this intention was already apparent even in the promulgation of martial law itself in July 1977. For the first time in Pakistan's history, martial law was formally extended to the Northern Areas, all of which was included in Martial Law Zone E. Martial law was not formally extended to Azad Kashmir, on the other hand, but even there it was at least tacitly introduced. The elected government of Azad Kashmir, under pressure from Islamabad, "temporarily" dissolved itself by constitutional amendment. The President was retained; but the Prime Minister was replaced, first by a retired army general, later on by a serving general (Brigadier, later Major General Mohammad Hayat Khan). All martial law regulations were introduced in the Northern Areas and in Azad Kashmir, albeit in the latter area under separate presidential ordinance. Political parties were banned and then later directed to reregister—as everywhere else in martial law-ruled Pakistan.

An additional step seemingly in the direction of the political integration of the Northern Areas occurred in April 1982, when the government gave three men from there (but none from Azad Kashmir) observer status in the Federal Advisory Council (Majlis-i-Shura), the nominated, quasi-legislative body introduced under martial law. Yet another step in the same direction occurred in November 1983, when President Zia hosted a dinner in Gilgit, the principal town and administrative hub of the Northern Areas, to which over forty foreign envoys based in Islamabad were invited. Not surprisingly, the Indian government protested both gestures as a departure from Pakistan's traditional stand and as a transparent strategy to build support for altering the status of the Northern Areas. Never before, the Indians pointed out, had these areas been represented in Pakistan's elected national assemblies nor had they been listed as part of Pakistan in the suspended 1973 constitution.[29]

India's allegations at that time were given at least partial confirmation with the publication in mid-1985 of the official *Atlas of Pakistan,* the first such publication in the country's history.[30] It was perhaps not a fortunate time for the *Atlas* to make its debut, since the sanctity of Pakistan's northern borders, on the east and west, was by then looming as a major political issue and a focus of media attention. What the *Atlas* did cartographically was to remove Gilgit Agency from the status of a disputed territory, as it had hitherto always been shown,[31] and to give it entirely separate standing. This left the disputed status of Baltistan (at whose eastern edge, according to Pakistan's claim, stands the Siachen Glacier) untouched; but it rid Gilgit of at least some of its ambiguity and, obviously, reduced the size of the territory still in dispute with India.[32]

Further confirmation of Pakistan's integration-oriented policy was given in July 1986 when President Zia, according to a report in an Islamabad-based daily, announced that the federal government was giving serious consideration to the matter of political representation of the Northern Areas in the National Assembly.[33] Precisely which territories were meant by "the Northern Areas" was not specified in the report.

The continuing ambiguity in Pakistan's position has provoked considerable controversy in Pakistan, in and out of government, not least in those parts of the nation most directly affected—Azad Kashmir and the Northern Areas. The ruling party in Azad Kashmir, the All Jammu and Kashmir Muslim Conference, opposed Zia's appointment of three observers from the Northern Areas to the Majlis-i-Shura as a threat to the integrity of Kashmir. The head of that party and then President of Azad Kashmir, citing the 1963 Sino-Pakistani border agreement's wording on the subject (and in seeming conflict with his close political ally, President Zia), stated categorically to the author that the Northern Areas, including Gilgit, were an integral part of Jammu and Kashmir state.[34] In this, he had the vocal support of virtually the whole of the political opposition in Azad Kashmir, including that of the late K. H. Khurshid, at the time opposition leader in the Azad Kashmir Assembly. Himself President of Azad Kashmir from 1959 to 1964, Khurshid stated to the author in 1986 that the Northern Areas (meaning Gilgit *and* Baltistan) were administratively separated from Azad Kashmir as the result of an agreement struck between the Muslim Conference leadership and the government of Pakistan in the chaotic environment that prevailed in the immediate postindependence period. The agreement's actual purpose, according to Khurshid, was to transfer responsibility for administration of the Northern Areas *temporarily* from Azad Kashmir to the government of Pakistan. That expedient arrangement, in Khurshid's judgment, had resulted in the permanent alienation of the Northern Areas from Azad Kashmir.[35]

Responding to Kashmiri demands for the restoration of Gilgit and Baltistan to Azad Kashmir, spokesmen for the Northern Areas, in turn, began generating a flurry of news items in the Pakistani press opposing merger with Azad Kashmir and demanding separate provincial status for the Northern Areas, or at least some form of representation in Pakistan's National Assembly.[36] Various Pakistani writers entered the fray, ransacking history for evidence that the Northern Areas were—or were not—entitled to political status separate from Azad Kashmir. Ayub B. Awan, who was Secretary in the Ministry of Home Affairs at his retirement in 1969, and who had earlier served that ministry as the Director of its Intelligence Bureau, concluded his survey of the historical background to the issue by saying that "the areas of the Gilgit Agency across the River Indus were never a part of the State of Jammu and Kashmir as evidenced from the categorical and authentic ruling of the late Government of India. As such, they are totally outside the Kashmir dispute between Pakistan and India. Their formal accession to Pakistan [following a local rebellion against the Dogra Maharaja in 1947] is legal, final and binding. This is the constitutional position."[37] Very little of an official nature appeared in the Pakistani press to clarify the government of Pakistan's own views on the subject, though the Surveyor General, reacting to a letter printed in an Islamabad daily complaining about the status of Baltistan shown in the new *Atlas,* gave assurances that the maps published in the *Atlas* showing Jammu and Kashmir state as disputed territory were "in conformity with the position that the question of accession of the State of Jammu and Kashmir is yet to be decided in accordance with the relevant resolutions of the United Nations through the democratic method of a free and impartial plebiscite."[38] His statement, unfortunately, did not offer an explanation for the diminishing size of the disputed territory in official publications.

While Islamabad's emerging Kashmir policy seemed to be provoking increasing resistance not only from India but also from the Kashmiri leadership within Pakistan, from outside the subcontinent Islamabad's territorial claim won some, perhaps unexpected, symbolic support. The 1974 edition of the operational navigation chart of the Kashmir area prepared by the U.S. Defense Mapping Agency depicted an Air Defense Information Zone (ADIZ) line separating India and Pakistan in the Karakoram Mountains. It ran from the terminal point of the LOC at NJ 9842 in a straight path northeastward about 60 miles to the Karakoram Pass. Over the next half-dozen years, this was followed by a stream of updated maps clearly favoring Pakistan printed in current editions of a number of highly regarded, commercial Western atlases. Among others, the National Geographic Society's *Atlas of the World,* the University of Chicago's *A Historical Atlas of South Asia,* and *The Times Atlas of the World,* published in London, all showed the CFL and/or LOC extending *beyond* map grid-point NJ 9842 in a clear northeasterly direction right up to the Karakoram Pass on the Chinese border.[39] This not even Pakistani maps had ever done. The National Geographic map was even more helpful to Pakistan in that, while noting India's claim to the Northern Areas in fine print, it depicted the Northern Areas in a color distinct from Indian-administered Kashmir but indistinct from Pakistan. Not the least reason for satisfaction among Pakistanis in regard to all this cartographic support was the fact that some of it, including a map of Northern Kashmir in a widely acclaimed book by one of India's best-known defense analysts, even came from India![40]

Another source of more or less symbolic foreign support for Pakistan's position came in the form of international mountaineering expeditions to peaks in the vicinity of the Siachen Glacier. These expeditions, Pakistanis claimed, had been undertaken solely with the permission of *Pakistani* authorities since as far back as the 1950s.[41] Foreign expeditions to the eastern Karakorams, including the Siachen, were banned by Pakistan from 1961 to 1974. With the ban's lifting in 1974, foreign expeditions returned to the area in larger numbers than ever. According to a listing supplied to the author by the Institute of Strategic Studies in Islamabad, twenty Pakistan-authorized foreign climbing and trekking expeditions to the general vicinity of the Siachen Glacier were carried out between 1974 and 1981.[42] Widely circulated international alpine journals and trekking guides generally accepted Pakistan's claim to be in control of the Siachen. A leading American journal, for instance, footnoted a report from India of an Indian army team's 1980 traverse of the Siachen Glacier and successful ascent of Apsarasas peak with the remark that it was "surprising that an Indian Army force should have crossed the Cease-Fire Line and entered into what is generally held to be Pakistan, although the Indians would dispute this."[43]

Such comments seemed to point in the direction of growing international acceptance of Pakistan's administrative control of the Siachen area. They may well have alerted Indian authorities, who until then had not encouraged international expeditions to that area to originate from the Indian side, to the dangers of what some were calling "mountain poaching" and others "oropolitics"—the politics of mountains and mountaineering.[44] Indeed, the military steps India ultimately took to secure its own claim to the Siachen stemmed at least in part from them. While one must question the accuracy of one Indian journalist's contention that the Siachen conflict "began when India became aware, towards the end of 1983, that Pakistan intended to support a big international expedition into the Siachen in 1984, and was preparing to man permanent outposts through the winter of 1983-84 to ensure non-interference by the Indians," there is no doubt that Pakistan's mountaineering policy had the potential to inch the country's territorial claim to the Siachen Glacier area toward international respectability.[45] In summer 1985, as if to balance things out, India threw open to international climbers sixteen of the better-known peaks around the glacier, with one condition—that each climbing team be led by an Indian.[46]

No detailed authoritative statement of Pakistan's position in regard to the underlying territorial issues of the Siachen dispute was published during the Zia period. Zia's own comments on the matter were sometimes obscure and at times contradictory. Aside from the obvious complexity of these issues, any attempt to define Pakistan's position during the Zia period was thus bound to fall short of precision. A rough approximation of Pakistan's official territorial claim is, however, possible. Judging from what the government chose to reveal to the press or in reply to parliamentary probes, from my own interviews with senior Pakistani army officers and government officials in autumn 1989 and summer 1990, as well as from long-standing positions taken by the government toward the Kashmir issue, the Siachen claim of Zia's government, I believe, ran something like this:

1. The act of accession to India by the state of Jammu and Kashmir in October 1947 is incomplete in law. It was conditioned upon conduct of a plebiscite to determine the state's future status, a fact acknowledged by India in its formal acceptance of the Instrument of Accession. Adherence of Jammu and Kashmir state proper, and of the *disputed* sector of the Northern Areas (that is, Baltistan, including the Siachen Glacier), to either India or Pakistan is thus a matter to be settled by internationally supervised plebiscite.[47] Pending conduct of a plebiscite, in other words, the Siachen Glacier falls under the strict territorial sovereignty neither of India nor of Pakistan.

2. The Siachen Glacier is situated at the eastern edge of Baltistan, a territory over which Pakistan has asserted continuous administrative control ever since independence. Of its control over the Siachen area, in particular, there is abundant evidence. International mountaineering expeditions have routinely sought Pakistani permission to enter the Siachen area; and prestigious international atlases virtually all conceded the area to Pakistan. Until recently, even India acquiesced in Pakistan's possession of the area.

3. The Siachen Glacier lies outside the formally delimited LOC in Jammu and Kashmir state;[48] but any ambiguity in the wording relating to the northern terminus of the line in either the 1949 or 1972 agreement does not constitute an argument against Pakistan's continued administrative control of the glacier. On the contrary, Pakistan's long-established and widely recognized administrative control of the area argues for an extension of the LOC running in a northeasterly direction to the vicinity of the Karakoram Pass. The logic of Pakistan's position in this regard is reinforced by the fact that

the Karakoram Pass was also the terminal point of the boundary delimitation agreed between Pakistan and China in 1963.
4. Indian military intrusion into the Siachen area in 1984 was an act of aggression in flagrant violation of the 1949 Karachi Agreement on the cease-fire and the 1972 Simla Agreement requiring the two sides to refrain from the use of force in their bilateral relations.
5. Peaceful settlement of the Siachen dispute would be best served by restoring administrative control of the area to Pakistan. At a minimum, India must pull its forces back to the positions they occupied prior to the outbreak of hostilities in 1984.

India's Siachen claim, as far as one could judge, was in most respects the mirror image of Pakistan's. Boiled down to its essentials, it looked something like this:

1. By virtue of the act of accession in 1947, all of Jammu and Kashmir, including the so-called Northern Areas, rightfully belongs to India. Pakistan's seizure of part of this territory in that year by force of arms was illegal. Aggressive Pakistani behavior since then and refusal to vacate the territory militarily have completely nullified any obligation for India to submit to popular plebiscite its territorial claim to all or any part of Kashmir.[49] The only issue that remains to be settled in the so-called Kashmir dispute is Pakistan's continued illegal occupation of Indian territory.
2. The Siachen Glacier and its environs lie outside the formally agreed LOC in Jammu and Kashmir state, hence outside the territory falling legally under Pakistan's administrative control as established by the 1972 Simla accord. That accord did not warrant the arbitrary extension of the LOC by *either* party to the agreement in *any* direction. Ambiguity in the wording of the agreement in regard to the northern terminus of the LOC could at least as well support Indian claims to glacial systems lying to the west of Siachen as any Pakistani claim to a straight-line delimitation bypassing Siachen on the east and running northeastward to the Karakoram Pass.[50] Pakistan's reluctance to make official public acknowledgment of its unilateral extension of the LOC is tacit admission of its illegality.
3. Pakistan's claim to permanent *administrative* control of the Siachen area since independence is without any foundation in fact. Its sponsorship of foreign expeditions to the area since 1974 is a deliberate tactic, involving promotional advertisement, eased application pro-

cedures, and waiver of royalties on some peaks, to gain international acceptance of its administrative authority in that area and, hence, of its unilateral and arbitrary extension of the LOC. The Siachen Glacier, in fact, forms the western boundary of the Nubra subdivision of Ladakh district, a territory which has been within India's administrative jurisdiction continuously since independence was gained. India has an obvious right to use force to defend itself against Pakistan's efforts to annex Indian territory whether by resort to military aggression or spurious claims of customary practice.

4. In accord with the Simla Agreement of 1972, the problem of delimiting the Siachen area must be settled bilaterally, through negotiation between India and Pakistan. The settlement must take into account the Kashmir boundary problem as a whole.

From the above, we can see that the positions taken by the governments of India and Pakistan in regard to the Siachen dispute were heavily influenced by the positions taken earlier by each side in regard to the preexisting conflict over possession of Kashmir. Thus, India claimed that the glacier lay within the jurisdiction of India's Jammu and Kashmir state and was, therefore, not disputed territory at all but an integral part of India. Pakistan, on the other hand, claimed that the glacier lay within the Pakistan-administered sector of the disputed territory of Jammu and Kashmir and that, pending final resolution of its status through an internationally supervised plebiscite in that territory, it must, therefore, be restored to Pakistan's control. Neither of these positions was airtight. As already pointed out, whether the territory in which the glacier is located ever fell within the legal jurisdiction of the prepartition princely state of Jammu and Kashmir was itself a subject of controversy. If it did not fall within that jurisdiction, then neither Pakistan's entitlement to the glacier by virtue of a prospective plebiscite in Jammu and Kashmir nor India's by virtue of Jammu and Kashmir's formal accession to India would stand inspection.

We have observed that the government of Pakistan, displaying diminished tolerance of persistent territorial ambiguity in its position on Kashmir, had over the years substantially shifted its ground. Initially under Bhutto and increasingly under Zia, Pakistan had moved haltingly but surely away from its earlier almost exclusive reliance on the UN resolutions calling for plebiscite in the disputed territory. These resolutions had reached an obvious dead end. No matter how often Islamabad invoked them, there were fewer and fewer people in or out of government who continued to believe that they either could or would ever be implemented.[51] In their place, Pakistan had clearly adopted a tacit policy of incremental annexation both of Azad Kashmir and of the Northern Areas which, if it continued, would eliminate the ambiguity in Pakistan's territorial claim and put it on much the same footing as India's. Indeed, to the extent that Pakistan's move toward fuller integration of territories under its administrative control represented the same sort of territorial "solution" adopted by New Delhi much earlier in regard to the territories under its administrative control, then India and Pakistan had for some years been moving quietly on a parallel course.

Available facts do not warrant the conclusion that Pakistan, in seizing the initiative to reduce the ambiguity in its territorial claim to Kashmir, was preparing to yield on its claim to the whole of Kashmir and to settle for the LOC as the permanent international boundary with India. If Pakistan's leaders ever had a definite plan of this kind, they have not revealed it. Apart from any such consideration, Islamabad already had ample justification to shift the grounds of its territorial claim. The regional security environment abounded in disturbing developments. Some of these developments, including Soviet military occupation of Afghanistan and a negative shift in the subcontinent's military balance, we have already reviewed in earlier chapters. By any measure, these developments were threatening enough to erode confidence in Pakistan's existing position on the territorial issue and to prompt serious soul-searching in regard to alternatives.

However, even if Pakistan's moves to harden its claim to Kashmir were motivated largely by threatening developments in the region's security environment, the relationship between these developments and the Siachen dispute itself were by no means crystal clear. To assert that Pakistan faced a worsening military balance with India was one thing. It was quite another, however, to build a convincing argument that India could use the Siachen Glacier as a permanent military base, intelligence listening post, or staging ground for launching military operations further afield. No doubt, India had made a huge commitment in men and resources to the fight over the Siachen; and that in and of itself unquestionably presented Pakistan with an additional threat to its security. But the magnitude of the threat thus presented defied easy reckoning. After all, how great the threat to Pakistan was depended very much on Indian intentions, and these proved especially difficult to infer from events occurring on the remote glacier itself. There the fighting seemed very quickly to have bogged down into a costly stalemate. Indeed, far more than any of Pakistan's earlier armed conflicts with India, this one struck many foreign observers, and even some Pakistanis, as basically pointless, as essentially "much ado about nothing."[52] Any definition of Pakistan's military-strategic stake in the Siachen conflict was thus bound to stir up objection. We move now to consider the issues involved.

II. THE MILITARY-STRATEGIC CONTEXT

What is publicly known of events leading up to the outbreak of hostilities in the vicinity of the Siachen Glacier in early spring 1984 does not supply unambiguous evidence that either India or Pakistan was technically the aggressor. Precisely who shot first is probably impossible to determine. So too, I suspect, is the precise sequence of decision-making—or mix of action and reaction—on both sides that preceded the fighting. Which of the two armed forces had the "right" to be on the glacier was a matter obviously open to disagreement, since (1) neither had hitherto occupied it and (2) the question of the legitimacy of the two sides' territorial claims had never been submitted to impartial adjudication. It is a bit perplexing, therefore, to find an American commentator describing India's intrusion into the Saltoro Range in 1984 as an act somehow consistent with the territorial status quo, Pakistan's as a forcible attempt to alter it.[53] On the contrary, there is ample evidence (actually, there is no argument about it) that Indian armed forces were the first to establish permanent posts in the strategic passes of the Saltoro Range and on the glacier and that they had prepared themselves longer and better for the task than had the Pakistanis. Published Indian accounts of Operation Meghdoot (Cloud Messenger), the deployment of specially trained units of the Kumaon regiment and the Ladakh Scouts onto the glacier in mid-April 1984, left little room for doubt, in fact, that the Pakistanis were caught napping and that their principal strategy for fortifying Pakistan's claim to the glacier—sponsoring foreign mountaineering expeditions to the area—had been a dismal failure.

The most authoritative of the Indian accounts was one by retired Lieutenant General M. L. Chibber, who headed the Indian army's Northern Command in 1984 and directed the Siachen operation, that was published in the *Indian Defence Review* in January 1990. In it, Chibber revealed that the Siachen Glacier had come to his notice as a "problem area" as early as January 1978, when he was Director of Military Operations at Army Headquarters in New Delhi. One of India's foremost mountaineers, Colonel Narinder ("Bull") Kumar, had at that time alerted Chibber to the existence of American maps showing the LOC extended to the India-China border at the Karakoram Pass. Kumar sought—and received—Chibber's support for an "operational reconnaisance patrol" into the Siachen Glacier area. The matter of the offending maps was brought to the attention of the Ministries of Defence and External Affairs; and, according to Chibber, he then

> initiated action to analyse the whole problem in depth, and bring together all the relevant facts so that we may have contingency plans to handle the situation whichever way it may develop....From an examination of all the relevant facts, one point stood out quite clearly, that we should open up the area to mountaineers, and also keep an eye on it to prevent intrusions by Pakistan-based expeditions.

Colonel Kumar's expedition to Terram Kangri in the Siachen area during the summer of 1978 thus became important from the security angle.[54]

It is thus quite clear, even if India's decision to take military control of the glacier was not taken until much later, that New Delhi's contingency planning and military-related expeditions to the vicinity of the glacier began in 1978—six years before Operation Meghdoot took place. A number of these expeditions were, in fact, widely reported in the Indian press. Especially noteworthy were two articles by Colonel Kumar, who was then Commandant of India's High Altitude Warfare School (HAWS) at Gulmarg, that appeared in *The Illustrated Weekly of India* in 1980 and 1982. In the first of these, Kumar reported on a 1978 HAWS expedition that successfully scaled the Teram Kangri II peak on the northern edge of the Siachen Glacier.[55] In the second, Kumar told of a massive 1981 HAWS expedition that traversed the entire Siachen Glacier and scaled three peaks in its vicinity.[56] Kumar made it abundantly clear in these articles that these expeditions were heartily supported by the top leadership of the Indian army and that he considered the Siachen Glacier and the surrounding peaks to be Indian territory.

New Delhi's seemingly calculated exposure, at least as early as 1980, of its keen military interest in the Siachen Glacier does not appear to have immediately set off alarm bells in Pakistan. For up to two years, no concrete steps either to buttress Pakistan's claim to the Siachen militarily or to prepare its army generally to meet the requirements of high-altitude mountain warfare appear to have been taken by the Zia regime; and whatever steps were taken thereafter were obviously inadequate. Given Pakistan's customary sensitivity in regard to the border dispute with India, this slowness to respond is puzzling. No doubt, Islamabad was preoccupied to an extent with the war in Afghanistan. One may suspect that part of the explanation lay also in the army's inability to discharge fully its military mission while at the same time running the government. Be this as it may, the report in a major

American newspaper in late 1987 that put the Pakistanis on the glacier ahead of the Indians and implied that the fighting was precipitated by a threatening Pakistani military offensive on the glacier to which the alarmed Indians were simply responding, besides having the order of events reversed, substantially overstated the war-readiness of the Pakistan army.[57] The truth, it appears, does not flatter the Pakistanis. It was they and not the Indians who were surprised on the Siachen.

The Pakistan government never claimed, of course, that its "administrative control" over the Siachen implied any more than the barest military presence. Interviews with a number of senior Pakistani army officers in autumn 1989 revealed, in fact, that until alerted by the Indian army's activities on the glacier in the early 1980s, the Pakistan army's own presence in that area was both very slender and strictly seasonal. As the commander of a brigade committed to the Siachen fighting put it, the army's mission in this area had heretofore been simply to protect areas of civilian habitation. Permanent habitation, he pointed out, was confined to the river valleys. Units of the paramilitary Gilgit Scouts had for many years manned small garrisons in these valleys; but only in the warm season, when local villagers ventured up the valleys as high as the snowline to pasture their flocks, did the Scouts patrol anywhere near the passes leading onto the glacier. The Pakistan army was thus *present* around Siachen from the start, he said, but only very modestly.

The absence of permanent military garrisons in the immediate vicinity of the Siachen Glacier may help to explain why Pakistan's awareness of the military implications of India's growing interest in the glacier developed rather late in the game. Indeed, it seems it was the Indian media and not Pakistani reconnaisance that supplied the earliest clues. According to Brigadier Syed Asif Riaz Bukhari, Chief of Staff, Headquarters, 10th Corps, an officer with several years' involvement in the Siachen fighting at both field command and staff levels, Pakistani suspicions were, in fact, initially aroused by Colonel Kumar's above-mentioned 1982 article in *The Illustrated Weekly of India*, in which the 1981 HAWS' expedition to the Siachen was described.[58] The article seemed odd to Pakistani analysts, said Bukhari, among other reasons because of the delay between the occurrence of the expedition and publication of Colonel Kumar's account of it.[59] It was only with publication of this account, Bukhari observed, that the Pakistanis came to know about the 1981 expedition. According to him, the Pakistani Foreign Office promptly lodged an official protest with India about this incursion into what Pakistan considered its own territory. The Indian reaction, he said, was to inspire a spate of articles in the Indian press claiming that India had sponsored a number of even earlier expeditions to the glacier. Projected by the Indian media as adventure training and orientation treks for the Indian army, at least some of these earlier expeditions, he said, were actually manufactured by the Indian government after the fact for political purposes.

In 1982 and 1983, Brigadier Bukhari explained, Pakistan organized proper army expeditions to the glacier, but these found no trace of the Indians. Then, in August 1983, a senior Pakistani officer flying reconnaisance noticed some soldiers on the glacier. Thinking they were members of the Pakistani expedition, he moved closer only to discover that they were Indian soldiers. The Pakistani troops were alerted. Helicopter reconnaissance of the area in which the Indians had been seen was ordered, and two or three Indian camps were spotted. There were Indian-constructed helicopter pads at these camps. All the camps, however, had been abandoned. At this point, according to Bukhari's account, Pakistan lodged a serious protest with New Delhi, firm in the knowledge that this time hard evidence was available of Indian incursions.

According to Brigadier Bukhari, Pakistan took no steps itself in the summer or autumn of 1983 to occupy the glacier militarily. "Pakistan," he said,

> had to make a difficult decision. Should it maintain a military presence on the glacier or not? It certainly *could* have remained: the Indian incursions originated near Dzingrulma, at the mouth of the glacier, at an altitude for which the Pakistan army even then was reasonably well-equipped. To have remained there, however, would have weighed against a negotiated solution with India. The government of Pakistan considered it a political rather than a military problem. Pakistan worried that occupation of the glacier by its military could have a snowball effect and lead to worse confrontations with India. Political implications proved to be overriding. It was decided that it was better not to have a permanent presence on the glacier. At the time, this seemed a good choice. The Indians gave vague assurances, obviously buying time, and agreed to discuss the matter with the government of Pakistan. Pakistan fell for it.

In April 1984, Pakistan became aware that the Indian army had occupied positions in the Saltoro Range over the entire length of the glacier. "When we saw Indians at those heights," said Bukhari, "we knew that they had come to stay....The Indians claimed that they had acquired information that the Pakistan army was itself preparing to occupy the glacier. In fact, what we had tried to avoid, they turned against us. After all, had we acted first we would not have chosen to occupy the heights. We would have blocked the entrance to the glacier. To hold the entrance requires defending only 2 kilometers, not 75." Pakistan rushed in troops and, in the latter part of June, launched an attack on forward Indian outposts in a fruitless endeavor to dislodge the entrenched Indian troops.

The Indian version of these events paints a somewhat different picture. According to Chibber, India's move onto the glacier in spring 1984 was an entirely preemptive action, precipitated in large measure by Pakistan's protest notes of 21 and 29 August 1983, complaining of Indian army intrusions into what Pakistan claimed was its own territory.[60] In those notes, according to Chibber, Pakistan made a unilateral and unacceptable claim that the LOC extended all the way to the Karakoram Pass. The 21 August note, as reproduced by Chibber, read:

> REQUEST, INSTRUCT YOUR TROOPS TO WITHDRAW BEYOND LINE OF CONTROL SOUTH OF LINE JOINING POINT NJ 9842, KARAKORAM PASS NE 7410 IMMEDIATELY. I HAVE INSTRUCTED MY TROOPS TO SHOW MAXIMUM RESTRAINT, BUT ANY DELAY IN VACATING OUR TERRITORY WILL CREATE A SERIOUS SITUATION. ASSURING YOU OF MY FULLEST COOPERATION IN MAINTAINING PEACE AND TRANQUILITY ALONG LINE OF CONTROL.

The 29 August note, replying to the Indian counter-protest note, read:

> ONE. YOUR REPLY TO OUR PROTEST NOTE OF TWENTY FIRST AUGUST, 1983 RECEIVED.
>
> ALPHA. YOUR TROOPS HAVE CARRIED OUT INTRUSIONS ACROSS LC [LOC] NORTH OF POINT NJ 980420—KARAKORAM PASS—NE 7410 (POINT NJ 980420—KARAKORAM PASS—NE 7410). THEY INTRUDED APPROXIMATELY TWENTY FIVE MILES INSIDE OUR TERRITORY IN SIACHEN GLACIER COMMA NJ 9797 COMMA NK 0689.
>
> BRAVO. LAST YEAR ALSO YOUR TROOPS HAD INTRUDED INTO THE SAME AREA FOR WHICH THE PROTEST HAD BEEN LODGED BY OUR GOVERNMENT STOP.
>
> TWO. THIS IS A SERIOUS VIOLATION AND UNLESS STOPPED FORTHWITH IS LIKELY TO DISTURB THE PEACEFUL CONDITION STOP THEREFORE PLEASE INSTRUCT YOUR TROOPS TO REMAIN SOUTH OF THE LINE—POINT NJ 980420— KARAKORAM PASS NE 7410.[61]

Intelligence reports, said Chibber, indicated that Pakistan was preparing to back up its claim militarily. They indicated

> that a column of about two companies supported by mortars was on the move in September/October 1983 to occupy passes on the Saltoro Range....Due to bad weather and possibly due to inadequate logistic support, the column could not

reach their objective. But the intention of Pakistanis across the Line of Control was quite clear. They were determined to support their unilateral cartographic claim by physical occupation of the area.

This conclusion was reinforced, Chibber pointed out,

> when we got further intelligence reports that the Pakistan Army was trying to procure large quantities of special snow and ski equipment from the UK and Europe to be available to the troops by January 1984. They also launched an intensive training programme for a force named "Burzil Force" to occupy Siachen Glacier.
>
> The decision was taken that we must prevent the Pakistani side from presenting us with a *fait accompli*. It was obvious in our discussions with Delhi that if they were to establish posts on the Siachen Glacier it would be very costly to evict them. The probability that we may not be able to do so at all was also very high.
>
> We considered at length and even war-gamed the best way to prevent the Pakistanis from establishing themselves in the glacier. We concluded that the only way would be to occupy the two proven passes, namely Bilafond La and Sia La.[62]

Pakistan's intent to occupy the area, said Chibber, left India with no other option than to act first. "The strategic importance of the area," he commented, "was not a major consideration, nor was our purpose to capture any territory. It was simply to ensure that we were not presented with a *fait accompli* like that in Aksai Chin in the early fifties."[63]

Neutral accounts of the developments leading up to the outbreak of fighting between Indian and Pakistani forces were nonexistent. Both sides maintained a news blackout on the gathering crisis until fighting had actually begun; and journalists were largely at the mercy of official spokesmen thereafter. Pakistan brought its concerns to the attention of officials of the United Nations Military Observer Group in India and Pakistan (UNMOGIP) in late summer 1983; but UNMOGIP was constrained by the nature of its mandate—and by the lack of Indian cooperation—from doing much about it. Established pursuant to the 1949 Karachi Agreement to supervise the cease-fire and the CFL,[64] UNMOGIP had no authority of its own either to initiate investigations or to maintain a presence in the undelimited area beyond the formally agreed terminus of the CFL. In fact, since the CFL's redesignation as the LOC in 1972, UNMOGIP teams on the Indian side had not been permitted even to approach the LOC itself in order to investigate Pakistani complaints of cease-fire violations.[65]

In striving to explain the underlying reasons for the outbreak of hostilities on the Siachen, Pakistani observers pointed to several different possibilities. Some of them, for example, suggested that the Indian intrusion on the glacier, at least in its early stages, may have resulted from purely military initiatives taken within the Indian army's Northern Command. Local Indian field commanders, in other words, noting the unoccupied and unclaimed territory, simply seized the opportunity thus afforded, producing cumulative unanticipated consequences that eventually committed both sides to protracted struggle. This interpretation of events placed more weight on military "accident," less on calculated political decision. Most Pakistanis, however, whether of military or civilian background, dismissed this "local initiative" theory, arguing that the Indian military maneuver to take control of the glacier, whatever its motivation, was too carefully planned and too heavily laden with political consequences to have been undertaken without the full concurrence of the central government.

Another explanation given in Pakistan for the outbreak of fighting on the Siachen emphasized the glacier's strategic importance. New Delhi, said some, seized the glacier in a coordinated move designed to bolster the Indo-Soviet alliance against its Sino-Pakistani rival. For this explanation, developments in the vicinity of the glacier clearly lent some support. Prominent among these developments was the fact that Soviet military forces had been introduced into Afghanistan only a few years earlier, bringing Soviet military power for the first time into direct geographic contact with Pakistan. Not the least peril imagined to stem from this was the potential for a joint Indo-Soviet military operation that would cement geographically their already close military ties while at the same time serving their mutual interest in cutting the land route that connected Pakistan with its Chinese ally. Soviet occupation in 1980 of the Wakhan Corridor, the panhandle of Afghanistan created in the nineteenth century as a buffer between Czarist Russia and British India, seemed to many Pakistanis to be a menacing step precisely in this direction. Not uncharacteristic of their views was the statement of the President of Azad Kashmir, Sardar Abdul Qayyum Khan, that India's military occupation of the Siachen Glacier "would not have meant anything had the Russians not earlier occupied the Wakhan Corridor."[66] From the easternmost edge of the Wakhan to the nearest point on the Karakoram Highway was, after all, hardly 20 miles. If the Soviet Union had actually annexed the Wakhan Corridor, as some contended, then not even the withdrawal of its forces from Afghanistan would fully relieve Pakistan of the pressure on its northwestern border or of the presumed danger to the Karakoram Highway of an Indo-Soviet pincers movement.[67] Even if Indian and Soviet leaders had nothing quite so drastic in mind, the pressure on Pakistan's northern boundaries stemming from the Soviet intervention in Afghanistan if nothing else may have reduced the constraints on India in its move to secure a military foothold on the Siachen.

Pakistanis seemed noticeably reluctant to admit it, but the growth of a close Sino-Pakistani relationship over the years had itself almost certainly contributed to India's strategic interest in the Siachen area. In view of China's geographic proximity to the glacier and India's strong resentment over the loss of the nearby Aksai Chin region of Ladakh in the 1962 border war, this development was hardly surprising. Indeed, Indians had a number of good reasons for considering the China factor.

First, China's military ties with Pakistan were both varied and extensive. China backed Pakistan in the 1965 and 1971 wars, its support then having included the threat of military intervention against India along the mountainous Sino-Indian border. Since the first Sino-Pakistani arms agreement was signed in 1966 for $120 million, China had developed into Pakistan's principal and indispensable supplier of conventional arms. Pakistan's air, ground, and naval forces were all heavily dependent on Chinese military equipment; and China had had a major hand in aiding the development of Pakistan's small indigenous defense production capability.[68] Apart from the supply of conventional military equipment, China was widely believed to have quietly assisted Pakistan in the development of a nuclear weapons capability.[69] Moreover, from the Afghanistan war's beginning in 1980, China and Pakistan worked together very closely in the struggle against the Soviet-backed Kabul regime. Large quantities of Chinese weapons reportedly were funneled covertly through Pakistan to the Afghan resistance forces.[70] Given a military association as large, long-standing, and comprehensive as this one, the possibility for Sino-Pakistani collaboration in seizing disputed territory in northern Kashmir certainly had to be considered.

Second, the potential for concerted Sino-Pakistani military action in the Northern Areas of Pakistan had been somewhat enhanced in recent years by dramatic improvements in ground transport and communication links both within each country and between them. Of particular note in this regard was China's close collaboration with Pakistan in the construction of a network of strategic highways linking Pakistan's Northern Areas with China's Xinjiang province. The backbone of the network was the spectacular 500-mile Karakoram Highway, a nominally all-weather artery that connected the two countries through the 15 430-foot Khunjerab Pass. China's agreement to aid in the construction of this road was acquired soon after the 1965 war. Construction was begun in June 1969. After nearly a decade of work involving thousands of Pakistani and Chinese technicians and laborers, the road was completed in 1978.[71]

New Delhi lodged a protest with Islamabad over the road when construction began in 1969 and continued to voice its objections as the road progressed. On the surface, India's complaint was simply that China and Pakistan had no right to be building a road through territory over which India had never relinquished its claim. Also of concern to New Delhi, presumably, was the road's potential for strengthening the existing strategic bond between India's two principal rivals. Its construction had improved ground communications between China and Pakistan, thus expanding opportunities for concerted frontier defense and helping to secure the land corridor between them. It also enlarged the access of both Pakistan and China to their remote, lightly populated and vulnerable hinterlands—China's Xinjiang province and Pakistan's Northern Areas—while, at the same time, it inevitably increased the military threat to India's own lines of communication in Kashmir. In the broadest terms, it served China's requirement to inhibit encirclement by the Soviet Union and Pakistan's urgent need to arrest the worsening asymmetry in the military balance with India.[72] The motives for building it had of course included the expansion of trade and commerce, the opening of remote areas to mineral resource exploitation, the promotion of tourism and mountaineering expeditions, as well as increased social integration of frontier populations. By no stretch of the imagination, however, was the Karakoram Highway's strategic and military significance, as one Pakistani writer put it, "incidental" to these other objectives.[73]

Reports circulated privately in Pakistan in 1987 that Beijing and Islamabad signed a secret agreement in that year to expand the existing strategic road network by constructing another strategic road crossing from China into Pakistan to the east of the Karakoram Highway. The new road was to provide alternative routing between the Aksai Chin road in Chinese-held Ladakh and the Karakoram Highway as well as improved access to the area immediately west of the Siachen Glacier.[74] The plan, if true, implied that the remarkable overlap in Sino-Pakistani strategic perceptions that had been present when the road was first conceived remained essentially intact.

The Karakoram Highway was clearly not ideal for military purposes. Firstly, it fell well short of its billing as an all-weather road: the stretch connecting Pakistan and China over the Khunjerab Pass was closed to all traffic, military included, for most of the winter months; and intermittent closure of the road due to rock and mud slides was common during the rest of the year. Secondly, the road's twenty-four major bridges undoubtedly made admirable targets for both saboteurs and precision aerial bombing.

Thirdly, the road joined Pakistan and China in an area extremely remote from centers of population and industry on either side; and one could certainly conceive of circumstances in which military supplies would be more safely, swiftly, or cheaply transported between China and Pakistan by air or sea. There was no question that the Pakistan army's ability to maneuver its ground forces in the Kashmir sector in the event of another war with India had been substantially increased by the road's construction; but the military benefit to Pakistan coming from the road's transstate linkage with China remained problematic. Convincing evidence had yet to surface, in any event, to buttress Ispahani's claim that the road's presence had "put India on the psychological defensive in Kashmir; brought China into the Kashmir quarrel on Pakistan's side; and enhanced Sino-Pakistani military cooperation. The decision to construct these northern routes, and the angry responses of the Soviet Union and India, suggest the regional political significance of the Karakoram Highway."[75] On balance, however, construction of the Karakoram Highway was undoubtedly a setback for India.

Third, China had a direct interest of its own in the territorial issues involved in the Siachen dispute. As we have already taken note of, India not only disputed Pakistan's right to the glacier but China's right to the area north of the glacier (including the 1050 square miles of the Shaksgam-Muztagh drainage basin) that was ceded by Pakistan to China in the 1963 Border Agreement. As we have seen, Pakistan in this pact did not claim ownership of the territory lying south of the newly agreed border with China, only that its defense was under Pakistan's control. Resolving the matter of ownership was left to future negotiations between India and Pakistan. India's response at the time was that Pakistan, owning *none* of the territory through which the new Sino-Pakistani boundary was supposed to run, lacked authority to give any of it away. Neither Beijing nor New Delhi had ever agreed, furthermore, that the general principle that would serve as the basis for a settlement of the Sino-Indian border dispute should be that of the main watershed—the basis for the 1963 Sino-Pakistan agreement. In fact, New Delhi had never conceded that it even had a border dispute with China, arguing instead (as it had in Pakistan's case) that China was in illegal occupation of Indian territory which it must vacate. The military seizure of the Siachen Glacier by India in 1984 was thus a matter of direct concern to China since it clearly affected, and could possibly unravel, China's 1963 border settlement with Pakistan.

Senior Pakistani military officers interviewed by the author in 1989 naturally scoffed at reports in the Indian press which suggested that Indian forces had seized the Siachen just in time to foil a Sino-Pakistani plan to slip a strategic noose around Indian Ladakh.[76] Pakistan, they all insisted, had no such intention. By any rational calculation, they pointed out, the territory to the east of the Siachen had no significant military value for Pakistan. New Delhi, they suggested, inflated the glacier's strategic value as a way to deflect attention from India's own act of aggression. Pakistan, they argued, simply lacked the capability to mount any such attack. "Anyone familiar with the terrain realizes the enormity of the logistical problems Pakistan faces even now," said a Pakistani brigadier with command experience in the Siachen fighting. Pakistan would be much better advised, he said, to attack Indian targets at a more southerly point on the Line of Control, where it holds ground closer to Indian supply routes and where it faces fewer logistical difficulties. "Only a madman," he observed, "would contemplate an attack on India via Siachen."[77]

The same sources were also frank to admit, however, that they could detect no strong *Indian* strategic motivation to seize the glacier, either. The Siachen, in their judgment, had no readily obvious military value for either side, neither as an intelligence listening post nor as a base for military operations. In spite of all that had been written in Pakistan to the contrary, the Siachen Glacier, they felt, was an extremely unlikely staging ground for an Indian attack on the Karakoram Highway. That road's nearest point lay about 125 miles from Conway Saddle at the westernmost edge of the Siachen Glacier, and in between lay some of the most rugged, impassable, and easily defended terrain on earth. If the Indian army was planning a pincers movement to sever the strategic highway linking Pakistan with its Chinese ally, then, from the point of view of these Pakistani officers, it had selected an odd way to accomplish it.

One senior Pakistani staff officer conceded that the Indian seizure of the Siachen Glacier was "related to the border settlement that Pakistan had worked out with the People's Republic of China." The glacier, he said, supplied India with an opportunity to disturb, perhaps even to nullify, the settlement. After all, he pointed out, if a portion of the Sino-Pakistani treaty were nullified, then the whole treaty would have to be redrafted. This time, he observed, India itself would be directly involved. From that, he contended, India would gain moral ascendancy over Pakistan, an opportunity to play Pakistan's "big brother." "The Indians," he asserted, "always want to cow down Pakistan, to bring political pressure to bear, to set precedents for Pakistan's neighbors. It could then show the other smaller countries that Pakistan too was bowing to pressure."[78] Insofar as direct Chinese involvement in the Siachen fighting was concerned, however, this officer insisted that India was not really worried. China was not directly affected by the fighting over Siachen, he argued, and would likely stay aloof so long as its own interests did not suffer. In regard to the Siachen dispute, he observed, China pursued its own calculated self-interest.

Most Pakistani military professionals interviewed about the Siachen dispute by the author seemed, in fact, genuinely skeptical of major military or strategic motivation in the Siachen fighting involving either the Soviet Union or China. And on this point, at least, they were not far apart from their Indian counterparts. The Pakistanis and Indians, observed Chibber in summer 1990, "stumbled into it." There was, he said, no Pakistani design on the glacier (via cartographic encroachment or mountaineering expeditions) or any collusion with the Chinese. The idea that the Siachen and Sino-Indian border disputes were interrelated, he suggested, was an after-the-fact concoction of Indian bureaucrats.[79] By far the more fundamental explanation for the Siachen dispute, so far as most Pakistanis were concerned, lay within the subcontinent itself. And there it was the still-smoldering boundary conflict over Kashmir that seemed, in Pakistani minds, the pivotal factor.

III. PAKISTAN'S COUNTERBOUNDARY POLICY IN KASHMIR

The Siachen Glacier has no obvious political importance of its own. Located in a distant corner of the subcontinent, it was until recently almost inaccessible. The territory surrounding it is sparsely populated and has often been characterized as a no-man's-land. Emotional ties to it by either Indians or Pakistanis—to the extent they exist at all—are likely to be recent in origin. For all practical purposes, the Siachen area has no political life; it can spawn neither a secessionist nor an irredentist threat. Whatever resonance it has in the political outlook of either India or Pakistan is thus bound to be derivative, arising almost solely from its connection with the parent Kashmir conflict. Among the consequences of that conflict, we have observed, were certain deficiencies in the original delimitation of the Cease-Fire Line and later the Line of Control in Kashmir. The connection goes deeper than this, however, to the very heart of Pakistan's boundary policy in Kashmir. What seemed, in fact, most at stake in the Siachen dispute during the Zia period was Pakistan's fundamental right to deny the permanence of the existing Indo-Pakistani boundary in Kashmir, the Line of Control, and to continue to contest the political status of Indian-controlled Kashmir.

This right was first exercised militarily in the first Indo-Pakistan war (1947-49), when Pakistan laid claim to the whole of Kashmir on grounds of its Muslim majority. It has been exercised continuously since then, of course, politically in the sponsorship of Azad Kashmir and diplomatically in the demand for a UN-supervised plebiscite to ascertain the Kashmiris' own political preferences. It has already been twice heavily qualified, however, first in the Karachi agreement of 1949 ending the first war between them, and then again in the Simla agreement of 1972, ending the third.

In 1949, Pakistan formally consented to the suspension of hostilities and creation of a cease-fire line in Kashmir in exchange for the guarantee of *multilateral* involvement by the United Nations both in policing the cease-fire between Indian and Pakistani forces and in determining the popular will of the Kashmiri people. This meant acquiescing to international mediation as a substitute for the unilateral use of force in the hope that that would suffice to correct what Pakistanis felt had been a monstrous violation of the spirit, if not the letter, of the partition agreement. It also meant acceptance of self-determination in place of communal majority as the overriding principle that was to govern the search for resolution of the territorial conflict. Unlike the principle of communal majority, which would automatically join mainly Muslim Kashmir with Muslim Pakistan, self-determination allowed for the possibility that the Kashmiris might either let stand the accession to India or opt for complete independence.[80]

In 1972, Pakistan yielded ground once again, this time committing itself to the *bilateral* resolution of all disputes between itself and India as well as to noninterference in internal affairs. The commitment was made under duress and was obviously halfhearted. Moreover, "the imprecision of the wording in the final act [of the Simla Agreement] on the principle of bilateralism left Pakistan with considerable room for 'creative interpretation.'"[81] Pakistan, in fact, did continue to raise the Kashmir issue in multilateral forums and to give moral (and, very likely, material) support to anti-Indian elements in the Indian Kashmiri population. Nevertheless, the Simla Agreement, insofar as Pakistan's right to contest the territorial status of Kashmir was concerned, was a defeat for Pakistan. While it did not call for the actual elimination of UNMOGIP or for abrogation of the demand for an internationally supervised plebiscite, it clearly undermined the authority of the former and considerably reduced moral pressure on India in regard to the latter. Its effect, overall, was to strengthen India's hand in any future negotiations over possession of Kashmir.

India's occupation of the Siachen area in 1984 threatened yet another setback for Pakistan's stand on the question of ownership of Kashmir. To Pakistanis, India's action looked like an attempt to redefine the LOC by force of arms. It was a *unilateral* action, in other words, and thus a major departure from the bilateralism India had itself vigorously espoused in 1972. It seemed to disavow India's commitment at Simla to the peaceful resolution of all disputes between itself and Pakistan; and it inevitably raised doubts about the sanctity of the rest of the LOC. More than that, however, it threatened to strip away whatever remained of Pakistan's right to contest ownership of Indian-held Kashmir. After all, if India were free to sweep aside Pakistan's territorial claim to the Siachen, over which India had never hitherto exercised any control whatsoever, what would prevent it from sweeping away *in toto* Pakistan's claim to that part of Kashmir that had always been in Indian hands? The Siachen could not be yielded, it seemed, without granting India the same unilateral rights in Kashmir that Pakistan had itself reluctantly given up in 1949. It could not be yielded, in other words, without retreating from Pakistan's long-standing counterboundary policy, that is, the maintenance of a "disputed" status for the whole of Kashmir and of Pakistan's right to contest for ownership of it.

Naturally, the threat of such a complete reversal of fortunes would be disturbing for Pakistanis; but it must have been particularly distressing for the Zia regime. India's seizure of the glacier, apart from any military or strategic threat it posed, was a major political embarrassment for the regime. Islamabad was helpless to explain the seeming failure of its armed forces to defend the Siachen against the Indians in the first place; and its military options in the wake of India's move onto the glacier seemed limited to a basically defensive response—the containment of Indian forces to the territory already occupied. Realistically, the regime could not hold out to Pakistanis any hope for a rollback of Indian forces. Already there were plentiful threats to Pakistan's security piled up on its western frontier; and there was every reason to avoid provoking a major military confrontation with India on the eastern frontier. In contrast with the Afghanistan war, there was no apparent silver lining for Islamabad in the struggle for Siachen.

There were powerful reasons, nevertheless, for the Zia regime to follow the path laid down by its civilian and military predecessors, all of whom had given high priority to the protection of Pakistan's counterboundary policy in Kashmir, and to recommit Pakistan at Siachen to that policy.

One reason was the fact that, by Zia's time, the Indian state of Jammu and Kashmir had lost none of its vulnerability to the idea of self-determination. The only one of India's twenty-five states to have a Muslim majority, its population of nearly 6 million was roughly 65 percent Muslim. In Kashmir Valley, with the heaviest concentration of Muslims in the state, the Muslim total was closer to 85 percent of the population.[82] Geographically isolated from the rest of India and historically oriented by its topography, economy, and culture mainly toward Pakistan, Kashmir had defied strenuous efforts by New Delhi over several decades to integrate it fully into the Indian union.

Pakistan, which since 1949 had been the principal upholder of Kashmiri self-determination, was obviously a leading potential beneficiary of India's failure.

In 1949, owing largely to the unusual circumstances of its accession to India, the state of Jammu and Kashmir won recognition of its autonomous status in the Indian constitution. Its special rights, enjoyed by no other constituent unit of India, were eventually spelled out in detail in an agreement worked out in July 1952 between Indian Prime Minister Jawaharlal Nehru and his friend and political ally Sheikh Mohammad Abdullah (the "Lion of Kashmir").[83] Provisions of the agreement sharply limited the central government's jurisdiction in the state and even included a bar on India's right to take emergency steps to curb domestic unrest in Kashmir without the concurrence of the state legislature. Championed at one time or another by practically every Kashmiri Muslim leader, the state's special standing in the Indian union was unpopular with the state's Hindu minority and with many other Indians as well. Almost immediately, in fact, confronted with its own political and security imperatives, New Delhi began encroaching on Kashmir's special rights. Sheikh Abdullah was driven from power and placed under arrest in 1953, and a leadership more favorably inclined toward the state's accession to India installed in his place. The state's formal integration into the Indian union moved ahead rapidly thereafter; and by the mid-1960s, when the central government's emergency powers were extended to Jammu and Kashmir, the apparatus of Indian government—administrative, judicial, economic, and financial—was well established in the state. To be sure, the state retained a separate constitution, a unique feature among Indian states; but within two decades of India's independence Kashmiris, in truth, had very little of substance to show of their autonomy.

New Delhi had never taken the permanence of the political bond thus fashioned between Kashmir and India for granted. On the contrary, it very early made clear its intention to combat by every means lingering separatist impulses in the state. These means included payment of heavy economic subsidies to the state;[84] tolerance of undemocratic and corrupt government in the state so long as the leadership pursued proaccession policies;[85] and, whenever Kashmiri state governments insisted upon trumpeting their independence of New Delhi or appeared unduly soft on "antinational" activities, direct interference in state government. In July 1984, for example, within months of India's seizure of the Siachen Glacier, the state's Chief Minister Farooq Abdullah (Sheikh Abdullah's son) was toppled by a New Delhi-engineered split in the ruling National Conference party, ostensibly because he was fanning Muslim communalism—perhaps also because he had proven more than a match for his Congress party rivals in the state elections held in Kashmir in June 1983.[86]

An added precaution against separatist inclinations in Kashmir that New Delhi had always taken was, of course, the maintenance of a powerful military presence in the state. In the mid-1980s, it stationed there about 100 000 regular army troops (8 percent of India's total armed forces) and about 45 000 paramilitary troops (50 percent of the country's total Border Security Force). These augmented an already large standing police force in a state containing well under 1 percent of the country's total population. This left little room for doubt in Kashmiri Muslim minds about New Delhi's willingness to enforce its claim to Kashmir.[87]

No matter whether New Delhi emphasized incentives or disincentives, the state of Jammu and Kashmir remained politically unstable and a breeding ground for separatist conspiracies. The atmosphere of political alienation and frustration produced a quicksand for Kashmiri politicians loyal to New Delhi. Indeed, they seemed to pay as heavy a political price in the 1980s for their collaboration with the central leadership as they ever had in the past. New Delhi's consent to a National Conference-Congress(I) alliance in the March 1987 state elections, for example, enabled Farooq Abdullah to stage a dramatic political comeback; but "the price he had to pay," according to one of India's most respected newsmagazines, "was to accept a ruling partner—identified in the Kashmiri mind as a coloniser—whom he himself had denounced as an oppressor two years before."[88] Within months of Farooq's landslide victory, his popularity appeared to be fading and his strongly pro-Indian and secular orientation already seemed a liability. His defeated rival, the state's former Chief Minister G. M. Shah, announced his retirement from politics in late August 1987, reportedly after making stunning pro-Pakistani comments at a public rally of the opposition Muslim United Front in Srinigar.[89] Kashmiri Muslims, in the judgment of many observers, continued to think of themselves mainly as Kashmiris and not as Indians.[90] After decades of effort by New Delhi to neutralize antiaccession forces in Kashmir, the idea of Kashmiri political self-determination was still very much an explosive domestic issue.

Some Indians held that New Delhi's stress on loyal rather than good government in the state of Jammu and Kashmir had helped to sustain a pervasive distrust of Indian intentions among Kashmiri Muslims and was thus responsible for the spread of separatist sentiments.[91] Other Indians contended that the political discontent of Kashmiri Muslims stemmed to an important degree from the spread of Islamic "fundamentalist" ideology and Muslim political self-assertion among India's huge (90 million plus) Muslim minority.[92] Still others argued that Kashmiri alienation was in large measure externally inspired. Pakistan's hand, in particular, was said to be guiding a clandestine program of destabilization involving not only Kashmiri Muslims but Punjabi Sikhs as well. "There seems to be a perception among certain quarters in Pakistan and their proxies in Kashmir," observed the noted Indian columnist Rajendra Sareen,

> that if the situation in the State [of Jammu and Kashmir] can be destabilized, the efforts to cut it loose from the Indian Union would stand a better chance of success than the tribal raids of 1947 and "Operation Gibraltar" followed by the 1965 war. Towards that end exacerbation of communal tensions, political instability and a massive effort to promote religious fanaticism among Muslims and the Sikhs have been undertaken.[93]

While there was thus considerable debate among Indians over the reasons for the political alienation of Kashmiri Muslims, there was little question toward the end of the Zia period that the alienation was widespread and gaining ground. Militant secessionist elements had remained for most of the Zia period on the fringes of Indian Kashmiri politics; and the discontent with India was certainly not proof of a popular upsurge among Kashmiri Muslims of pro-Pakistani sentiment. Of this, and notwithstanding ex-Chief Minister Shah's statements, there was little unequivocal evidence. Nevertheless, India's serious vulnerability to appeals for Kashmiri self-determination was indisputable and clearly growing. So too was the opportunity this gave Islamabad to pursue its own goals in Kashmir, whether these were actually irredentist in inspiration or aimed simply at offsetting some of India's military advantage over Pakistan by lending a hand to Kashmiri dissident movements. By reasserting at Siachen Pakistan's counterboundary policy in Kashmir, the Zia regime helped to keep this opportunity alive.

A second reason lay within the domestic politics of Pakistan itself. In sharp contrast with India, Kashmir had never been for Pakistan a divisive political issue. On the contrary, it had always stood as a symbol of collective national injury suffered at the hands of the Indians and as a spur to patriotism. Every national leader since partition had relied on it to rally popular support. There had been a consensus in Pakistan over it that was to be found in regard to practically no other issue. Any concession to India in regard to Kashmir always put this consensus at risk.

In the Zia regime's case, the amount of political risk involved in the Siachen episode was substantial. India, in establishing its military grip on the Siachen Glacier, had clearly undermined the credibility of the Pakistan army as guardian of Pakistan's claim to all of Jammu and Kashmir state. Not only had the army been unable to make good the country's claim, after 40 years, to the Indian-controlled sector of the state, but, in failing to prevent India's seizure of the glacier, it was vulnerable to complaints that it was unable even to defend territory that Pakistan insisted (and many international atlases appeared to confirm) fell under its *own* administrative control. The Siachen dispute had exposed not only Pakistan's military weakness vis-à-vis India but the weakness of its military leaders' presumption that only they were fit to rule Pakistan. Already suspected in some quarters of Pakistan of having abandoned the cause of Kashmiri reunification, the Zia regime found itself the target of charges that it had failed to defend even its own territory.[94] No wonder, then, that the Zia regime, saddled already with mounting domestic political discontent and the seemingly insurmountable problem of its own unpopularity, decided to fight for the Siachen.

We should note here, by the way, that the consensus over Kashmir that existed within Pakistan also existed between Pakistan and its Azad Kashmiri client. Although pocket-sized Azad Kashmir (5134 square miles) qualified in the Zia period no better than India's Jammu and Kashmir state as a model of autonomous, democratic, or incorruptible government, its population displayed few if any traces of the deep-seated political alienation from its political master that was so characteristic of Indian-controlled Kashmir. On the contrary, in most respects Azad Kashmiris seemed indistinguishable from—and not at all inferior to—the Pakistani population.

Azad Kashmiris are nearly 100 percent Muslim. There is neither any sectarian difference between Azad Kashmiri Muslims and the dominant religious community of Pakistan nor is there any sectarian difference *within* Azad Kashmir to parallel the Hindu-Muslim rivalry within Indian Kashmir. The language of Azad Kashmiris is mainly Punjabi, the language of the numerically largest and politically most powerful group in Pakistan.[95] Azad Kashmiris have been quite successful within Pakistan itself. No restrictions, formal or informal, or apprehensions of communal hostility against them impeded Kashmiris from moving and resettling wherever they wished in Pakistan.[96] They were numbered among Pakistan's leading business and industrialist families; and their representation in Pakistan's federal bureaucratic establishment, while probably less than proportional to the population of Azad Kashmir, had steadily improved.[97] They boasted, moreover, a rate of progress for Azad Kashmir in many sectors of socioeconomic development (education, health, rural electrification) that was at least equal to, in some sectors (adult literacy, for example) better than, the record achieved in many parts of Pakistan itself.[98] No doubt, there was deep resentment among Azad Kashmiris against the curbs on political democracy imposed during the Zia period. In this, however, they were scarcely distinguishable from their counterparts elsewhere in Pakistan. Azad Kashmiris had never manifested any interest in joining up with *Indian*-controlled Kashmir; and few of them had ever shown much excitement over the prospects of Kashmiri independence from *both* India and Pakistan. Whatever reservations they may have had about Pakistani government, rarely did they protest continued affiliation with it.[99] For all practical purposes, in fact, Azad Kashmiris seemed to think of themselves as—and in most respects were—Pakistanis.

A third and final reason for the Zia regime to adhere to the counterboundary policy laid down by its predecessors was rooted in Pakistani fears that any diminution in Pakistan's defense of its right to contest the ownership of Kashmir might result in India's eventual preemption of that right by armed force. Against odds that included the glacier's seeming unimportance and, consequently, the world's indifference to its ownership, Pakistan was in danger, in other words, of losing not only its right to contest for possession of Indian-held Kashmir but even its right to hold the disputed territories still in its own physical possession.

Pakistan's fears in this regard were far from groundless. As we saw in the preceding chapter, India's military capabilities relative to Pakistan had grown substantially since the 1971 war and, by the time fighting broke out on the Siachen, Pakistan's ability to arrest its gradual military decline relative to India seemed to most observers fairly slight. Side by side with the mounting imbalance in the subcontinent's military capabilities had grown the belief in Pakistan that New Delhi's political willingness to exercise those capabilities had also increased substantially. This belief had, of course, been nourished for years by Pakistan's own propaganda focused on alleged Indian hegemonism. In Zia's day, however, accusations of Indian saber-rattling and military brinkmanship were appearing with nearly equal frequency among Indians concerned that New Delhi's assertion of its military clout in the region—in Sri Lanka and along the Chinese and Pakistani borders—was unnecessarily adventurous and dangerously provocative. The issue was pointedly addressed shortly before Zia's death in an article in *India Today* assessing the impact of General Krishnaswami Sundarji, India's just-retired Chief of Army Staff, on the Indian army's operational planning, strategy, and tactics. The article included among his various legacies "an infinitely more aggressive military posture (called 'forward posture') vis-a-vis Pakistan and China as part of the new 'dissuasive and deterrent' policy."[100] This policy, according to the article, found expression not only in the much-publicized military exercises of 1986-87 (Operation Brass Tacks), India's largest-ever, but also in the much less publicized struggle for the Siachen Glacier.

Indeed, the article seemed to suggest that the two events were not unconnected. In part, it said, Operation Brass Tacks was intended simply to warn Pakistan of the power and strength of Indian armed forces. Citing sources in the Indian Defence Ministry, however, it claimed that an additional aim "was to provoke Pakistan into some action which would then give the Indian Army an excuse to launch its own offensive." This offensive, it said, was codenamed Operation Trident, involving an assault across the Line of Control in Kashmir. Quoting Ravi Rikhye, a well-known Indian defense analyst, the article said that "Trident called for an attack, with Skardu (in Pakistan-occupied Kashmir) as the first objective and Gilgit as the second....Brass Tacks was originally intended as a massive strategic deception to focus Pakistani attention on Sind while India went for the northern areas."

Rikhye's book, entitled *The War That Never Was*, had itself unquestionably given Pakistanis new grounds for suspecting Indian intentions. In it, Rikhye, a self-professed hawk, made an astonishingly frank appeal for the immediate military defeat of Pakistan. His belief, he said, "is that India should, at the earliest opportunity, incorporate Pakistan into the Republic, followed by all the territories that composed the India before independence."[101] Written, according to Rikhye, by June 1987, the book alleges that key Indian leaders, including not only General Sundarji but Prime Minister Rajiv Gandhi, Arun Singh ("de facto Defence Minister"), and Natwar Singh ("de facto foreign policy advisor to the Prime Minister"), were "trying to get a war with Pakistan going" via the mechanism of Operation Brass Tacks. "Not for any final solution," said Rikhye, "not a last war that would reunite India and Pakistan, but for narrower ends: these included the destruction of Pakistan's nuclear enrichment facility at Kahuta, the recovery of as much as possible of Northern Pakistan Occupied Kashmir, and the detachment, if possible, of Sind from Pakistan."[102] Rikhye upbraided India's political leadership for having failed, in the end, to follow through with the plan, and, in prose that was unusually blunt and often inelegant, called them stupid, degenerate, effete, and corrupt. But in the course of over 200 pages of detailed discussion of Operation Brass Tacks, Operation Trident, and the military capabilities and current deployments of India and Pakistan, Rikhye, the author of an earlier and equally provocative book, managed nevertheless to supply Pakistan with at least some justification for the military reaffirmation at Siachen of its counterboundary policy in Kashmir.[103]

By the time of Zia's death in August 1988, efforts to resolve the Siachen conflict through negotiations had made little apparent headway. An initial agreement to hold talks on the Siachen issue was reached on 17 December 1985, at a brief meeting in New Delhi between President Zia and Prime

Minister Rajiv Gandhi. This agreement resulted in two rounds of negotiations during 1986, the first in Rawalpindi in January, the second in New Delhi in June, between fairly high-level delegations led by the defense secretaries of the two countries. These produced expressions of joint commitment to seek a negotiated settlement in accordance with the spirit of the 1972 Simla Agreement. They accomplished nothing concrete, however, and remained suspended until particularly heavy fighting on the glacier in September-October 1987 apparently revived interest on both sides in the search for a settlement.[104] At a meeting in Kathmandu early in November 1987, Prime Minister Junejo and Prime Minister Gandhi were reported to have discussed the Siachen problem and to have agreed to resume the talks. After a lapse of nearly 2 years, the third round was held in Islamabad in May 1988. The joint statement issued at the conclusion of this session noted only the two sides' acceptance of the need to pursue a negotiated settlement and their agreement to meet again later in the summer. The fourth round was held in New Delhi in late September 1988, but by that time Zia was dead and custody of Pakistan's counterboundary policy in Kashmir passed to his successors.[105]

In my judgment, there is very little likelihood that the dispute, had Zia lived, would have moved any more speedily toward resolution than has actually been the case. The issues at stake in the dispute, as we have seen, were far from trivial. The two countries' territorial claims were wide apart; and over 40 years of unyielding conflict had bred into the leaders of both a deep suspicion of one another's motives. At the time of his death, moreover, Zia's hold on power was growing increasingly shaky; and it seems most unlikely that he would have ventured very soon to make any concessions to India over the glacier that might have weakened his grip still further. Added to this was Zia's recognition that the Indian army, once having occupied positions on the glacier, had made no further progress to speak of. After 4 years of fighting, there had been very little change in the location of either side's line of forward deployment. The Indian army was unquestionably "on top" in this fight; but its actual military advantage in the two passes it clearly dominated seemed, in fact, quite marginal. The Pakistan army was well dug in; and for the Indian army there didn't seem to be any place to go. The Indian government was increasingly being asked by its critics to justify the costs of fighting. The Pakistan government, in contrast, was asked only why it had failed so far to throw the Indians out.

There was, of course, some risk for Pakistan inherent in the lengthening stalemate over the Siachen. The Indians were likely to grow impatient and there was no guarantee that when they sought relief it would not be at

Pakistan's expense. A correspondent for *The Hindu* wrote, for example, that "the deadlock is imposing a heavy cost on India, both in terms of men and money. Presumably, it is doing so for Pakistan as well. If there is no progress in talks, the Indian Army may well be forced to go down to Saltora [Saltoro] river valley and occupy positions that will not be so punishing in terms of climate and natural hazards."[106] Since the Saltoro River valley is a main staging area for Pakistani military operations in the Saltoro Range, an Indian descent into it would amount to a direct challenge to Pakistan's hold on its Northern Areas.[107] Such action by the Indian military, on the other hand, was infinitely easier for journalists and professional analysts to recommend than for the army to implement.

President Zia and his advisors, one suspects, probably felt that the risk inherent in continued stalemate was unavoidable and, moreover, that relaxing Pakistan's counterboundary policy by conceding India's demands was not the best way, in any event, to alleviate it. Reports cropped up in India in 1989, in fact, that in the final months of his life Zia was actually taking moves in Kashmir to stiffen Pakistan's Kashmir policy. With the Soviet pullout in progress in Afghanistan diminishing pressure on Pakistan's western frontier, Zia, it was said, had given the go-ahead to the Pakistan army's intelligence body, the ISI, to step up Pakistan's support of an armed underground separatist movement operating in the Indian-controlled Kashmir Valley.[108] There were grounds for suspecting that at least the more alarmist of these reports were the product of creative imaginations in Indian intelligence. Nevertheless, meddling in Kashmir may well have seemed to Pakistani leaders the best available means for offsetting the natural advantages of Pakistan's better-endowed adversary. Of course, any such activity was hardly likely to accelerate progress toward a negotiated settlement of the Siachen dispute. That, Pakistanis may well have reasoned, was at best a very distant prospect.

NOTES

1. Parts of this chapter draw upon the author's serialized article, "The Siachen Glacier Dispute—I: The Territorial Dimension; II: The Domestic Political Dimension; III: The Strategic Dimension," *Strategic Studies* (Islamabad) 10:1 (Fall 1986) 49-66; 11:3 (Spring 1988) 83-97; 12:1 (Fall 1988) 38-54. For further discussion of the dispute, see the author's forthcoming book, *Confrontation in Kasmir*.
2. India began its helicopter airlift of troops to the Saltoro Range on 13 April 1984. On 25 April occurred the first skirmish between these troops and a

small advance force of Pakistani troops at Bilafond La. The Pakistanis, apparently surprised to find the Indians already in position in the pass, quickly withdrew. On 23 June a large task force of Pakistani Northern Light Infantry and the Special Services Group sought to retake positions at key points occupied earlier by the Indians. For background on the origins and development of the dispute, see Joydeep Sircar, "Siachen Glacier: Who Is On Thin Ice?", *Telegraph* (Calcutta), 23 June 1985; "The 'Meghdoot Operation,'" *The Hindu* (Madras), 29 October 1985; Shekhar Gupta, "Mountain Marauders," *India Today* (New Delhi), 30 September 1984, p. 140; Manoj Joshi, "Blood on Throne Room of Gods," *Frontline* (New Delhi), 20 April-3 May 1985, pp. 76-84; Zulfikar A. Khalid, "The Geopolitics of the Siachen Glacier," *Asian Defence Journal*, November 1985, pp. 44-50; Shabbir Hussain, "Siachen Glacier—Fact and Fiction," *The Pakistan Times* (Lahore), 6 September 1985; and Edward W. Desmond, "War on High Ground," *Time International*, 17 July 1989, pp.18-25.

3. One right-wing Indian newspaper reported that over 1000 Pakistani troops had been killed in attacks launched by them to retake the Siachen. *Organiser* (New Delhi), 23 June 1985.

4. Casualty figures given out from time to time on both sides were extremely unreliable. According to news reports, the Pakistan National Assembly was officially informed in August 1985 that Pakistani casualties up to that point had been 18 killed and 22 wounded. *Dawn* (Karachi), 18 August 1985. For roughly the same period, Indian press reports indicated 54 Siachen-related deaths on the Indian side. Manoj Joshi, "Solution to Siachen Tangle," *The Hindu*, 7 January 1986. Indian killed-in-action were estimated unofficially in mid-1988 at 250 per year. Inderjit Badhwar and Dilip Bobb, "Disputed Legacy: General K. Sundarji," *India Today*, 15 May 1988. In September 1989, General Mirza Aslam Beg, Pakistan's Chief of Army Staff, reportedly stated in a press briefing that Pakistan had lost a total of 297 officers and men since the fighting began in 1984, most of them (200) due to harsh weather and environmental conditions. India, he said, had lost 1200 officers and men in the same period from fighting, and several hundred more due to weather and environment-related conditions. *The Muslim* (Islamabad), 14 September 1989. According to senior Pakistani military officers interviewed by the author at the Siachen in October 1989, Pakistan's noncombat casualties in the first few years of fighting accounted for over 80 percent of total casualties suffered by the Pakistan army.

5. Pakistan's forward lines were more readily accessible, hence its logistics were considerably easier. Pakistan's army chief reportedly claimed in 1989 that the cost of supporting India's troops on the Siachen was nine or ten times as great as Pakistan's. *The Muslim*, 14 September 1989. See also Arun Chacko, "The High Price of Siachen," *The Indian Express* (New Delhi), 2 July 1989.

6. "Agreement Between Military Representatives of India and Pakistan Regarding the Establishment of a Cease-Fire Line in the State of Jammu and Kashmir, 27 July 1949 (S/AC.12/TC.4)," in K. Sarwar Hasan (ed.), *The*

Kashmir Question: Documents on the Foreign Relations of Pakistan (Karachi: Pakistan Institute of International Affairs, 1966) p. 229.
7. See, for example, Jasjit Singh, "Siachen Glaciers: Facts and Fiction," *Strategic Analysis* (New Delhi) 12:7 (October 1989) esp. 703-4; K. Subrahmanyam, "Kashmir," *Strategic Analysis* 13:2 (May 1990) 135-6; and "Siachen: India for Peaceful Solution," *The Hindu* (International edition), 19 March 1988.
8. In spite of the somewhat ambiguous wording in the 1949 agreement, the thrust of that document leaves very little doubt that its authors did not contemplate delimitation of the CFL beyond NJ 9842.
9. Indian writers, obviously pained by the Indian government's failure in 1972 to exploit its superior negotiating position to better advantage in regard to delimiting the northern boundary, were quick to point out that "eastwards joining the glaciers" fell well short of endorsing an extension of the line all the way to the Karakoram Pass. See Joshi, "Solution to Siachen Tangle"; and A. G. Noorani, "Fire on the Mountain," *Illustrated Weekly of India* (New Delhi), 30 June 1985, pp. 40-1. Joshi subsequently reported that the 1972 delimitation agreement terminated the LOC at NJ 9842, leaving the rest of the area untouched. However, he continued to hold, wrongly I think, that the 1949 agreement had extended the line vaguely northward beyond NJ 9842. Manoj Joshi, "Siachen: India for Peaceful Solution," *The Hindu* (International edition), week ending 19 March 1988.
10. "Boundary Agreement Between the Governments of the People's Republic of China and Pakistan, 2 March 1963," in Hasan (ed.), *The Kashmir Question*, p. 384.
11. Ibid., p. 388.
12. "Letter of the Representative of India Addressed to the President of the Security Council, 16 March 1963 (S/5263)," in ibid., pp. 388-91. For additional discussion of the Sino-Pakistani border pact, see Anwar H. Syed, *China and Pakistan: Diplomacy of an Entente Cordiale* (Amherst: The University of Massachusetts Press, 1974) pp. 82-93; and Yaacov Vertzberger, *The Enduring Entente: Sino-Pakistani Relations 1960-1980* (New York: Praeger, 1983) pp. 15-83. See also Mahnaz Z. Ispahani, *Roads and Rivals: The Political Uses of Access in the Borderlands of Asia* (Ithaca: Cornell University Press, 1989) pp. 180-5.
13. Personal interviews with government officials in Islamabad, June-July 1990.
14. Nehru himself stated in the Lok Sabha on 26 May 1956 that Chitral was a part of Jammu and Kashmir state and that Pakistan's sovereignty over that area would no longer be recognized. Sisir Gupta, *Kashmir: A Study in India-Pakistan Relations* (Bombay: Asia Publishing House, 1966) pp. 305-6. See also the White Paper, *Statement of Facts on Gilgit, Hunza, Nagar, Yasin, Ponial, Chitral and Skardu*, produced in Srinagar by the Government of Jammu and Kashmir state (1983?). The British scholar Alastair Lamb speculates that in laying claim to Chitral, Nehru may have been "hoping to make the plebiscite less attractive in Karachi. After all, if

Chitral really was a part of Kashmir, and if Pakistan did lose the plebiscite as it was then envisaged by the United Nations, then the consequences would be even more disastrous. It is possible that here was another Indian argument for the recognition, at any rate tacitly, of the cease-fire line as the legal boundary." *The Kashmir Problem: A Historical Survey* (New York: Praeger, 1966) pp. 90-1.

15. Dixon reported to the Security Council that "India was willing that the following areas should go to Pakistan, viz., Gilgit, Gilgit Agency, Gilgit Wazarat, political districts and tribal territory and Baltistan, and so much of the Jammu province as lies to the west of the cease-fire line as corrected." "Report Submitted by the United Nations Representative for India and Pakistan, Sir Owen Dixon, to the Security Council, 15 September 1950 (S/1791/Add.1)," in Hasan (ed.), *The Kashmir Question,* p. 268. See also Jyoti Bhusan Das Gupta, *Jammu and Kashmir* (The Hague: Martinus Nijhoff, 1968) pp. 160-1.

16. See Y. D. Gundevia, *Outside the Archives* (Hyderabad: Sangam Books, 1984) pp. 233-310.

17. See, for example, G. S. Bhargava, *South Asian Security after Afghanistan* (Lexington, Mass: Lexington Books, 1983) p. 120.

18. Rosalyn Higgins, *United Nations Peacekeeping, 1946-1967, Documents and Commentary, II: Asia* (London: Oxford University Press, 1970) p. 317. Nehru qualified the commitment, however, by insisting that the restoration of peace had to come first. India would later argue that Pakistan's failure to withdraw its armed forces from Kashmir ("to vacate its aggression") nullified any obligation upon India to conduct a plebiscite. See Gupta, *Kashmir: A Study in India-Pakistan Relations,* pp. 203-54.

19. The article enumerated certain "temporary" provisions safeguarding the state of Jammu and Kashmir's separate constitutional status. It stipulated that laws enacted by the Indian parliament could not be introduced or applied there without the concurrence of the Kashmir provincial government.

20. Lamb, *The Kashmir Problem,* p. 86.

21. See, for example, *Organiser,* 11 May 1986. The right-wing, pro-Hindu Bharatiya Janata Party, which won 88 of 525 seats in the Indian Parliament in the November 1989 general elections, was formally opposed to giving special constitutional status to the state of Jammu and Kashmir. Barbara Crossette, "Party Crucial to Opposition Bloc in India Rearranges Its Leadership," *The New York Times,* 1 December 1989, p. A13.

22. The administrative organization of Pakistan's Northern Areas has changed a number of times since independence. The agency system introduced by the British in the nineteenth century was formally dropped in 1972. At that time, Gilgit and Baltistan were redesignated as districts and a third district, Diamar, was formed. The new districts, as in the past, continued to be separately administered by the federal government through a Commissioner for Northern Areas. The arrangement was further modified near the end of 1989, when two additional districts (Ghizar and Ghanche) were carved from

the area, a subdivision of the latter reportedly containing the Siachen Glacier. *The Muslim*, 27 November 1989. For details, see Ahmad Hasan Dani, *History of Northern Areas of Pakistan* (Islamabad: National Institute of Historical and Cultural Research, 1989) pp. 408-29. Both in popular usage and on Pakistani maps, Gilgit continues to be designated as Gilgit Agency.

23. See, for example, the Government of Pakistan's publication *Kashmir in Maps* (Rawalpindi: Public Relations Directorate, Ministry of Kashmir Affairs, 1955).

24. Khan Zaman Mirza, Director of the Institute of Kashmir Studies, University of Azad Jammu and Kashmir, interview with the author, Muzaffarabad, June 1986.

25. Khurshid Hasan Meer, interview with the author, Islamabad, February 1986. Zulfikar Bhutto's intent, according to Sardar Muhammad Ibrahim Khan, three-time President of Azad Kashmir, was to merge the Northern Areas into the North-West Frontier Province and to make Azad Kashmir a "unit" of Pakistan with representation in the National Assembly. According to Ibrahim, Bhutto considered a number of ad hoc arrangements to move the country in that direction, but took no concrete steps. His motive, said Ibrahim, was "to make Pakistan's jurisdictional hold on the area legal and constitutional." Ibrahim, President of the Azad Kashmir section of the People's Party of Pakistan since 1984 and for long a member of the party's Central Executive Committee, contends that Bhutto wanted Pakistan to be a factor to be reckoned with in international affairs. For that reason, said Ibrahim, Bhutto sought closer relations with China. That, he knew, risked placing the Northern Areas in greater jeopardy from the Soviet Union and India. Hence, the legitimacy of Pakistan's claim to that area had to be strengthened. Interview with the author, Islamabad, January 1986. That Bhutto acted in keeping with a "secret deal" over Kashmir struck with Prime Minister Gandhi at Simla has often been alleged; but no hard evidence of such a deal has ever surfaced. Imtiaz H. Bokhari and Thomas Perry Thornton, *The 1972 Simla Agreement: An Asymmetrical Negotiation* (Washington, D.C.: Foreign Policy Institute, School of Advanced International Studies, The Johns Hopkins University, 1988) pp. 33-4.

26. This was the view of retired Colonel Mansha Khan, in recent years Vice President of the Azad Kashmir branch of the People's Party of Pakistan and member of the national unit's Central Executive Committee. Interview with the author, Rawalpindi, June 1986. Khan was elected to the Azad Kashmir Assembly on a PPP ticket in 1975, and served as Speaker until its dissolution in August 1977. Khan says that he tried a number of times, without success, to persuade Bhutto that Jammu and Kashmir state included Gilgit and Baltistan.

27. V. P. Dutt, *India's Foreign Policy* (New Delhi: Vikas, 1984) p. 167.

28. Ibrahim was interviewed by the author in Islamabad in January 1986.

29. *The Statesman* (New Delhi), 13 November 1983; and *Hindustan Times* (New Delhi), 11 November 1983. President Zia was quoted in the Indian

press at this time as having stated to a visiting Indian journalist that the Northern Areas—including Baltistan—"were not disputed areas but part of Pakistan." *The Times of India* (New Delhi), 10 November 1983. After the outbreak of fighting on the Siachen Glacier, however, Zia was reported to have acknowledged in a press conference at Quetta that the Siachen Glacier lay in *disputed* territory and that it was considered a no-man's-land. *The Muslim*, 25 September 1986.

30. *Atlas of Pakistan*, first edition (Rawalpindi: Director of Map Publication, Survey of Pakistan, 1985).
31. See Government of Pakistan, *Kashmir in Maps*.
32. See *Atlas of Pakistan*, esp. pp. vi, 23, 26, 61. The *Atlas* is hardly a monument to consistency. Some maps appear to show the Northern Areas, including Gilgit Agency, as falling entirely within the disputed territory of Jammu and Kashmir state (pp. 3 and 4), while others show the Northern Areas and Jammu and Kashmir state as a part of Pakistan (pp. 17 and 22). On the page (vi) listing the jurisdictional divisions of Pakistan, however, Gilgit Agency and Jammu and Kashmir state are listed separately, and only Jammu and Kashmir as "disputed." See also *Ferozsons Atlas for Pakistan* (Lahore: Ferozsons Ltd., 1986), especially the map showing Pakistan's administrative divisions (p. 2). This widely used edition carries the imprimatur of the office of the Surveyor General of Pakistan.
33. *The Muslim*, 21 July 1986.
34. Sardar Abdul Qayyum Khan, interview, Islamabad, January 1986.
35. K. H. Khurshid, interview with the author, Lahore, May 1986.
36. See, for example, *Dawn*, 4 November 1985 and 15 March 1986; and *The Muslim*, 17 January, 16 February, and 14 March 1986.
37. Ayub B. Awan, "'Northern Areas' Constitutional Status," *Dawn*, 4 October 1985. See also Ahmad Hasan Dani, "Gilgit Scouts Win the Battle of Freedom," *The Muslim*, 2 November 1984; and Mir Abdul Aziz, "Northern Areas: A Case for Representation," *The Muslim*, 8 April 1986. The most scholarly effort thus far to explore the circumstances surrounding the Northern Areas' joining of Pakistan in the immediate postindependence period is by Dani, *History of Northern Areas of Pakistan*, esp. pp. 326-407.
38. *The Muslim*, 25 March 1986.
39. National Geographic Society, *Atlas of the World*, fifth edition (Washington, D.C.: National Geographic Society, 1981) pp. 184-5; Joseph E. Schwartzberger, editor, *A Historical Atlas of South Asia* (Chicago and London: The University of Chicago Press, 1978) pp. 87-8; and *The Times Atlas of the World*, sixth edition (London: Times Books, 1980) plate 31.
40. Ravi Rikhye, *The Fourth Round: Indo-Pak War 1984* (New Delhi: ABC Publishing House, 1982) map facing p. 68. Rikhye's map shows the CFL running northeastward all the way to the Karakoram Pass on the Chinese border, in effect ceding the contested area of the Siachen Glacier to Pakistan with room to spare. Even more pleasing to Pakistanis, perhaps, were the maps of Jammu and Kashmir shown in a 1984 book published in India by retired Lt General K. P. Candeth, *The Western Front: The Indo-Pakistan*

War 1971 (New Delhi: Allied Publishers, 1984). In that war, Candeth commanded the Indian army's Western Command, which then included Kashmir. His maps, including a close-up of the Nubra River valley immediately adjacent to the Siachen, all supported the Pakistani claim to Siachen.

41. See, for example, Hussain, "Siachen Glacier—Fact and Fiction."
42. The climbing teams were mainly from Japan and Western Europe. For contrasting interpretations of these expeditions, see ibid. and "The Stakes in Siachen," *The Hindu*, 11 June 1985.
43. *The American Alpine Journal 1981*, p. 298. Describing the Nubra River valley, the author of a popular American trekking guidebook wrote in 1982 that "just to the north [of Rimo Glacier] is the Karakoram Pass, now the official meeting point of Pakistan, India, and China." Hugh Swift, *The Trekker's Guide to the Himalaya and Karakoram* (San Francisco: Sierra Club Books, 1982) p. 157. See also the comments on Pakistan's administrative control of access routes to Mount K-2 by Galen Rowell, a member of a 1975 American expedition, in *In the Throne Room of the Gods* (San Francisco: Sierra Club Books, 1977) pp. 16-23.
44. Sircar, "Siachen Glacier: Who Is on Thin Ice?"
45. Ibid. Another Indian journalist has written that "New Delhi first became suspicious in 1983 when an American map showed the Siachen Glacier and places like Lyogme and Lagonma as part of Pakistan. Subsequently, the Indian army came to know that a Japanese mountaineering expedition team was seeking Islamabad's permission to scale certain mountains in the area. The Indian Embassy in Tokyo told the team that it was New Delhi which had to give the permission. Consequently, the Japanese called off the expedition." Kuldip Nayar, "Pak's No to Joint Survey," *The Tribune* (Chandigarh), 15 December 1985.
46. "Indo-Pak 'Mountain Diplomacy,'" *Telegraph*, 9 June 1985.
47. The Kashmiris' right of self-determination expressed through plebiscite was reportedly reaffirmed emphatically by then Prime Minister Mohammad Khan Junejo in September 1986 at a public rally at Muzaffarabad. *The Muslim*, 21 September 1986. It is a part of stock phrasing appearing on all authorized maps published in Pakistan. In the post-Zia period, of course, its constant articulation by Pakistani leaders became a major issue between the two countries.
48. Pakistan's Foreign Minister Sahabzada Yakub Khan was reported to have told the National Assembly in June 1985 that the Siachen Glacier, while a part of the Northern Areas of Pakistan, was situated to the north of the terminus of the LOC. *Dawn*, 9 June 1985.
49. Indian Prime Minister Rajiv Gandhi bluntly reminded Pakistanis of the Indian point of view in this regard in a joint press conference held with Pakistani Prime Minister Benazir Bhutto in Islamabad at the conclusion of an official visit in July 1989. Replying to a question about the status of Jammu and Kashmir, the Indian leader reportedly told his listeners that the

Simla agreement of 1972 had superseded all past actions and that "the question of a plebiscite is out." *The Muslim*, 18 July 1989.

50. Jasjit Singh, Director of New Delhi's government-supported Centre for Defence Studies and Analyses observed, for example, that "the fallacy of [Pakistan's straight-line] claim is obvious since the lines of control or boundaries in lofty mountainous regions could hardly be expected to run along a straight line cutting across mountain ranges and valleys." "No Pak Claim to Siachen," *The Times of India*, 19 May 1988. Singh argued in the same article, on the other hand, for a formula of territorial delimitation that seems no less provocative and self-serving. The line should be drawn, he says, following the high crest line of the Saltoro Range in a northwesterly direction from map gridpoint NJ 9842 all the way to Mount K-2. The world's second-highest peak, K-2 lies fifteen to twenty miles northwest of the westernmost edge of the Siachen Glacier (i.e., Conway Saddle). Singh's argument, which would leave the Pakistanis without the barest scrap of a claim to Siachen, seems less than foolproof. Correctly drawn in accordance with the Karachi and Simla agreements, he says, the LOC would run *due* north to the glaciers. "The glaciers implied," he insists, "are undoubtedly those on the *western* slopes of the Saltoro range" [emphasis added]. Notwithstanding Singh's inferences, the treaty-makers seem, in fact, to have given no guidance at all in regard to the direction in which the boundary was to go after NJ 9842. See also Jasjit Singh, "Siachen: Search for a Just Solution," *The Times of India*, 22 March 1989, and "Siachen Glaciers: Facts and Fiction."

51. The development of a powerful Kashmiri Muslim separatist movement in Indian Kashmir since Zia's death may have altered at least some Pakistani expectations in this regard.

52. Syed Rifaat Hussain, "Siachen Glacier: Much Ado About Nothing?", *The Muslim*, 15 June 1986.

53. Douglas C. Makeig, "War, No-War, and the India-Pakistan Negotiating Process," *Pacific Affairs* 60:2 (Summer 1987) 281. Makeig wrote that "even though India has never renounced its claim to all Pakistan-controlled Kashmir, India generally supports the territorial status quo with all its neighbors except China. Pakistan's forcible attempts to alter the status quo—in Kashmir in 1948 and 1965, in the Rann of Kutch in 1965, *and in the northernmost reaches of the line-of-actual-control along the Siachen Glacier in the past three years*—are seen by India as proof of its expansionist designs."(Emphasis added.)

54. Lt. General (Retd.) M. L. Chibber, "Siachen—The Untold Story (A Personal Account)," *Indian Defence Review* (January 1990) 146-7. See also the account of these events by Manoj Joshi, "The Siachen Tangle," *The Hindu*, 6 October 1987.

55. Colonel Narinder Kumar, "A New Peak of Achievement," *The Illustrated Weekly of India* 101:21 (25 May 1980) 33-40.

56. Colonel Narinder Kumar, "Conquering Karakorams," *The Illustrated Weekly of India* 103 (6 June 1982) 10-17. Described as part of the training

for the HAWS Advance Course, the 1981 expedition was apparently one of the biggest ever attempted in the Karakorams. According to Kumar, the team consisted of fifteen instructors and forty students.
57. "Fighting first erupted in 1984," it said, "when Pakistani troops reportedly set up camps in a no-man's-land in the inhospitable upper reaches of the strategic glacier that overlooks India's sensitive military installations. India, alarmed by what it saw as a threat to its security, mounted a major offensive and seized control of the upper glacier, analysts say." Brahma Chellaney, "Fighting Flares Anew on Long-tense India-Pakistan Border," *The Christian Science Monitor*, 2 October 1987. To say the least, this report grossly understated the difficulties involved in mounting a major offensive on the Siachen Glacier!
58. Interview with the author, Rawalpindi, October 1989.
59. There was an even greater delay between the 1978 HAWS's expedition to the Siachen and publication of Colonel Kumar's account of it in 1980.
60. As was customary, the protest notes were passed to Indian army officers at a border checkpoint near Kargil in the Northern Sector of Jammu and Kashmir.
61. Chibber, "The Untold Story," 149-50.
62. Ibid., 150.
63. Lt. General (Retd.) M. L. Chibber, "Siachen Solution Will Help India, Pak," *The Times of India*, 13 June 1989. The Aksai Chin lies to the east of the Siachen Glacier in Ladakh. India claims it, but China successfully asserted its control over it in the 1962 border war.
64. The Karachi Agreement authorized creation of a United Nations Military Observer team, which was converted to UNMOGIP in 1951.
65. UNMOGIP's neutrality in the Siachen dispute was questioned in the Indian media. See, for example, B. L. Kak, "Peace-keepers Turn Spies?", *Sunday* (Calcutta), 30 June 1985. India has not reported violations of the LOC to UNMOGIP since 1972.
66. Interview, Islamabad, January 1986. For additional Pakistani views on the strategic meaning of the Siachen dispute, see Brigadier (Retd.) M. Shafi Khan, "Siachen and the Indian Designs," *The Nation* (Lahore), 25 December 1987; Rasul B. Rais, "China and Pakistan: The Strategic Link," *The Muslim*, 27 June 1987; and Khalid, "The Geopolitics of the Siachen Glacier."
67. An American analyst commented in summer 1988, for example, that the Wakhan Corridor had been converted into an important Soviet military enclave and that Moscow would be very reluctant to vacate it. "The U.N. General Assembly's call for a commitment to Afghanistan's territorial integrity," she observed, "is negated by the refusal of both Moscow and Kabul to acknowledge the Soviet annexation of the Wakhan Corridor, which occurred de facto in May 1980 and was confirmed by a secret treaty in June 1981. It was announced on Kabul Radio, then hastily denied, but an Italian journalist managed to get into the Wakhan and photographed the Soviet flag flying over government offices." Rosanne Klass, "Afghanistan:

The Accords," *Foreign Affairs* 66:5 (Summer 1988) 938. Developments in Afghanistan since Klass wrote this article do not seem to offer any confirmation of her argument.

68. The best recent discussion of the Sino-Pakistani strategic relationship is Yaacov Y. I. Vertzberger, *China's Southwestern Strategy: Encirclement and Counterencirclement* (New York: Praeger, 1985).

69. See ibid., pp. 102-4; and Carnegie Endowment for International Peace, *Nuclear Weapons and South Asian Security*, Report of the Carnegie Task Force on Non-Proliferation and South Asian Security (Washington, D.C.: Carnegie Endowment, March 1988) pp. 40-2.

70. See John G. Merriam, "Arms Shipments to the Afghan Resistance," in Grant M. Farr and John G. Merriam (eds.), *Afghan Resistance: The Politics of Survival* (Boulder: Westview, 1987) pp. 71-101.

71. For background and an excellent discussion of the road's geopolitical implications, see Ispahani, *Roads and Rivals*, pp. 185-213. See also Nazir A. Kamal, "Karakorum Highway: A Nation-Building Effort," *Strategic Studies* 2:3 (Spring 1979) 18-31.

72. See Vertzberger, *China's Southwestern Strategy*, esp. pp. 1-19.

73. Kamal, "Karakorum Highway," p. 30.

74. Interview with the author, Islamabad, December 1987.

75. Ispahani, *Roads and Rivals*, p. 201.

76. For examples of such reports, see O. P. Sabherwal, "Siachen: Snow-bound Frontier," *Mainstream* (New Delhi), 22 June 1985; Yusuf Jameel, "India Ready Even for Sino-Pak Offensive," *Telegraph*, 23 June 1985; Shekhar Gupta, "Gunfire on the Glacier," *India Today*, 31 July 1985, pp. 132-5; Sahdev Vohra, "Siachen's Strategic Location," *Mainstream*, 28 November 1987; and Jasjit Singh, "Siachen: The Himalayan Battlefield," *The Hindustan Times*, 18 October 1987.

77. Interview with the author, October 1989.

78. Interview with the author, Rawalpindi, October 1989.

79. Interview with the author, New Delhi, June 1990.

80. The UNCIP resolution of 5 January 1949 did not provide for the choice of independence.

81. Bokhari and Thornton, *The 1972 Simla Agreement: An Asymmetrical Negotiation*, p. 39.

82. Hindus predominated in Jammu, the larger but more lightly populated of the state's three regions. In it Muslims accounted for about 34 percent of the population. Mainly Buddhist Ladakh was the third and least populated region of the state.

83. For background, see Josef Korbel, *Danger in Kashmir*, revised edition (Princeton: Princeton University Press, 1966) pp. 223-6. See also Das Gupta, *Jammu and Kashmir*.

84. Ever since independence, per capita resource transfers in the form of loans and grants from the center to the state of Jammu and Kashmir had consistently exceeded those to virtually every other Indian state. See P. K. Bhargava, "Transfers from the Center to the States in India," *Asian Survey* 24:6 (June 1984) 665-87. Coincidentally, Jammu and Kashmir was also the least-taxed state in India. Balraj Puri, "Jammu and Kashmir," in Myron Weiner (ed.), *State Politics in India* (Princeton: Princeton University Press, 1968) pp. 225-6.
85. No state in India had a worse reputation when it came to the conduct of elections. Ventilating a widespread public judgment of the March 1987 state elections in Jammu and Kashmir, a major New Delhi-based daily editorialized, for example, that "such is the State's murky record in this sphere [vote-rigging and other election malpractices] that barring the 1977 poll not a single election could be said to have reflected the people's will truly and faithfully." *The Hindustan Times*, 15 April 1987.
86. See Mohan Ram, "In Search of Power," *Far Eastern Economic Review*, 2 October 1986, p. 31.
87. For discussion of internal security and the use of force in India, see Raju G. C. Thomas, *Indian Security Policy* (Princton: Princeton University Press, 1986) pp. 51-85. The extraordinarily large forces based in Jammu and Kashmir state are there, of course, primarily for external security purposes.
88. Inderjit Badhwar, "Farooq Under Fire," *India Today*, 15 September 1987, p. 22.
89. Mr. Shah reportedly declared that he and everyone else in Kashmir considered themselves Pakistanis and that he did not accept Kashmir's accession to India. *The Hindustan Times*, 3 September 1987; *Indian Express*, 10 September 1987.
90. See, for example, Robert L. Hardgrave, Jr., *India Under Pressure: Prospects for Political Stability* (Boulder: Westview Press, 1984) p. 36.
91. An article in a major New Delhi fortnightly commented, for example, that "the alienation that the Kashmiris suffer is partly because ever since 1953, elections have been either uncontested or rigged and have failed to draw Kashmiris into India's emotional mainstream. The backlash has always been a flight to obscurantist or secessionist causes." Inderjit Badhwar, "Jammu and Kashmir: A Tarnished Triumph," *India Today*, 15 April 1987.
92. See, for example, Arun Joshi, "Rise of Fundamentalism in Kashmir," *The Hindustan Times*, 7 July 1987. Though still located on the political fringe of Indian Islam, Kashmiri Muslims in the 1980s were much less isolated from the Muslim mainstream in India than they once were. They naturally sympathized with widespread Muslim demands for a larger slice of the country's economic and political power; and they could hardly ignore the steady increase in communal violence and bloodshed—in which Muslims were commonly the chief victims—that had taken its toll in recent years of Hindu-Muslim relations in many parts of India. For a summary of the problem of communal violence, see Thomas, *Indian Security Policy*, p. 69. See also James Manor, *Collective Conflict in India*, Conflict Studies 212

(London: The Centre for Security and Conflict Studies, June 1988). The threat of contagion of Kashmiri Muslims by these developments was undoubtedly already a major worry for New Delhi and its political allies in Jammu and Kashmir by the middle of the 1980s. Thus, when enraged Muslim mobs made unprecedented assaults on several Hindu temples in Kashmir Valley in February 1986, New Delhi reacted by sacking Chief Minister Ghulam Mohammad Shah—the second chief minister to have been removed from office in two years—and by imposing Governor's Rule in March. *The Statesman,* 8 March 1986; and Steven R. Weisman, "Kashmir Muslims—Disenchantment with New Delhi," *Dawn,* 13 June 1986. Among the first steps taken by Farooq Abdullah upon resuming the post of chief minister of the state on the lifting of Governor's Rule one year later (March 1987) was to propose a state takeover of Muslim "fundamentalist" schools as well as to implement a ban on distribution in the state of Urdu-language papers from New Delhi. Farooq reportedly justified the ban with the argument that news of Muslims being massacred elsewhere in the country threatened to bring a violent response in Jammu and Kashmir. *Indian Express,* 27 April 1987.

93. Rajendra Sareen, "J & K: Beyond G. M. Shah," *The Tribune,* 19 March 1986.

94. *The Christian Science Monitor,* 2 October 1987, p. 7; and Kamran Shafi, "The Truth?, Please," *The Muslim,* 10 October 1987.

95. In 1986, Azad Kashmir's population was officially estimated at 2.3 million. According to Mir Abdul Aziz, a well-known Kashmiri journalist and erstwhile political figure, barely 10 percent of this number was "true" (i.e., Kashmiri-speaking) Kashmiri. The President of Azad Kashmir in recent years, Sardar Abdul Qayyum Khan, was Punjabi-speaking, born (as was Azad Kashmir's first President, Sardar Muhammad Ibrahim Khan) in Poonch district in what is now Azad Kashmir. Of Qayyum Khan's seven cabinet ministers in early 1986, none was a native Kashmiri-speaker. Of the forty-two members of the Azad Kashmir Assembly at that time, only five (12 percent) were native Kashmiri-speakers—and all of them were elected from outside Azad Kashmir in the special "refugee" constituencies in Pakistan proper. Interview with the author, Rawalpindi, February 1986. Aziz claimed that there was only relatively light migration into Pakistan in the period 1947-49 from the densely Kashmiri-speaking area of Jammu and Kashmir state—i.e., the valley of Kashmir. Many of the Kashmiri-speaking migrants, he pointed out, did not settle in Azad Kashmir, preferring to settle elsewhere in Pakistan or to journey abroad. Migration from the Indian side was mainly from Punjabi-speaking Jammu.

96. An estimated 1.0-1.5 million Kashmiris (between 30 to 40 percent of the total combined Kashmiri populations in Azad Kashmir and Pakistan) have settled in Pakistan proper. Hundreds of thousands more have migrated to the Gulf and to the United Kingdom. According to Mohammad Abdul Jabbar, Additional Chief Secretary for Development in the Government of Azad Jammu and Kashmir, virtually every family in Azad Kashmir had at

least one member abroad or resident elsewhere in Pakistan. Interview with the author, Muzaffarabad, June 1986.

97. See Charles H. Kennedy, *Bureaucracy in Pakistan* (Karachi: Oxford University Press, 1987) pp. 193-7. In Azad Kashmir's own bureaucracy, Azad Kashmiris appear to be overwhelmingly dominant. According to Chaudhary Khurshid Ahmad, an Azad Kashmiri-born Section Officer in the General Services Division of the Secretariat, Government of Azad Jammu and Kashmir, fewer than 1 percent of bureaucrats posted in Azad Kashmir are Pakistani. Interview with the author, Muzaffarabad, 23 June 1986. In 1986, there were a total of five officers from the All-Pakistan Unified Grades on deputation in Azad Kashmir. They included the Chief Secretary, the Additional Chief Secretary, and the Inspector General of Police.

98. In 1981, Azad Kashmir's literacy rate stood at 25.7 percent, Pakistan's at 26.2 percent. The NWFP had a rate of 16.7 percent, Baluchistan, 10.3 percent, and *rural* Sind, 15.5 percent. Government of Pakistan, Population Census Organization, *1981 Census Report of Pakistan* (Islamabad: Statistics Division, December 1984) p. 28; Azad Government of the State of Jammu and Kashmir, Planning and Development Department, *Azad Kashmir at a Glance 1985* (Muzaffarabad) p. 2.

99. None of the parties that have expressed support for the full independence of a united Kashmir (e.g., the Jammu and Kashmir Plebiscite Front and the Jammu and Kashmir Liberation Front) has ever held any seats in the Azad Kashmir Assembly.

100. Badhwar and Bobb, "Disputed Legacy: General K. Sundarji."

101. Ravi Rikhye, *The War That Never Was: The Story of India's Strategic Failures* (New Delhi: Chanakya, 1988) p. 2.

102. Ibid.

103. Rikhye's earlier book was *The Fourth Round: Indo-Pak War 1984*. A serving Indian army brigadier had this to say (paraphrased) about Rikhye's allegations: The contention Rikhye makes in regard to Operation Trident is preposterous. So too is his contention that Operation Meghdoot had a larger objective than merely seizure of the Siachen. No doubt there are individuals in the Indian army who would propose such plans. But they have no credibility unless given confirmation by other sources, or by the actual course of events. The actual course of events, in this case, in fact does *not* confirm Rikhye's thesis. His argument flies in the face of geographical limits nature has placed on any military operations in that area. Indian army expeditions and patrols on the Siachen beginning in 1978 were a reaction to Pakistan's mountain poaching (via mountaineering expeditions and cartographic claims). It may be that India's expeditions and patrols were themselves not fully in the spirit of the Simla accords (i.e., peaceful settlement of all disputes); but neither were Pakistan's activities in the vicinity of the glacier entirely peaceful. These included provision of military "guides" to accompany mountaineering expeditions. Who can say that *such* activities had no *military* purpose? It is, in fact, probable that Pakistan took no *significant* military steps vis-à-vis Siachen until late 1983, when it

was alerted to Indian army activities. But Pakistan's role, cartographic and otherwise, was definitely not innocent. Why, for instance, did it waive fees on some of the higher peaks? Indian army intrusions do not add up to a *design,* carefully executed. They *were* meant to establish India's claim to the territory. They were not forerunners either of Operation Meghdoot, which was hastily contrived upon receipt of intelligence reports of planned Pakistani military deployment in the area, or of anything even more spectacular (i.e., Rikhye's suggestion that an attack down the Shyok River valley was planned). Had Operation Meghdoot been planned all along, the Kumaon regiment wouldn't have been used. It happened that a battalion of this regiment was in reserve outside Srinagar. In other words, it was available. Of course there were efforts made to acclimatize these troops, but they were hasty. There simply had not been a lengthy and systematic effort to marry troops to terrain prior to the Operation. One assumes this would have been done had an Indian "grand plan" been under way. Interview with the author, New Delhi, June 1990.

104. See *The Christian Science Monitor,* 2 October 1987, p. 7; *The Hindu* (International edition), 10 October 1987; *The New York Times,* 1 October 1987, p. A3; and *The Muslim,* 1, 2 and 10 October 1987.
105. For a more thorough discussion of the negotiations between India and Pakistan over Siachen, see the author's article, "The Siachen Glacier Dispute: Can Diplomacy Untangle It?", *Indian Defence Review (July 1991).*
106. "Siachen Deadlock Costs India, Pak. Dear," *The Hindu,* 1 October 1987.
107. There was at least a hint of similar thinking in the comment of Jasjit Singh, Director of New Delhi's Centre for Defence Studies and Analyses, who commented in late 1987 that

> India's options at present are restricted to holding the ground and trying to seek an agreement with Pakistan. However, the previous talks of 1985-86 had already reached an impasse. Over a period of time holding the line of control militarily against tremendous odds of terrain, climate and frequent attacks will extract a heavy price from India, politically and otherwise. *Withdrawal, of course, would be disastrous. Serious thoughts may have to be given in future to a defensible line of control which would safeguard strategic interests at lesser costs, while working for a mutually agreed line of control* (emphasis added).

Singh, "Siachen: The Himalayan Battlefield."
108. These reports detailed the late Pakistani president's alleged plan (codenamed Op Topac) to destabilize the Indian state of Jammu and Kashmir by funneling sophisticated weapons and other aid to Kashmiri militant groups such as the Jammu and Kashmir Liberation Front. These groups launched the most prolonged, widespread, and well-armed campaign of domestic violence in the state's history in July 1988, roughly one month before Zia's death. See IDR Research Team, "Op Topac: The Kashmir Imbroglio," *Indian Defence Review* (July 1989) 35-48. See also Devsagar Singh, "Centre May Seal J-K Border with Pak," *Indian Express,* 11 July 1989; "India

Must Respond," *Economic & Political Weekly* (Bombay), 8 July 1989; and Barbara Crossette, "Islamic Militancy Called Threat to an Indian State," *The New York Times,* 3 May 1989, p. A7.

5

CONCLUSION: THE PERSISTENCE OF INSECURITY

The years from Zia's seizure of power in 1977 to his death in 1988 were witness to momentous developments in Pakistan's security policy. In these years, Pakistan organized and led a massive program of covert military intervention in Afghanistan, fought a miniwar with India, made major advances toward nuclear weaponization, joined the ranks of the nonaligned nations, helped to found the South Asian Association for Regional Cooperation, and—not least—revived its security relationship with the United States. These developments involved unquestionably weighty decisions. In more than a few instances, they carried with them a heavy political price. Most of them were highly controversial. This book's assessment of these developments reveals, however, that on the whole the Zia period was not a major turning point in Pakistan's foreign security policy. Continuity with the past, in fact, was one of its most visible characteristics.

There were important differences, of course, between Zia and his predecessors both in background and in general approach to the making of security policy. Zia himself was less Westernized, more ideologically Islamic, and more naturally at home in the Muslim Middle East than had been any of them. He was certainly more narrowly military and less experienced with diplomacy than had been most of them. His manner of presenting Pakistan's case to the world tended to be blunt and unadorned, lacking the polish and elegance of Ayub Khan and the dash, brilliance, and keen sense of drama of Zulfikar Ali Bhutto. Zia's security decision-making was certainly more cautious, less driven by xenophobia, and more consensus-based than had been true of at least some of those who preceded him in office. But these were differences largely in personality, rhetoric, and style, not in how Pakistan's leaders have conceived of the nation's fundamental interests and strategic requirements. In regard to them, there was little, in fact, to distinguish between Zia and his predecessors.

No less than they, Zia had to contend with a domestic political situation whose chronic instability impaired Pakistan's prestige abroad, exposed it to covert projects of destabilization from its neighbors, and undermined the government's capacity to rally mass support for foreign policy objectives. No less than they, he also had to contend with a bundle of strategic "givens"—a severe imbalance of power relative to India, heavy dependence on international material and political support, and the marked ambivalence of its allies about the virtues of Pakistan's friendship—that set severe limits on the range of policy choice. While it is probably true that Zia was not a particularly imaginative leader, regional circumstances at the time were even less congenial than usual to policy innovation and experimentation. Mainly, they appeared to require prudence and pragmatism, qualities which Zia and his principal advisors seemed to possess in ample quantity. Encumbered with enormous handicaps, internal and external, and lacking the means to push Pakistan along unfamiliar paths, they wisely kept to well-established policies.

Examination of these policies, which in this book have been clustered together as "imperatives" of intervention in Afghanistan, territorial irredentism in Kashmir, and engagement in a conventional and nuclear arms race with India, shows that they were not executed in blind conformity with the past or with anything approaching uniform commitment. Zia's security policies were by no means simply a carbon copy of what had gone before. The Soviet invasion of Afghanistan, together with the collapse of the Pahlavi dynasty in Iran, presented Zia's Pakistan with a far greater threat to its western borders than had been experienced at any time in the past. The Zia regime was thus bound to pay greater attention to this threat—and at the same time to play down and to seek to allay the traditional Indian threat—than had its predecessors. As Ispahani put it, "peace with India—however cold—was a military necessity."[1] Nevertheless, Zia's Pakistan followed policy paths very largely consistent with the past. Interregime differences in security policy were almost exclusively matters of emphasis and not of core principles and direction.

The point of view taken in this book obviously minimized the impact of the Zia regime's political coloration—its militaristic and authoritarian inclinations—on the country's security policy. This policy, it was argued, was best understood mainly as a prudent response to Pakistan's threatening external environment, not as an offshoot of the country's failure to build democratic institutions or as an artful disguise for the various distasteful

Conclusion: The Persistence of Insecurity

appetites of its entrenched elites. This was not to say that the Zia regime was without inherent weaknesses, or that the country's lack of political accountability or the glaring inequalities of its socioeconomic structure had no effect on security decision-making. There was little doubt, for example, that Zia's lack of legitimacy in the eyes of many Pakistanis created serious handicaps in building sustained public support for the government's risky Afghan policy. Zia's capitulation in the Geneva talks to a set of accords that conspicuously omitted provision for an interim government to replace Najibullah in Kabul may well have resulted in part from this factor. It was certainly true, moreover, that Pakistan's unattractive reputation for political instability, government mismanagement, heavy-handed techniques of maintaining public order, and official corruption was earned in no small measure under the auspices of President Zia. Throughout his time, the sometimes unconscionable greed of Pakistan's privileged elites manifested itself with painful regularity. However, deficiencies of these kinds had debased the political order for most of Pakistan's history and under virtually all of its leaders, military or otherwise. Their relationship to the security policies of the Zia regime was often vastly overdrawn; and they unquestionably stemmed from causes that went far deeper than the regime's political complexion.

The argument of this book also expressed skepticism in regard to the ability of either of the superpowers to superimpose its strategic will on Pakistan, in effect to subordinate Pakistan's security policy to its own. Obviously, the global superpowers, even before the entry of Soviet troops into Afghanistan in 1979, were both key players in the region. Whether as adversary or ally, their "presence" in the region in the years thereafter shadowed practically every security decision taken by Islamabad. This book has maintained throughout, however, that regional rivalries, in particular that between India and Pakistan, easily retained a commanding role in the shaping of Pakistan's security outlook. India remained the principal threat. At all times, acquiring the means to counter Indian power loomed the largest in Islamabad's security calculations. The superpower rivalry, in addition to other consequences it held for Pakistan, both compounded the Indian threat while at the same time generating opportunities for Pakistan to counter it. Driven mainly by the imperatives of its own environment, Islamabad actively courted Washington. In the 1980s as in the years immediately following independence, it "was most definitely not pulled reluctantly into an American empire."[2] Pakistan's security policy, in other words, was largely its own. Far from being simply a pawn in the strategic rivalry of the superpowers, Pakistan was, in fact, a more than willing recruit to that rivalry.

Developments in Pakistan's domestic and regional security environment since Zia's death provide few reasons for expecting Zia's successors to be any less conservative than he was in setting the country's security policy. In the immediate post-Zia period, this environment seemed to be on the threshold of major change. Zia's demise was followed by the stunning electoral victory of Benazir Bhutto and the establishment at the end of 1988 of the first fully and freely elected government in Pakistan's history.[3] The emergence of a popular and democratically elected leader, conceivably more responsive to popular aspirations for peace and economic prosperity, promised to bring greater political stability to the country. The departure of the last Soviet troops from Afghanistan early in 1989 removed the direct threat of Soviet military pressure from Pakistan's border on the west; and a flurry of diplomatic activity at about the same time between New Delhi and the new government in Islamabad over the Siachen Glacier dispute raised the possibility that the newfound compatibility of their youthful, modern-oriented, and democratic governments might put an end to the military confrontation between them along the disputed border on the east. At the global level, Sino-Soviet rapprochement and the astonishing warming in U.S.-Soviet relations set in motion by Soviet leader Mikhail Gorbachev's stunning overhaul of Soviet society and policy promised to increase opportunities and incentives for regional peace initiatives.

These events indicated to some observers that Zia's security policies, even if they had been reasonably suited to his times, were now clearly out of date; that the profound changes on Pakistan's borders, especially in Afghanistan, required correspondingly substantial adjustments in Pakistan's regional threat assessments; and that, with the rapid and precipitous decline in Cold War rivalry, Pakistan should no longer count on the West in whose front line against Soviet expansionism it was no longer required. American writers, in particular, seemed keen that Washington not miss the opportunity to scale down the U.S. commitment to Pakistan. With the winding down of the war in Afghanistan, they said, the overlap in outlook between Washington and Islamabad was bound to diminish. Hence, Pakistan's oversized share of Washington's budgeted security assistance could be pared down to more realistic dimensions and there could be a substantial conversion from military to economic assistance. Moreover, hitherto muted differences between the United States and Pakistan in regard, for example, to the desirability of a "fundamentalist" takeover in Afghanistan, could be brought out in the open and squarely faced; Washington's "permissive" nonproliferation policy toward Pakistan could be stiffened; and a fresh look could be taken at India,

Conclusion: The Persistence of Insecurity

which was likely now gradually to become America's more important partner in the South Asian region.[4]

Few such writers recommended that the United States abandon its longtime association with Pakistan. Nevertheless, their arguments in regard to the "exaggerated" quantities of U.S. military aid to Pakistan in the 1980s and the "ideal" of a shift by Washington to India implied an unmistakable downgrading of it.[5]

By the second anniversary of Zia's death, it no longer seemed so obvious that the changes in Pakistan's security environment were so positive or Zia's security policies so obsolescent as in the immediate wake of Zia's passing. In fact, the same nagging problems persisted, in some respects even worsened. One reason for this lay in the resistance to resolution of the Afghanistan problem. The withdrawal of Soviet armed forces from that country in time substantially lessened the intensity of the war, but it did not succeed in bringing it to a swift end. Kabul soon settled down to a basically defensive posture, while the resistance proved equally unable either to unify the various mujahideen groups around a central leadership or to mount strong and sustained military operations against the well-fortified urban garrisons of the Kabul regime.[6] For a host of practical as well as political reasons, very few refugees had made the decision to return to their stricken and inhospitable homeland.[7] With both the United States and the Soviet Union continuing heavy arms shipments to their Afghan clients, the war hardened into a stalemate which neither side seemed prepared to break.

The government of Benazir Bhutto introduced only subtle modifications to its predecessor's Afghan policy. It shuffled the leadership of the army's Inter-Services Intelligence Directorate, the agency responsible for overseeing the war, reduced government patronage of Gulbuddin Hekmatyar, and was noticeably warmer to the concept of a "broad-based" Afghan government involving a more restricted role for the Peshawar-based mujahideen than had been Zia.[8] But it did not reopen negotiations with the Kabul regime, seeming content to wait on the diplomatic sidelines for a breakthrough in periodic U.S.-Soviet talks on the subject.

Even if a superpower agreement on Afghanistan were reached, it wasn't clear that Pakistan would be among the beneficiaries. For one thing, there did not seem to be much likelihood that agreement at that level would translate very quickly into a stable political situation inside Afghanistan. Powerful animosities generated by eight years of brutal warfare; tribal, sectarian, and ideological differences among the various contenders for power; and the clashing interests of the Afghan rivals' remaining foreign supporters were bound to interfere with that. There were no guarantees, moreover, that a superpower-arranged settlement would produce a regime in Kabul sympathetic to Pakistan's regional point of view. Islamabad lacked the means to ensure a position of dominance in any new political setup for its political allies in the resistance; and even they could not be depended upon to prevent impulses toward Afghan nationalism from surfacing that might be inimical to Pakistan's long-standing interest in a secure and agreed western border. Afghanistan's potential movement into the ranks of the nonaligned, a seemingly benign development on its face, might well occur side by side with the growth of Indian—and the eclipse of Pakistani—influence on developments in that country.[9] Were Soviet-United States collaboration in an Afghan settlement to stimulate policy differences between Washington and Islamabad, as many predicted, Pakistan's leaders might well find themselves nearly as isolated after the war as they had been immediately before it.[10]

A second reason for doubting that post-Zia Pakistan stood on the threshold of major improvements in its security environment, hence that its security policy stood in need of major overhaul, was the remarkable downturn in Pakistan's relations with India that occurred within hardly more than a year of Zia's passing. Springing to a large extent from the grave separatist unrest in strategically critical areas along their common border, especially in Indian Kashmir and in East Punjab, it had led by the spring of 1990 to grave allegations by New Delhi of Pakistani interference and subversion, to major troop buildups and stockpiling of weapons on both sides of the border, as well as to the eruption in both countries of unusually fierce jingoism and saber-rattling rhetoric.

Since the Bangladesh war, nothing had so shaken the region's delicate regional peace as the Kashmiri separatist uprising. It had occurred in one of India's strategically most sensitive areas; and the temptation for Pakistan to exploit the uprising for its own purposes was unquestionably powerful. India and Pakistan had routinely charged one another with covert acts of intervention throughout the Zia period. Indeed, the alleged acts (by India, in the Sind; by Pakistan, in Indian Punjab) were frequently cited among the chief barriers to normalized relations between the two states. But the resort to violence of Kashmiri Muslims in January 1990, when New Delhi launched its crackdown on the separatist movement, put a whole new and unusually vexatious face on the matter of foreign interference. Alienated by what even most Indian observers conceded had been decades of economic neglect, police-state tactics, and cynical manipulation by New Delhi of the Kashmiri government, Kashmiri Muslims by the tens of thousands openly threw their support to the militant separatists. By mid-August 1990, over 1000 people

Conclusion: The Persistence of Insecurity

had been slain in the Kashmiri uprising.[11] No easy political solution presented itself; and the crisis inevitably took an increasingly international turn. New Delhi accused Pakistan of deliberately fanning the flames of separatism; and both countries rushed troops to the border. There ensued in New Delhi a lively debate among analysts over the relative importance in the Kashmir crisis of internal and external factors, with a far from negligible number insisting that India's political mismanagement—and not Pakistan's sinister designs—bore the lion's share of responsibility for the nearly complete collapse of Indian authority in the valley.[12] Nevertheless, in the midst of all this India took steps to seal the border against terrorist infiltration from Pakistan and announced a major increase in its annual defense outlay.[13] The threat of another war over Kashmir, according to some even nuclear war, hovered menacingly over India-Pakistan relations.[14]

The crisis promised few tangible gains for Pakistan. For one thing, many, perhaps most, Kashmiri Muslims seemed to prefer the goal of Kashmiri independence over that of absorption by Pakistan. For another, achievement of either independence or union with Pakistan seemed highly unlikely to most observers since India appeared determined to take whatever measures were necessary to crush the separatists. Moreover, Pakistan's efforts to mobilize international support for its stand on Kashmir had had very divided results, with some key allies, including China and the United States, appearing highly reluctant to antagonize New Delhi over the issue.[15] Nevertheless, New Delhi's deep embarrassment over the Kashmiris' exposure of serious shortcomings in the practice of Indian secularism, federalism, and democracy, together with India's evidently heightened political weakness and vulnerability to foreign interference, obviously gave a needed boost, both symbolic and material, to Pakistan's traditional counterboundary policy in Kashmir. The Kashmir issue was clearly not moribund; indeed, India and Pakistan seemed even more distant from a solution of it in 1990 than at any time in the preceding decade. The conflict in South Asia, as one analyst suggested, was one of a number of regional conflicts around the world for which the preconditions for conflict resolution simply had not been met.[16] For the time being, at least, the festering of the territorial dispute in Kashmir would stand in the way of any significant progress toward the normalization of relations. There was very little chance, therefore, for a significant softening in Pakistan's security policy toward its eastern neighbor.

Pakistan's security environment looked equally unpromising on its southwestern flank. Iraq's sudden invasion and subsequent annexation of Kuwait in August 1990 dramatized the extreme volatility of the whole Gulf region as well as the vulnerability of Pakistani interests in it.

With well over 100 000 Pakistanis reportedly stranded in Kuwait and Iraq, Islamabad was instantly affected by Iraq's action. The effects went beyond humanitarian concerns, obviously, since Pakistan's economic dependence on the conservative Arab sheikhdoms of the Gulf, both for oil and as a source of remittances from Pakistani migrant laborers, had been massive for years.[17] Any prolonged disruption in the flow from the Gulf either of oil or the remittances was certain to have a catastrophic impact on the delicate Pakistani economy. The Iraqi action also threatened to disrupt Pakistan's military ties with the conservative Arab states. Although these had been drastically curtailed following the December 1987 agreement with Riyadh to repatriate the bulk of Pakistani military contract personnel from Saudi Arabia, they still betokened a significant level of military exchange and cooperation.[18] Saudi Arabia and Kuwait had long been significant contributors to the cause of the Afghan resistance; and there had been rumors that they were supplying covert assistance to the Kashmiri militant groups fighting in Indian Kashmir.

Pakistan's current diplomatic exertions to focus world attention on what it said was New Delhi's ruthless repression of Kashmiri self-determination were an immediate casualty of the Iraq crisis. The Kashmir issue was swept from the front pages, at least temporarily, by the more spectacular events in the Gulf. A more serious problem for Pakistan, however, stemmed from the deep intra-Arab divisions that were surfacing in the Middle East. Pakistan's traditional neutrality in regard to these divisions no longer seemed practicable. In its swift commitment of several thousand Pakistani troops to join with the U.S.-led multinational force in the defense of Saudi Arabia, Islamabad appeared to tie Pakistan's fate more than ever to that of its conservative Gulf allies.

Pakistan's active military intervention in the Gulf crisis was not without its own problems. Avoiding the ire of its West-baiting Iranian neighbor was obviously one of them. It was not a new problem. From 1980 to 1988, Iraq had sustained a major military challenge of Iran, an important ally of Pakistan in Pakistan's previous wars with India; but Iraq's Saudi and Kuwaiti backing in that conflict had necessarily engendered a strong ambivalence in Islamabad's own outlook and behavior. Iraq's aggressive action against Kuwait in 1990, although more or less opposed both by Iran and the Saudis, eased the requirement for circumspection in Pakistani policy only slightly. Another problem lay in the uncertainty surrounding India's reaction to the Gulf crisis. On the one hand, India's potential economic loss from the crisis was hardly likely to be much less than Pakistan's. Almost 200 000 Indian citizens had been trapped in Iraq and Kuwait; and up to the crisis India had been dependent on these two countries for about 40 percent of its imported

Conclusion: The Persistence of Insecurity

petroleum supplies.[19] On the other hand, India's ties with Iraq, quite in contrast with the often thorny relationship between Iraq and Pakistan, had been India's closest in the Arab Middle East for many years.[20] Iraq and India stood first and third, respectively, among the world's arms importers in 1987.[21] They were the two largest recipients of Soviet military hardware outside the Warsaw Pact; and they were the first to receive the advanced MiG-29 fighter aircraft. There was a significant level of exchange between their armed forces; and they unquestionably had a common interest in restraining any Pakistani ambition to intrude as the Arab states' Big Brother in the Gulf region. Equally animated by the threat to their secular political ideologies posed by Islamic fundamentalism, they had a common interest too in containing its spread. Baghdad, incidentally, had gone further than most states in expressing support for India's stand on the Kashmir crisis.

It was conceivable, of course, that events in the Gulf would revive Pakistan's flagging status in the West's strategic calculus. Western writers even before the Iraq-Kuwait crisis had been arguing that post-Afghanistan Pakistan, given its geographic proximity, growing naval strength, and close political and military association with both Iran and the conservative Arab states, could play a useful, stabilizing role in Southwest Asia and the Indian Ocean.[22] It was now inescapably apparent that, with or without the presence of the Soviet Union, this area remained a very dangerous place. Pakistan might no longer have a role to play as an anchor in the chain of Western containment of the Soviet Union; but there were now perhaps clearer grounds for believing that Pakistan could help to contain the turbulent forces that threatened the stability of practically every state on the Soviet Union's southern periphery. The change in the regional balance of power spurred by the Iraqi action might boost Pakistan's role in the Gulf. Cutbacks in U.S. military aid to Pakistan might no longer seem cost-effective. It was at least equally conceivable, however, that differences between Washington and Islamabad held in check this far—over Afghanistan, for instance, or over the nuclear issue—might not remain in that state indefinitely. The renewal in early autumn 1990 of congressional demands for an aid cutoff in the face of Pakistan's apparent continuing refusal to back off from its nuclear weapons program, and President Bush's failure to meet the 1 October deadline for certifying Pakistan's eligibility for continuing aid, seemed clearly pointed in this direction.[23]

Events in the post-Zia period made it equally clear that Pakistan's efforts to build a secure regional environment would continue to be handicapped by its unresolved domestic political situation. On 6 August 1990, within days of the second anniversary of Zia's death, Pakistan's President Ghulam Ishak

Khan dismissed the government of Benazir Bhutto, dissolved the National Assembly, appointed a caretaker government led by the ex-Prime Minister's political foes, and promised fresh elections on 24 October. The President's step ended twenty months of People's Party rule. His dissolution order charged the Bhutto government with nepotism, unparalleled political horse-trading and corruption, usurpation of the authority of the provinces, undermining of the constitutional order, and with indecisiveness in the face of grave civil disturbances in the province of Sind.[24] Speculation was rife that the real reason was that Benazir had gradually antagonized the army's top generals, who had tolerated her leadership only so long as it suited their purposes. The dismissal had been rumored for months and came as no surprise to a population grown disillusioned with its leaders, both military and civilian, and used to periodic coups. Coming only 4 days after the Iraqi invasion and takeover of Kuwait, and clearly aided by the world's (especially American) preoccupation with that crisis, the President's military-supported "constitutional coup" caused barely a ripple of criticism abroad.

Benazir's dismissal confirmed what many analysts had already concluded—that the army remained a principal arbiter of Pakistan's political destiny and that the Bhutto regime had "failed to distinguish itself from an undistinguished tradition of civilian rule."[25] Once again, "change from below" had proven as ineffective in stabilizing Pakistani politics as had Zia's "change from above." Beset with powerful foreign threats, a severe economic crisis, radicalized ethnic sentiments, and the rampant spread of a socially poisonous drug-and-gun culture inherited from her military predecessor, Benazir proved unable to move Pakistan from its characteristically unstable and authoritarian political path. Her brief tenure as Prime Minister made clearer than ever that democracy would not come easily to Pakistan, that the country's instability had roots that went well beyond mere differences in regime, and that Pakistan's security policy in the 1990s would very likely continue to be undermined by the failures of its domestic political order. Instability was a constant, it seemed, and Pakistan was thus bound to remain vulnerable to its enemies while continuing to bear a flawed reputation among its friends.

In all of these developments, there was nothing that supplied unambiguous evidence that Pakistan's security imperatives were on the brink of fundamental revision. The liabilities that went along with Pakistan's status as a peripheral Asian power—its weakness vis-à-vis its Indian neighbor, its dependence on foreign support, its inherent lack of appeal as an ally—all remained firmly in place. Pakistan seemed fated to pursue security policies that would antagonize its adversaries and keep its allies aloof; that would

Conclusion: The Persistence of Insecurity

make it a target simultaneously of foreign subversion and unrelenting foreign demands for both domestic political reform and demilitarization of its security policy; and that would expose it to the constant dangers of war and even territorial dismemberment. Zia's Pakistan had shown itself capable of a realistic, canny, and sometimes brilliant security policy. By any fair standard, it had coped responsibly and with reasonable skill with an extraordinarily inhospitable regional environment. It had found permanent solutions to none of the country's fundamental security problems; but their solution lay well beyond the reach of any Pakistani regime.

It was always possible, of course, that Pakistan's persistent insecurity might soon be ameliorated, and that its amelioration would be brought about mainly by changes from within. It has been the burden of this book, however, to suggest that any positive development in relation to Pakistan's security, absent significant change in its situation from without, remained highly improbable. For the foreseeable future, at least, Pakistan seemed most likely to be guided by the same policy imperatives that had guided Zia and all other Pakistani leaders.

NOTES

1. Mahnaz Z. Ispahani, *Pakistan: Dimensions of Insecurity*, Adelphi Papers 246 (London: International Institute of Strategic Studies, Winter 1989/90) p. 43.
2. Robert J. McMahon, "United States Cold War Strategy in South Asia: Making a Military Commitment to Pakistan, 1947-1954," *The Journal of American History* 75:3 (December 1988) 840.
3. Benazir's father, Zulfikar Ali Bhutto, was the only earlier national leader chosen in a free election (1970) based on universal adult suffrage. His victory was qualified, however, by its having been made possible only by the violent repartition of the country in 1971. Bhutto's People's Party had been defeated by the Awami League of East Pakistan in the 1970 national elections. It had won a majority of seats, however, in West Pakistan.
4. Among those calling for change in American policy toward South Asia were Paul Kreisberg, "The United States, South Asia and American Interests," *Journal of International Affairs* 43:1 (Summer/Fall 1989) 83-95; Thomas P. Thornton, "The New Phase in U.S.-Pakistani Relations," *Foreign Affairs* 68:3 (Summer 1989) 142-59; and Gerard C. Smith and Helena Cobban, "A Blind Eye to Nuclear Proliferation," ibid., 53-70. Recommendations were not uniform on all issues. Kreisberg, for instance, took a more accommodating view of the proliferation problem than did most others. "There is no turning back the Indian nuclear clock," he said, "and no disinventing or dismantling of Pakistan's achievements,...U.S. policy must live with what

has happened, encouraging both countries to develop ways to assure that neither ever uses nuclear weapons against the other....It is probably time for the United States to take another look at its nonproliferation policy strategy, at least so far as it relates to the subcontinent, and retune it for changing circumstances"(91-2).

5. A common assumption was that there would be a corresponding upgrading in Indo-United States relations. Kreisberg wrote, for example, that while Washington would continue "to work with Pakistan as a quasi-ally,...India will steadily become the more important partner for the United States with respect to the most central issues for U.S. policy in South Asia—security, economics, the environment and technology." "The United States, South Asia and American Interests," 94. Some analysts, however, were more equivocal. Thornton, for example, argued for reduction of U.S. arms supply to Pakistan to a level that was "tolerable to India," moreover that Washington's South Asia policy ideally "should grow out of [its] relationship with India, even more than with Pakistan." He conceded, however, that improving U.S. relations with independent-minded India would be problematic. "The New Phase in U.S.-Pakistani Relations," 152-3, 158.

6. Following Soviet withdrawal of its troops from Afghanistan in February 1989, not a single town fell to rebel forces until early October 1990. *The New York Times,* 6 October 1990, p. A5.

7. See Marvin G. Weinbaum, "The Politics of Afghan Resettlement and Rehabilitation," *Asian Survey* 29:3 (March 1989) 287-307.

8. Ispahani, *Pakistan: Dimensions of Insecurity,* pp. 46-7.

9. See Robert G. Wirsing, "The Soviet Role in South Asia: Potential for Change," in Leo E. Rose and Kamal Matinuddin, (eds.), *Beyond Afghanistan: The Emerging U.S.-Pakistan Relations* (Berkeley: Institute of East Asian Studies, 1989) pp. 295-6.

10. Thornton, "The New Phase in U.S.-Pakistani Relations," 155-6; and Ispahani, *Pakistan: Dimensions of Insecurity,* pp. 46-7.

11. "India Sends Soldiers to the Pakistani Border," *The New York Times,* 22 August 1990, p. A5.

12. For a sampling of Indian viewpoints on the Kashmir crisis, see Tapan Bose et al., "India's 'Kashmir War,'" *Economic and Political Weekly* (Bombay), 31 March 1990, pp. 650-62; Inderjit Badhwar, "Kashmir: Perilous Turn," *India Today* (International edition), 30 April 1990, pp. 10-16; Shekhar Gupta, "Benazir Bhutto: Playing With Fire," *India Today,* 31 May 1990, pp. 22-9; K. Subrahmanyam, "Kashmir," *Strategic Analysis* (New Delhi) 13:2 (May 1990) 111-98; Samuel Baid, "Self-Determination for Kashmiris: A Camouflage for Pak's Own Claim," *Strategic Analysis* 13:3 (June 1990) 327-55; Anand Sahay, "Kashmir's Dilemma," *Frontline* (New Delhi) 7:12 (9-22 June 1990) 4-11; B. G. Verghese, "Kashmir: Way to Recovery," *Mainstream* (New Delhi), 5 May 1990; Prem Shankar Jha, "Frustrated Middle Class: Roots of Kashmir's Alienation," *The Times of India,* 28 May 1990; and K. S. Bajpai, "Kashmir: A Question of Nationhood," *The Hindustan Times,* 28 June 1990. Following a week's visit to Srinagar in autumn

1989, I. K. Gujral, soon to be named India's Foreign Minister, seemed to side with those who placed greater emphasis on internal factors. "While the foreign hand is discernible," he wrote, "some knowledgeable people believe that it is being exaggerated as a cover-up for political lethargy and administrative lapses. The armed forces, by all accounts, have a firm grip on the border and their vigilance evokes confidence." "Kashmir: Challenge of Alienation," *The Times of India,* 13 October 1989.

13. In March 1990, New Delhi announced an 8.6 percent increase in the defense budget for 1990-91. This was the first increase in three years. "Sharp Increase in Defence Outlay," *The Telegraph,* 20 March 1990. In April, Prime Minister V. P. Singh was said to have told reporters that the government planned to restore the two-to-one military superiority over Pakistan which he claimed had been lost by the previous government of Rajiv Gandhi. "India to Restore Military Superiority," *The Statesman,* 25 April 1990.

14. See, for example, Leonard S. Spector, "India-Pakistan War: It Could Be Nuclear," *The New York Times,* 7 June 1990, p. A23; Mushahid Hussain et al., "War Threat" [Cover story], *Globe* (Karachi) 3:5/6 (June 1990) 14-71; and Shekhar Gupta et al., "Defence: Are We Prepared?" [Cover story], *India Today,* 30 June 1990, pp. 73-83.

15. Pakistan's most significant public support came in a strongly pro-Pakistani resolution adopted by the Organization of the Islamic Conference (OIC) Foreign Ministers' meeting in Cairo on 4 August 1990. F. J. Khergamvala, "Pak. Carries Day at OIC Meet," *The Hindu,* 5 August 1990. Pakistan was also given strong backing by neighboring Iran. Iraqi strongman Saddam Hussein and PLO Chairman Yasir Arafat openly backed India. Both Indians and Pakistanis, apparently convinced that Prime Minister Bhutto's Middle East diplomacy had been a failure, seemed to have been surprised by the OIC tilt to Pakistan. See Manvendra Singh, "Arabs and Kashmir," *Indian Express,* 26 May 1990; F. J. Khergamvala, "Benazir's Futile Bid to Influence OIC," *The Hindu,* 23 May 1990; K. K. Katyal, "Neutral Perspectives," *Frontline* 7:12 (9-22 June 1990) 13-15; and the editorial, "Kashmir & Diplomacy," *The Muslim,* 24 June 1990.

16. Richard N. Haass, *Conflicts Unending: The United States and Regional Disputes* (New Haven: Yale University Press, 1990).

17. There were reports that half or more of Pakistan's petroleum imports at the time of Iraq's invasion came from Kuwait alone. Sultan Ahmed, "The Oil Crunch for Pakistan," *The Muslim,* 5 August 1990.

18. Ispahani, *Pakistan: Dimensions of Insecurity,* p. 51. Of late, the government of Pakistan had admitted only to the deputation of military technicians and training personnel to Saudi Arabia.

19. Barbara Crossette, "New Delhi Hopes Gulf-Aid Ship Can Unload," *The New York Times,* 18 September 1990, p. A9.

20. India's relations with most of the conservative Arab states of the Gulf had always been fairly cool. New Delhi's refusal to condemn the Soviet military occupation of Afghanistan had alienated them even further. New Delhi's

friendship with Baath-socialist Iraq, however, had survived all earlier crises. See Bhabani Sen Gupta, "India's Relations with Gulf Countries," in Alvin Z. Rubinstein (ed.), *The Great Game: Rivalry in the Persian Gulf and South Asia* (New York: Praeger, 1983) pp. 148-75; and Robert G. Wirsing, "India and the Gulf," in Hafeez Malik (ed.), *International Security in Southwest Asia* (New York: Praeger, 1984) pp. 107-39.

21. U.S. Arms Control and Disarmament Agency, *World Military Expenditures and Arms Transfers 1988* (Washington, D.C.: U.S. Government Printing Office, June 1989) p. 8.
22. See, for example, Rodney W. Jones, "Pakistan and the United States: Partners After Afghanistan," *The Washington Quarterly* (Summer 1989) 65-87; and Lieutenant Mark Montgomery, "The U.S.-Pakistani Connection," *Proceedings* (July 1989) 67-73.
23. Michael R. Gordon, "Bush Urged to End Pakistan Aid Over Issue of Nuclear Arms Plan," *The New York Times,* 25 September 1990, p. A4; Neil A. Lewis, "Key Congressman Urges Halt In American Aid to Pakistan," *The New York Times,* 3 October 1990, p. A7; Stuart Auerbach, "Pakistan Tried to Buy Nuclear Aids," *The Washington Post,* 10 October 1990, p. A1; R. Jeffrey Smith, "Administration Unable to Win Hill Support for Continued Aid to Pakistan," *The Washington Post,* 10 October 1990, p. A14; Salamat Ali and Frank Tatu, "Nuclear Fallout," *Far Eastern Economic Review,* 25 October 1990, pp. 11-12; and R. Jeffrey Smith, "U.S. Stiffens Policy on Nuclear Arms, Pakistan Aid," *The Washington Post,* 20 November 1990, p. A11.
24. Tariq Butt, "Benazir Government Dismissed," *The Muslim,* 7 August 1990.
25. Ispahani, *Pakistan: Dimensions of Insecurity,* p. 15. See also Anthony Hyman, *Pakistan: Towards a Modern Muslim State?,* Conflict Studies 227 (London: Research Institute for the Study of Conflict and Terrorism, January 1990).

INDEX

Abdullah, Farooq, 173-4
Afghanistan, 9-10, 13-14, 15-16, 18, 20, 30-3, 102, 103, 107, 109
  and Geneva negotiations, 63-71
  interference in Pakistan by, 32
  Marxist coup in (1978), 33, 54
  after Soviet withdrawal, 199-200
  See also Afghan refugees; Afghan resistance movement; Pakistan; People's Democratic Party of Afghanistan
Afghan Refugee Commissionerate, 46-7
  criticism of, 56-7
Afghan refugees
  and Afghan Refugee Commissionerate, 46-7, 56-7
  and Awami National Party, 47-8
  attitudes toward in Pakistan, 47-8, 49, 52-3
  in Baluchistan, 49-50, 53
  distribution of in Pakistan, 46
  economic burden on Pakistan of, 37, 43-4, 48
  international support of, 42-4
  and Jama'at-i-Islami party, 46-7
  and King Zahir Shah, 70
  and law enforcement, 48
  in North West Frontier Province, 45-8, 53
  in Pakistan's domestic politics, 44-53
  in Punjab, 51-3
  repatriation of, 43-4
  See also Afghan resistance movement
Afghan resistance movement
  attitudes toward in Pakistan, 47-8, 49, 52-3
  and diversion of arms supplies, 55-7
  fundamentalist influence on, 57-62
  international support of, 40
  and Inter-Services Intelligence Directorate, 55-6
  Pakistan's support of, 14, 26-8, 30-1, 33, 34, 35, 38, 40-2, 53-63, 107-8
  and Zia ul-Haq, 57-63, 68
  See also Afghan refugees
Agni missile, 96
Ahmad, Professor Khurshid, 58
Aid India Consortium, 120
Air Defense Information Zone (ADIZ), 153
air force, Indian, 91-2
air force, Pakistan, 105-6
Aksai Chin, 148, 164, 166, 167
All Jammu and Kashmir Muslim Conference, 152
Amin, Prime Minister Hafizullah, 25
Andropov, Yuri V., 66
Apsarasas peak, 154
Arif, Lieutenant General K. M., 58
arms control
  impediments to, 99-101
  Pakistani proposals for, 99
arms race, India-Pakistan, 102
  and arms imports, 94-5
  compared with other countries, 87-8
  and human resources, 96-7
  Indian perceptions of, 85-9
  and indigenous arms production, 95-6
  and military balance, 89-92
  and military expenditures, 93-4
  nuclear, 83, 122-6
  in space technology, 96

Index

and superpower rivalry, 82-3, 197
army, Indian
  in Kashmir, 174
  Northern Command of, 165
  in Siachen Glacier dispute, 159-70, 179-80
army, Pakistan, 92, 105-6
  corruption in, 56-7
  in Siachen Glacier dispute, 159-70, 176
  support of Afghan resistance, 54-7
Arnold, Anthony, 18
Article 370, 148
Atlas of Pakistan, 151, 153
Atlas of the World (National Geographic Society), 153
Awami National Party (ANP), 47-8, 52
Awan, Ayub B., 152-3
Ayoob, Mohammed, 17
Azad Kashmir, 145, 148, 149, 150-2, 158, 170
  relations with Pakistan, 176-7

Babar, Major General Naoirullah, 31
Baghdad Pact (CENTO), 6, 36
Baltistan, *see* Northern Areas
Baluch/Baluchistan, 9, 13, 30, 44, 49-50, 52, 105-6, 118
  Afghan refugees in, 49-50, 53
  insurgency (1973-7), 49
Bangladesh, 13, 81, 86, 92
Barnds, William, 6
Bhutan, 86
Bhutto, Prime Minister Benazir, 117, 198, 199
  dismissal from government of, 203-4
Bhutto, Prime Minister Zulfikar Ali, 1, 34, 35-6, 105, 113, 114,115, 149-50, 195
  execution of, 10
  policy toward Afghanistan of, 30-3
Biharis, 50-1
Bilafond La (Saltoro Pass), 144, 164
Bizenjo, Mir Ghaus Bux, 15-16
"bomb in the basement", 125
Border Security Force (BSF), 174

Brass Tacks, Operation (1986-7), 99-100, 123, 177-8
Brzezinski, Zbigniew, 101
Buckley, James L., 101-2
Bukhari, Brigadier Syed Asif Riaz, 161-2
Burma, 86
"Burzil Force", 164
Bush, President George, 203

Canada, 119
Carnegie Endowment for International Peace, 105
Carnegie Task Force on Non-Proliferation and South Asian Security, 112, 122-3
Caroe, Olaf, 30
Carter, President Jimmy, 8-9, 34, 36, 38, 101
Cato Institute, 11
cease-fire line (CFL), 149, 153, 154, 164, 170, 171
  description of, 145-6
Central Intelligence Agency (CIA), 123
Central Treaty Organization (CENTO), *see* Baghdad Pact
Chaghai district, 49
Chah Bahar, 36
Chamalang battle, 105, 106
Chibber, Lieutenant General M. L., 159-60, 163-4, 170
China/Chinese, 54, 92, 93, 94, 100, 110, 201
  "counter-encirclement" strategy of, 8
  military aid to Pakistan, 166
  relations with Pakistan, 6, 8
  See under Siachen Glacier dispute
Chinook helicopters, 106
Chitral district, 148
Chopra, Pran, 85
Chulung Group (mountains), 146
CIRUS reactor, 114, 119
Clausen, Peter, 120
Cohen, Stephen P., 11, 12, 18, 125, 126
Comprehensive Test-Ban Treaty, 99
Congress (I) party, 174

Index

Congress, U.S., and Pakistan's nuclear program, 120, 203
Conway Saddle, 169
Cordovez, Diego, 63, 64, 65, 66, 68

Defence Research and Development Organisation (DRDO), 97
Defense Mapping Agency (DMA), 153
Desai, Prime Minister Morarji, 115
"deterrence by bluff", 125, 126
Dixon, Sir Owen, 148
Dunbar, Charles, 40
Duncan, Peter, 39
Durand Line, 9, 28-9, 32, 33
Durand, Sir Henry Mortimer, 28
Dzingrulma, 143, 162

Egypt, 40, 54, 82
Exocet missiles, 89

Federal Advisory Council (Majlis-i-Shura), 151, 152
Federally Administered Tribal Area (FATA), 30, 46
F-6 (MiG-19) fighter-interceptor, 91-2, 95, 106
F-16 fighter-bomber, 38, 91, 101-2, 104, 107
F-86 fighter-bomber, 106
flash x-ray equipment, 110, 111
Ford, President Gerald, 8
France, 94, 120

Gandhi, Mohandas, 29
Gandhi, Prime Minister Indira, 1, 10, 98, 115
Gandhi, Prime Minister Rajiv, 99, 116, 178, 179
Geneva accords (1988), 44, 197
  negotiation of, 38, 63-71
Germany (West), 110
Ghaus, Abdul Samad, 32
Gibraltar, Operation (1965), 175
Gilgit/Gilgit Agency, *see* Northern Areas
Gilgit Scouts, 161

Girardet, Edward R., 60-1
Glenn amendment, 109, 120
Gorbachev, President Mikhail, 39, 41, 66, 69, 198
Gromov, Lieutenant General Boris V., 64
Gulf crisis (1990-1), 201-3
Gyong La (pass), 144

Haass, Richard N., 113, 121
Hari Singh, Maharaja, 147
Harpoon missiles, 89
Harrison, Selig S., 66, 67-9, 105-6
Hasan, Mubashir, 117
Hekmatyar, Gulbuddin, 67, 199
  and Zia ul-Haq, 59-62
  See under Afghan refugees; Afghan resistance movement
Hezb-i-Islami Afghanistan party, 59-62, 67
High Altitude Warfare School (HAWS), 160, 161
Hindu, The (New Delhi), 180
Historical Atlas of South Asia, A (University of Chicago), 153
Hoover Institution, 18
Huey-Cobra attack helicopters, 105-6
humanitarian aid program (U.S.), 38
Hunza, 150
Hyderabad, 51

Illustrated Weekly of India, The, 160, 161
Inam Ul-Haq, Brigadier, 111
Independent Planning Commission (Lahore), 84
India/Indian, 13, 27, 28, 29, 34, 37, 38, 39, 70
  arms imports, 94-5
  arms production, 95-6
  and Gulf crisis, 202-3
  import of Soviet arms, 10, 82
  and Kashmiri separatism, 172-5
  military expenditure, 93-4
  nuclear program, 3, 114-16, 119-22
  regional dominance, 3-4, 87
  relations with United States, 103, 106-7

and Soviet intervention in Afghanistan, 10
strategic cooperation with Soviet Union, 36, 39, 165-6
strategic perceptions, 93
strategy of "limited deterrence", 93
strategy of "sufficient defense", 93
technological lead over Pakistan, 96-7
See also Arms race, India-Pakistan; Siachen Glacier dispute
Indian Atomic Energy Commission, 114
Indian Defence Review, 159
Indian Ocean, 90, 203
Indian Space Research Organization (ISRO), 96
India Today, 177
Indira Col (Saddle), 143
Indo-Pakistan wars,
 (1947-48), 7, 145, 170-1
 (1965), 7, 146, 148, 166
 (1971), 143, 146, 148, 166, 171
Indus River, 51
Institute for Defence Studies and Analyses (IDSA), 17, 85-6
Institute of Regional Studies (Islamabad), 15
Institute of Strategic Studies (Islamabad), 15, 154
Integrated Guided Missile Development Programme, 96
International Atomic Energy Agency (IAEA), 99
International Military Education and Training (IMET) program, 82
international nuclear nonproliferation regime,
 deficiencies in, 119-22
Inter-Services Intelligence Directorate (ISI), 55, 180, 199
Iran, 36, 105, 106, 202
Iraq, 82, 94, 201-3, 204
Isakhel (subdistrict), 51
Islamic Bomb, 114, 119
Islamization, 105
Ispahani, Mahnaz Z., 168, 196

Israel, 82, 104, 119
Israeli lobby, 119

Jaguar bomber, 91
Jama'at-i-Islami Pakistan (JIP) party, 46-7, 58, 59, 117
Jamiat-ul-ulema-i-Islam (JUI) party, 52
Jammu and Kashmir State, *see* Kashmir
Jang (Lahore), 15
Jinnah, Governer General Mohammad Ali, 5, 7
Jones, Rodney, 103, 114, 116, 125
Junejo, Prime Minister Mohammad Khan, 67, 68, 70, 100, 179

Kahuta, 113, 123, 178
Kapur, Ashok, 88, 125
Karachi, 50-1, 52, 56
Karachi Agreement (1949), 146, 156, 164, 171
Karachi Nuclear Power Plant (KANUPP), 110
Karakoram Highway, 165-8, 169
Karakoram Mountains, 81, 143, 153
Karakoram Pass, 28, 147, 153, 155-6, 159, 163
Karmal, Babrak, 65
Kashmir, 7, 28, 39, 81, 86, 92, 143, 145, 147, 172, 180, 202
 accession of to India, 155-6
 constitutional autonomy of, 173
 ministerial-level talks on (1962-3), 148
 Pakistan's policy motivations toward, 172-8
 separatist uprising in, 200-1
 and UN-sponsored plebiscite, 148, 149, 153
 See also Siachen Glacier dispute
Kashmir Council, 150
Khalis, Yunus, 59
Khan, Abdul Qadir, 110, 111, 113, 123
Khan, Abdul Wali, 48, 52
Khan, Air Chief Marshall Asghar, 117
Khan, Amir Abdur Rahman, 28

Index

Khan, Lieutenant General Akhtar Abdul Rahman, 55, 58, 68
Khan, Major General Mohammad Hayat, 151
Khan, Munir Ahmad, 113
Khan, President General Mohammad Ayub, 2, 107, 149, 195
Khan, President Ghulam Ishak, 203-4
Khan, President Mohammad Daoud, 25, 30-1, 32, 36
Khan, Sahabzada Yakub, 65-6
Khan, Sardar Abdul Qayyum, 165
Khan, Sardar Mohammad Ibrahim, 151
Khan, Sheikh Mohammad Abdullah, 47, 59, 173
Khunjerab Pass, 166, 167
Khurshid, K. H., 152
Khyber Pass, 101
Kissinger, Henry, 8
krytron switches, 110
Kumaon regiment, 159
Kumar, Colonel Narinder, 159-60, 161
Kurram Agency, 46
Kuwait, 201-3, 204

Ladakh, 145, 147, 148, 157, 166, 167, 168
Ladakh Scouts, 159
Lahore, 52
Libya, 82
Line of Control (LOC), 28, 148, 149, 150, 153, 155-7, 158, 159, 163-4, 169, 170, 171-2, 178
 description of, 146, 147

Manila Pact (SEATO), 6
maraging steel, 110, 111
Marri, Sardar Khair Bux, 49
Mazagaon Dockyard (Bombay), 96
Meghdoot, Operation ("Cloud Messenger"), 159, 160
Mianwali district, 51-2
MiG-21 interceptor, 91
MiG-29 fighter bomber, 203
Military balance, India-Pakistan
 conventional, 89-92
 nuclear, 124-5
Mirage III/V fighter bombers, 91, 95
Mirpur, 150
Mishra, Brajesh, 10
Mohajirs, 50-1
Mohammad, Mian Tufail, 117
"mountain poaching", 154
mujahideen, *see* Afghan resistance movement
Muslim United Front (MUF), 174
Mutual Defense Assistance Agreement (1954), 6, 82
Muzaffarabad, 149, 150

Najibullah, 67, 69, 197
National Conference-Congress (I) alliance (1987), 174
National Conference party, 173-4
navy, Indian, 89-91, 96
navy, Pakistan, 89-91
Nayar, Kuldip, 85, 111
Nehru, Prime Minister Jawaharlal, 98, 148, 173
New York Times, The, 111, 112
nonalignment, 108
Non-Aligned Movement (NAM), 27, 35, 103, 107
Northern Areas, 145, 147, 148, 149, 150-3, 155, 156, 158, 166-7, 178, 180
 martial law in, 151
North West Frontier Province, 29, 30-1, 44, 50, 51, 52, 118, 148
 Afghan refugees in, 45-8, 49, 53
 terrorist bombings in, 13-14
No-War Pact (1981), 99, 100
Nubra subdivision, 157
nuclear nonproliferation
 and the United States, 8-9, 108-13, 120
 See also nuclear weapons program, Pakistan; arms race, India-Pakistan
Nuclear Nonproliferation Act (1978), 120
Nuclear Non-Proliferation Treaty (NPT), 98, 99, 100, 118
nuclear-weapon-free zone (NWFZ), 98, 99

nuclear weapons program, Pakistan
  capabilities of, 122-6
  and China, 166
  clandestine record of, 109-11
  deterrent value of, 125-6
  motivations for, 113-16
  popular consensus on, 116-19
  See also nuclear nonproliferation

Organization of the Islamic Conference (OIC), 27, 35, 37
"oropolitics", 154

Pakistan Aeronautical Complex (Kamra), 95
Pakistan/Pakistani
  arms imports, 82, 94-5
  arms production, 95
  and border dispute with Afghanistan, 28-34
  and decline in superpower rivalry, 198-200
  and domestic political constraints, 10-16, 17-18, 20-1, 40-1, 44-53, 103-4, 116-19, 175-7, 203-4
  and Geneva negotiations, 63-71
  and Gulf crisis, 202-3
  Kashmir policy of, 145-59, 170-80
  and the Middle East, 7, 8, 9
  and military balance with India, 89-92, 124-5
  military expenditure, 93-4
  and normalization of relations with India, 85
  perspectives on Afghanistan war, 37-42
  policy options in Afghanistan, 26-8
  in post-Zia period, 198-205
  and problem of foreign interference, 12-14
  and problem of international prestige, 11-12
  relations with Afghanistan, 9-10, 30-3
  relations with China (PRC), 6, 8, 28, 147, 166-70
  relations with India, 10, 13, 19-21, 200-1
  relations with Iran, 9, 202
  relations with Saudi Arabia, 202
  relations with Soviet Union, 6, 82
  relations with United States, 5-10, 11-12, 34-7, 38, 40, 101-13, 197-200
  security decision-making in, 17-18, 196-205
  security policy debate in, 16-21
  and Soviet intervention in Afghanistan, 34-7
  strategic dependence of, 5-7
  strategic thinking, 35-6
  and superpower rivalry, 19-21
  support of Kashmiri separatists, 175, 180
  terrorist bombings in, 13-14, 45
  See also Afghan refugees; Afghan resistance movement; arms race, India-Pakistan; Kashmir; military balance, India-Pakistan; nuclear weapons program, Pakistan; Siachen Glacier dispute

Pakistan Atomic Energy Commission (PAEC), 113, 114
Pakistan Institute of Public Opinion (PIPO), 47-8
Pakistan Muslim League (PML) party, 70
Pakistan Philosophical Congress, 117
Panjsher/Panjshir incident (1975), 32, 61
Partial Test Ban Treaty, 98
Pashtunistan 9, 28-34
  definitions of, 29
Pashtuns, 29-30, 32, 47, 50, 51, 52, 59
"peace offensive", 98
People's Democratic Party of Afghanistan (PDPA), 33, 49, 64-7, 69-71
  and Baluch nationalists, 49-50
People's Party of Pakistan (PPP), 150, 204
Pervez, Arshad, 111
Peshawar, 46, 48, 56, 58
plebiscite (UN), 155, 157-8, 171
Pokharan (nuclear test site), 83
positive symmetry, 64
Pressler amendment, 112
Prithvi missile, 96
"proliferation ladder", 122-3

Index

Punjab, 50
  Afghan refugees in, 51-3

Rabbani, Burhanuddin, 59
Reagan, President Ronald, 38, 40, 63, 124
Rikhye, Ravi, 178
Roy, Olivier, 59, 61-2

Saltoro Range, 143, 144, 146, 159, 162, 180
Saltoro River, 180
Sareen, Rajendra, 175
Saudi Arabia, 34, 40, 59, 94
Sayyaf, Professor Abdul Rasul, 59
Schultz, George, 69
Schulz, John, 125
Sen Gupta, Bhabani, 85
Seth, S. P., 125
Shah, G. M., 174, 175
Shah of Iran, 9, 34, 105, 106
Shah, King Zahir, 36, 58, 70
Shahi, Agha, 26-8, 35, 36-7, 65, 69, 98, 104, 107-8
Shaksgam-Muztagh drainage basin, 168
Shastri, Prime Minister Lal Bahadur, 98
Shevardnadze, Eduard A., 70
Shyok River, 146
Siachen Glacier, 39, 81
  Pakistan's administrative control of, 154-8, 161
Siachen Glacier dispute, 198
  casualties in, 144
  China's role in, 147, 166-70
  impact on India-Pakistan relations of, 144
  Indian territorial claims in, 147-9, 156-7
  Indo-Pakistan negotiations on, 178-80
  and international atlases, 153-5, 170
  and international climbing expeditions, 154-7, 159, 170
  and Karakoram Highway, 165-8
  military-strategic motivation for, 165-70
  Pakistani territorial claims in, 149-59
  relation to Kashmir conflict of, 145-59, 170-80

  role of armed forces in, 144, 159-70
  role of UNMOGIP in, 164
Sia La (pass), 144, 164
Simla Agreement (1972), 81, 87, 98, 146, 156, 157, 171, 179
Sind, 118, 178, 204
  Afghan refugees in, 50-1, 53
  foreign interference in, 13
Singh, Arun, 178
Singh, Natwar, 178
Singh, Sardar Swaran, 146
Sino-Indian war (1962), 148
Sino-Pakistani Border Agreement (1963), 147, 149, 152, 156, 168, 169
Skardu, 178
Smith, Hedrick, 111
Sohrab Goth (Karachi), 51
Solarz amendment, 112
South Asian Association of Regional Co-operation (SAARC), 85, 195
Soviet Central Asia, 68
Soviet Union, 94
  and Geneva negotiations, 63-71
  and military aid to India, 82
  and military aid to Pakistan, 82
  and war in Afghanistan, 9-10, 20, 34-7
Special Services Group (SSG), 54
Spector, Leonard, 115
strategic ambivalence, 7-8
strategic asymmetry, 3-4
"strategic consensus", 107
strategic dependence, 5-7
Subrahmanyam, K., 17
  on Pakistan's security situation, 85-9
Sundarji, General Krishnaswami (COAS), 177, 178
Symington amendment, 9, 109, 120
Syria, 82

Tarapur reactors, 120
Tashkent Agreement (1966), 146
Taxila, 95
Tehrik-i-Istiqlal party, 47, 117
Teram Kangri peak, 160

terrorist bombings, 13-14, 45, 52
Thomas, Raju G. C., 93, 116
Thornton, Thomas, 103
Time, 111
Times Atlas of the World, The (London), 153
Treaty of Peace and Friendship (1982), 100
Trident, Operation, 178
Trishul missiles, 96
Trombay Atomic Research Center, 114
Truman, President Harry S., 7
Turkey, 82

United Kingdom, 94
United Nations, 27, 35, 37, 98
   and Geneva negotiations, 63-71
United Nations Commission on India and Pakistan (UNCIP), 145
United Nations High Commissioner for Refugees (UNHCR), 43, 47
United Nations Military Observer Group in India and Pakistan (UNMOGIP), 164, 171
United States, 54
   and Afghan resistance movement, 35, 55, 56
   attitudes toward Pakistan, 104-13
   and Geneva negotiations, 63-71
   military aid to India, 82
   military aid to Pakistan, 35, 38, 82, 94, 101-13
   nuclear nonproliferation policy of, 108-13, 119-22
   and Siachen Glacier dispute, 145, 153
   suspension of aid to Pakistan by (1990), 203
   See under India; Pakistan
United States Embassy, attack on (1979), 34, 104
United States Nuclear Regulatory Commission (NRC), 120

Vietnam, 106
VOLAGS (Voluntary agencies), 42

Wakhan Corridor, 39, 165
Warsaw Pact, 203
War That Never Was, The, 178
World Food Programme (WFP), 43

Xinjiang province, 147, 166-7

Zia ul-Haq, President Mohammad, 1-3, 14-15, 32-3, 40, 55, 84, 99, 108, 101, 103, 104-5, 111, 115, 117, 118, 125, 126, 150, 151, 152, 155, 178-80, 197, 198, 205
   and Afghan resistance movement, 57-63, 68
   compared with predecessors, 195-6
   and Geneva negotiations, 66-71
   and Pakistan's nuclear weapons program, 122-6
   See also Pakistan
zirconium metal, 110